PERSONAL VALUES IN PUBLIC POLICY

PERSONAL VALUES IN PUBLIC POLICY

Essays and Conversations in Government Decision-Making

Edited by
John C. Haughey, S.J.

PAULIST PRESS
New York/Ramsey/Toronto

Political ethics.
Christianity and politics.
Social values.
United States -- Politics and government.

Library of Congress
Catalog Card Number: 79-84401

ISBN: 0-8091-2201-4

Published by Paulist Press
Editorial Office: 1865 Broadway, New York, N.Y. 10023
Business Office: 545 Island Road, Ramsey, N.J. 07446

Printed and bound in the
United States of America

Contents

PART II: THEOLOGY AND GOVERNMENT DECISION

Foreword

Senator Charles McC. Mathias, Jr.

It is both my opinion and my experience that most people in the political world want to do "the right thing" to the extent that they have the light to recognize what is right. At times the light fails. Occasionally other forces are strong enough to overwhelm better instincts. But these moments represent the exceptions rather than the aspirations of political life.

I think, too, that there is a moral advance, however small, in the way the world conducts its affairs. Not all, of course, are as optimistic as I am. The skeptical say that we have abandoned gunboat diplomacy because even undeveloped countries will not tolerate it, or that we have suppressed business piracy because it ultimately preyed on consumers, who have revolted with their pocketbooks. Some may lead good and pure lives simply because they have found it is less likely to lead to complications.

Notwithstanding my over-all optimism about our slow gain in moral sensitivity, human motives are frequently complex and multi-faceted. While many in public life may be content merely to reach a right decision without regard to the reasoning that got us there, or to the deeper motivations for apparently unselfish conduct, it would be better if we were more in touch with the forces competing within us and recognized honestly which of them are dominating our lives. I think this volume should help us to grow in clarity about these elements.

In my own life, a recent example of competing forces at work beneath the surface is provided by the struggle for Congressional representation for the people of the District of Columbia. When I came to Congress in 1960, I had little interest in home rule for the District of Columbia let alone equal representation in Congress.

1

Certainly the issue of equal representation for the District arouses all of the unhappy political emotions. Racism plays a part, diffusion of power is involved, the selfish side of human nature—"I've got mine and I'm going to keep you from getting yours"—is revealed. So the issue is fraught with difficulty.

But, as I lived with the problems as a member of the House and then the Senate District of Columbia Committee, I became acquainted with the problem in a way that made it impossible for me to avoid a deeper contemplation of what was right. That inevitably led to the conclusion that our ideal of equality before the law for every American citizen could not be achieved without giving the people of the District of Columbia the same political rights, including representation, that the citizens of the states enjoyed.

I honestly believe that it was the moral force of the argument and that alone which converted me from a posture of serious doubt to the point of being a supporter of and sponsor for Congressional representation for the District of Columbia. There was simply no way in which a refusal even to make an effort to obtain political equality for the population of the District could be squared with the injunction to "love thy neighbor as thyself."

The opening chapter of this book deals with the external forces that govern our decisions and actions and the final chapter deals with the internal forces that influence us. The pages between traverse the complex terrain of human experience, exploring the question of how a person like myself works his sense of values into the public order, realizing that one will never be more than partially successful, but holding on in the attempt because otherwise the reality becomes ugly and distorted. I like the outside-inside scope of the work. "Two things fill the mind with ever new and increasing wonder and awe," Immanuel Kant has noted, "the starry heavens above me and the moral law within me."

The final essay extends to the reader "an invitation to a degree of introspection that we modern people are not sufficiently versed in doing." Its invitation is grounded in the hope that "public servants' responsibilities will be performed with more objectivity if they are more aware of their subjectivities which are replete with 'illusions and addictions', motivations and aversions, judgments and attachments, opinions and predispositions." It's an invitation well worth accepting.

I have no taste for conspicuous morality but who in political life couldn't use a little more awareness of the forces that drive us? I am reminded of an anecdote my colleague, Senator Russell Long of Louisiana, tells about asking his uncle, the late Governor Earl Long, to help him with a high school debate.

"What's the topic?" the Governor asked.

"Whether ideals should be used in politics," replied his nephew.

"Which side are you taking, son?"

"The affirmative."

"Why hell yes you use ideals," the Governor exploded, "you use anything you can get your hands on in politics."

This tale—and I'm assured it's not apocryphal—tells better than sermons the basic fact that we are often in great moral danger either when we cloak ourselves in morality or when everything becomes grist for our own purposes.

I think this book will be helpful to everyone who leads a busy and pressured life in a materialistic environment because it provides a way to analyze the influences that shape our decisions. It makes the reader aware of dimensions of personality and levels of consciousness that enter into public life in subtle undetected ways. It inevitably produces the introspection that can bring the reader to perceive beyond the thicket of "subjectivities," a glimmer of the moral law within.

Introduction

John C. Haughey

This volume is an effort on the part of theologians and philosophers to cast some light on the virtually opaque process of decision-making that takes place in government circles in our time. The particular area this study seeks to illumine is the point at which personally appropriated values flow, or might flow, into public policies carried there by decision-makers' judgments and choices. Of all the areas of government decision-making that have been the object of scrutiny or analysis, this particular area has seemed to us to be the least examined or the most neglected.

The determination to focus on decision-making in general and value-insertion in particular has grown out of several years of discussion between members of the Woodstock Theological Center and government officials. The Woodstock Center was set up in Washington, D.C. in 1974 by the Maryland and New York Provinces of the Society of Jesus with the mandate to undertake theological reflection on contemporary human issues. Members of the Woodstock Center soon developed specific ways of responding to this general mandate, one of which is generically called "Government as a Vocation." This section of the Woodstock Center is concerned to be in dialogue with and in service to those government officials who bear the main responsibilities for our country's handling of complex social issues. Dialogues between career civil servants as well as elected or appointed officials from various agencies and branches of the Federal government and members of the Woodstock Center have been going on for the last three years. Sometimes these took the form of seminars which dealt with such issues as the Ethics of Intervention, the Law of the Seas, U.S. Policy on Disarmament, etc. Classes for government personnel have also been conducted by members of the Woodstock Staff over the past three years. The recurring point of greatest interest in all of these interchanges was the one which this volume seeks to address. The need for this study, therefore, grew out of the experience of Woodstock staff persons with government officials.

This volume seeks to build bridges between the world of academe and the day to day execution of governmental responsibilities. The distance between these worlds has always been wider than is good for either population. Also, the distance between the day to day business of government and the world of religious professionals such as clergymen and scholars, is too vast to be satisfactory to either. Each of the authors appearing in this volume, in addition to holding doctorates in either theology, philosophy or political science, has also been ordained a clergyman of the Catholic Church in the Society of Jesus. This volume, therefore, since it conjoins the expertise of government professionals with that of academically and religiously trained professionals, should serve to narrow these distances.

The process by which these studies were developed could help the reader see how this volume has attempted to bridge these aforementioned worlds. In the spring of 1977, after a year and a half of close association with career civil servants and the dilemmas they face, we chose a small number of these officials and committed ourselves to spending many hours in learning about their respective responsibilities, the pattern of their decisions, and the approach each developed in arriving at these. From these intensive interviews each member of the Woodstock staff began to plumb the area of his own competence and the insight which he felt could in some way illumine the problematic of government insofar as he came to know this.

Having drafted initial reflections about the process of decision-making the authors critiqued one another and arrived at a further degree of unity (far short of unanimity, of course). The project then moved into the classroom where in October, 1977, the staff conducted a series of classes on the same matter with government employees, seeking to be of service to those who attended while at the same time seeking to grow in a greater awareness and depth of the peculiar problematic faced regularly by government personnel. The consequence of these sessions was a re-working of the same material on the basis of the additional experience and further exposure to the many sides of government decisions. The titles in the Table of Contents will give the reader a quick overview of the specific areas chosen by the authors because they felt they could bring some light to them and thereby illumine that patch of the murky terrain of government decision-making.

The penultimate stage of this development can be found under the rubric of conversations in this volume. These portions of our volume are edited conversations held in the spring of '78 between the authors and twelve government officials from nine different government agencies and a member of Congress. These conversations serve to concretize even further the analysis of personal values and their relationship to public policies. They can be read alone simply as interesting conversations or they can be read in conjunction with the essay which inspired the conversation. Our intention in recording them and including them in this volume was that one would serve to illumine the other.

It should be obvious immediately that the areas covered by the essays are few, while the terrain itself is infinitely broader. The first limitation of this volume, therefore, that the reader must appreciate is that while government decision-making is a continuum which is virtually infinite not to mention complex, the studies herein contained touch only a few points along that continuum. But the selection of the area of decision-making which concerns itself with the values operating in the decision-makers who are performing for the public the tasks for which they were employed, serves to narrow the vast field to a more containable subject.

The body of the volume divides into two parts depending on whether the author chose to address the subject of values and decisions as such or those particular kinds of values which have religious faith as their source or raison d'être. This choice, of course, also was dictated by the specializations of the authors. Essays in the first half use ethics, philosophy and political science. Those appearing in the second half are all theological.

The conversations, too, are between two different sets of government personnel. Those appearing in the first set impressed us at Woodstock in the course of previous associations with them especially for the ethical sensitivity they took to the performance of their professional tasks. Those in the second part of the volume, that which deals with religious faith values and the theological questions attendent on it, had likewise impressed us at the Center for the depths of their Christian faith.

The opening essay, written by the political scientist on the Woodstock staff, Brian Smith, attempts to create a map tracing the main routes which decisions ordinarily take in order to pass from velleities to public policies in our country. It is at pains to point out the varied types of input which go into creating policy, the resources that affect its shaping and the modes of its implementation. The reactions to this overview found in the conversational complement which follows the essay begin to give the reader an appreciation of the complexity of the federal bureaucracy. Essay and conversation together are a good beginning in deciphering the seemingly indecipherable.

The second essay is done by the philosopher on our staff, John Langan. The area he chooses to examine is what we mean by the term value in our study. Should our government be run and its decisional processes executed by officials who would follow rules rather than personally appropriated values? The bulk of the conversation on this study concentrated on a decision of one of the participants who is the Executive Director of the Inter-American Development Bank and the value questions it raises.

The following essay by David Hollenbach, formerly a member of the Woodstock staff and presently a professor of social ethics at Weston School of Theology, Cambridge, Massachusetts, unravels the issue of conflicting loyalties. Loyalties are carriers of values. The on-going attempt to resolve loyalty pulls when dealing with one's responsibilities to the public is the major reason for Hollenbach's describing government work as more than a job. He situates it in the category of a vocation. The subsequent discussion, among other things, shows both the richness and the amount of play there is in the notion of vocation as well as value-harboring loyalties.

The prickly question of reason, rationality and reasonableness in relationship to government decisions is dealt with by Langan's second essay. Are government decisions the product of human reason; should they be? How do reason and value interweave? The essay provoked much rich reflection on the part of government officials whose experience of the decision-making process shows in surprising ways how the rational and the nonrational combine in the affairs of government.

A whole series of decisions have to be made by the bureaucrat when he or she is faced with a policy that has harmful consequences. This issue is handled by Brian Smith in his essay on dealing with morally objectionable government decisions or situations produced by them. The discussion centered on the Kitty Genovese case because it sharply highlights the basic principles for action to be taken by an on-looker on behalf of those who are being wronged.

The first essay in the theological section of the volume is done by Richard McCormick, a noted moralist who is a research associate of the Woodstock Center and a member of the Kennedy Institute for Bioethics. His thesis, if subscribed to, has considerable consequences for the civil servant who is also a person of religious faith. Will that faith add any ethical insight, not in principle accessible to the non-believer, to the public issues they weigh in common? From the conversation which follows we can appreciate how novel McCormick's position was to many of the discussants.

The following essay moves away from discrete decisions and poses the question of the civil servant's view, presumably implicit, of the relationship between the enterprise of government and the enterprise believers call salvation. This issue is analyzed by Robert Mitchell, theologian, past president of the Jesuit Conference and director of the Woodstock Theological Center, because the world view of the civil servant consciously or unconsciously affects the way he or she approaches each decision and responsibility. The paper introduces three different world-views which theologize about the meaning of political development and its religious significance. The discussion centered largely on the role theology itself plays or can play in enlargement of the perspective of the government person.

From all that precedes, the question naturally arises about

the method the Christian civil servant employs for relating to the decision-making processes of government. Thomas Clarke, a theologian on the Woodstock staff, reflects on Christian discernment which is a formal process and method developed in the course of the Church's history for reaching personal and communal decisions. Its applicability for the Christian with a role in government is the concern of his study. The conversation which ensues should dispel any doubts one might have about the propriety or relevance of employing a religious tradition born in a wholly other moment and place for modern government decision-making.

The final essay seeks to do several things. It is presented as an exercise in examining one's own consciousness about a number of things that pertain to the execution of his or her governmental responsibilities. In presenting more than one way of seeing similar items, the examiner can become more conscious of alternatives to his/her own consciousness. It is also meant to serve as a way of recalling some of the book's insights and prolonging some of its questions.

The epilogue was done by a friend of a number of Woodstock staffers. He is a political scientist from Governors State University in Park Forrest, Illinois. Our long relationship with John Rohr was renewed last year while he was on a sabbatical leave in Washington, D.C. While here he did a training manual for the Civil Service Commission on "Ethics, Values and Administrative Responsibility for Government Managers." By reason of his familiarity with government, he has been able to add to our volume from his knowledge of the vast field of analyses of governmental decision making so that the reader can be somewhat more informed of the nature of these studies.

The book was composed with several audiences in mind. The most obvious is the civil or public servant whether local, state or federal. The mixture of reflection and experience it contains is intended especially for such a person. But those whose professional life has taken them in the direction of business will, presumably, see analyses here which pertain directly to their lives as well. They, too, have to "make straight" the routes between company policy and personal values as do their counterparts in government work. Those, too, who are in the position of having to achieve mastery of the field of either psychology or government, philosophy or theology should find the fare in this volume satisfying because it touches all four fields without becoming mired in any one of them. Although it is interdisciplinary, finally, educated citizens who have made themselves conversant with the affairs of government in recent years should find much in this volume that satisfies their curiousity about its processes.

The readers of this volume will be disappointed if they expect it to deliver something it is not intended to provide. It is not out to give answers. It is attempting to illuminate the process of personal values' insertion into public policies. It is not addressing the issues themselves that policies attempt to cover. It is not, furthermore, intended as a handbook of intermediate principles of public decision-making. If such a handbook could be written it would doubtless assist decision-makers who were looking for usable, concrete means for executing their responsibilities; but such an undertaking is unlikely.

The experience of participants in our discussions should be helpful in indicating the carry-away effects our approach is meant to have. They were quite appreciative and indicated the amount of reflection the whole process provoked in them. It heightened their awareness of new dimensions of a process they had been involved in, in many cases, for years. It got them thinking. It did not tell them what to think. It heightened consciousness; it didn't instruct them. Insofar as it does this to the reader it will have its intended effect.

The expected expressions of appreciation that inhabit book introductions can in the case of this volume disguise the degree of dependency that I as editor and we as authors have had on a number of people. First of all, Betty Mullen, an indefatigable mainstay on our staff at the Woodstock Center, has labored through a number of versions of all the material between these covers with a generosity and a thoroughness that has sustained all of us who were involved in the long process of creation. Secondly, the people who are listed in the conversations, when invited, left their already preoccupying chores and reflected trenchantly and humbly about themselves and their tasks. A special note of gratitude is due to John Ahearne and Frank Hennigan, because from the very beginning of the process of reflection on government decision-making they have encouraged, contributed to and critiqued our reflections. Several others who are not among the listed participants but who contributed much at an early stage of the project were Dr. Victor Alessi of the S.A.L.T., Dr. Robert Dowling of the D.O.E., and Mr. Philip Verveer of the Federal Trade Commission.

Part I
Ethics and Government Decision

1
The Topography of Government Decision-Making

Brian H. Smith

I
INTRODUCTION

The design and execution of governmental policies are not made by single agents or groups acting alone. They are the product of complex interactions of individuals and organizations having different inputs into the process and subject in varying degrees to outside pressures from interested publics. Responsibility and accountability are dispersed throughout the web of government and there are countless ways in which individuals, groups or agencies can exercise influence in the formation of policy as well as in the ongoing process of its execution and refinement.[1]

Since it is the purpose of this series of essays to clarify the role of moral and religious values in public decision-making, it is important to begin by providing a map or grid reference of various types of responsibility, resources for influence and ongoing tensions that exist along the continuum of the policymaking process as a whole in government. The topography that I shall present in this first essay is perhaps overly schematic. Nevertheless, the purpose of this initial descriptive sketch is to illustrate that individuals and groups throughout the government have very different types of input into the final outcome of a policy, and also experience different conflicts, depending upon their position in the legislature or bureaucracy.

The other four essays in the first part of the volume will deal with questions of when and how such choices and conflicts involve moral values, what the role of rational and non-rational factors is in decision-making, how ethical choices are made, and what options are available to persons when they encounter morally "bad" policies.

II
ELECTED OFFICIALS AND POLITICAL APPOINTEES

The 535 elected members of the Congress and the approximately 2,000 appointed executives in the bureaucracy are the ones most directly responsible in setting the overall direction for public policies. They are involved in articulating fundamental priorities, shaping legislation and allocating public resources. Their choices have a visible and direct impact on the public, and they create an important tone or atmosphere for executive departments and agencies.

Persons often aspire to these offices in order to have a major impact on public policies, and the principles and values they bring to such tasks can have a crucial bearing on the types of programs that an administration or Congress produces. People come to these positions with a feeling that they can accomplish something very significant and immediate for society or for the interested publics with whom they identify.

Their terms in office, however, are limited by law or by the pleasure of the one who appoints them, and they are also subject to far more direct political pressures than are career civil servants. Their choices are made amidst a series of very strong interacting influences coming both from their constituencies and from within the government itself.

Congressmen and Senators must think about re-election from the day they begin to serve in office. The demands from their districts or States are frequently made by organized groups with narrow goals that often do not reflect the interests of the voters as a whole but these wield disproportionate influence (especially in re-election campaigns) due to their resources and access to media. Elected officials who come to Washington with high ideals and enthusiasm to serve the public needs frequently find that they are approached primarily by those with very specific monetary interests and clout while seldom hearing from vast numbers of their constituents who are unorganized and silent. Much of their own time and that of their staffs is taken up in mediating between such constituents and government agencies and providing individual services to important individuals or groups. Their focus on overall legislative goals and the public interest is frequently limited or blurred by these pressures.

One freshman Congressman told us in a course for public officials conducted by the Woodstock Center several years ago, that he was elected in 1974 predominantly on an anti-war platform. He was strongly supported and assisted by groups in his district very much opposed to the Vietnam conflict. Once he came to Washington, however, he seldom heard from these people again, but was constantly barraged with requests from labor and business lobbyists focusing only on issues pertaining to their own interests.

Another Representative with more experience in Congress explained in the same course that one cannot avoid dealing with these special interest pressures. He said, however, that it is still possible and necessary to vote according to one's conscience and be re-elected regardless of the pressures. There are certain reasonable requests from special interests to which an elected official can accede, but it is also possible to say "no" at other times and also vote according to what one feels is right without jeopardizing one's career.

He also remarked that the public at large is much more intelligent and sensitive to moral issues than members of Congress sometimes acknowledge. There are, he said, a whole range of problems around which public opinion has not yet crystallized and where a Representative or Senator can and should provide leadership for his or her constituents.

"We need", he said, "public officials and candidates who will lead and who are not just public-opinion poll watchers. One can take unpopular stands on moral grounds," he concluded. "The public is better than we think."

Another problem limiting an elected official's ability to influence fundamental policy issues has resulted from changes over the past forty years in the functions of Congress. Since the New Deal and the Cold War much initiative in legislation and policy-making has shifted away from Congress. By the mid-1960's for example, 80% of the bills enacted into law originated in the executive branch of government, not in the House or Senate. Congressional influence in setting priorities and goals has diminished, and its function has become largely one of delay and amendment, or oversight of the activities of departments or agencies in the executive branch of government.[2]

Within the Congress itself the necessity for specialization has reduced the capacity of any elected member to keep abreast of the implications and consequences of many crucial pieces of legislation. He or she must rely on the opinion of colleagues or technical experts, and also must be willing to trade support in order to gain backing for his or her own preferred programs.

Although the seniority system has undergone some modification in recent years, those who have been in Congress longer still wield preponderant influence in affecting the outcome of legislation and resource allocation. Informal procedural rules of the club prevail on many issues, and those with less seniority must yield and learn how to compromise and abide by long-standing customs in order to have any impact in the legislative outcomes.

Appointed officials in departments, agencies, bureaus and commissions are not subject to the same political pressures as are elected officials concerned about re-election. They experience conflicts, however, when the policies they pursue antagonize public groups or organizations that wield influence either in Congress or at higher levels of the administration. They frequently bring with them skills developed outside of government and advisers and staffs inexperienced in government procedures. Tense relationships can thus develop between themselves and the civil servants under them, leading to ineffective management or a lack of policy coordination. Furthermore, they fully expect to move on soon; the average term in office of an appointed official is less than two years. All of these factors place limitations on the choices and the impact of an appointed official during his or her time in public service.[3]

Hence, although the potential for shaping fundamental

policies and influencing the direction of government by elected and appointed officials is considerable, the limitations and pressures are also very intense. Value conflict is a constant possibility. The desire to be re-elected must be weighed against voting for what one believes is right. Working for programs one considers crucial must be balanced with trading off support and making compromises. Responding to particularistic demands and oversight responsibilities limits the time and energies available to articulate overall goals and fundamental purposes of government. Exercising imaginative leadership clashes with bureaucratic procedures or unwritten customs.

In dealing with all of these conflicts, one must weigh what is politically feasible and effective, but one must also know the difference between legitimate compromise and the betrayal of fundamental principles.

III
CAREER CIVIL SERVANTS

The overwhelming majority of those in federal or local government are neither elected nor appointed officials. They are the more than 2.7 million career civil service employees responsible for the implementation of laws, regulations and policies authorized by the Congress, the President or department and agency heads.

Their actions are less visible to the general public, but their positions are more clearly defined and protected by legal procedures and it is difficult to fire them or force their resignations. They generally have a deeper commitment to the long-term functioning of public institutions than do elected persons or political appointees, and they act as carriers of traditional practical wisdom necessary for the day-to-day operations in government. The process and context of their work are also less hurried and less subject to outside pressures than those of elected officials.

Their attitudes and behavior shape more the quality and effectiveness of program performance than the content of goals and priorities. Nevertheless, although the original purpose of U.S.

civil service reform begun in the late nineteenth century was to remove the bureaucracy from politics and make the work of career personnel a purely technical matter, today there is a great deal of administrative discretion exercised by civil servants that goes beyond mere efficiency or obedience to regulations. The influence of partisan politics within the bureaucracy has been curtailed by civil service reform, but value-laden judgments in the execution of policies are and will always be part of the work of the bureaucrats. These clearly have political consequences in the sense that they affect the distribution of power and resources in society at large.[4]

Not only is there a certain amount of leeway available to civil servants in interpreting and applying commands of political superiors, they also participate in the formulation of those commands themselves now that the bureaucracy has a greater role in providing the initiative and information for policymakers. New emphases on management by objectives (MBO), organizational development (OD), and participative management further allow for considerable influence to be exercised in both directions along the vertical chain of command in the bureaucracy.[5]

John Rohr in his training manual for the Civil Service Commission summarizes the range of discretionary activities of a civil servant which affect the governing process:

> . . . He governs by means of administrative discretion which in a narrow sense involves interpretation of laws and regulations and in a broader sense refers to the fact that he advises, reports, responds, initiates, informs, promotes, retards, and mediates in a way that has a serious impact on American life.[6]

Hence, the context, the visibility and the public accountability of choices made by career civil servants are quite different from those of persons who serve by appointment or election. The impact on the overall performance of government which these people make, however, is not only crucial but the grounds for their choices are based on much more than scientifically established technical criteria. The something more, insofar as that is values, will be dealt with in Chapter 2; insofar as that is the product of reason will be dealt with in Chapter 4.

There are various functions of civil servants, each involving different types of responsibilities and choices, many of which include discretionary and prudential judgments with underlying value assumptions—e.g., deciding upon norms for supervising and critiquing public programs, applying general regulations or guidelines to particular cases, gathering and evaluating pertinent information for policymakers, improving the quality of services for the public, maintaining positive and constructive attitudes in the day-to-day ambience of the bureaucracy. These can be exercised by individuals with executive responsibility, by persons acting collegially in staff positions, by technical experts, or by secretarial personnel with no direct input into the decision-making process itself.

(A) Individuals with Executive Functions

(Program directors, middle-level managers, branch supervisors, agents in field offices)

Those persons responsible for overall program performance or the application of laws and regulations enjoy a certain flexibility for setting standards, choosing means to meet goals and interpreting general guidelines. The complexities of a modern industrial society have deterred Congress and department or agency heads from becoming too specific or detailed in writing laws and regulations. Much is left to the discretion of those who have to manage programs in determining the meaning of guidelines in concrete instances and in selecting the most practical methods to achieve desired ends.

Deciding what is "unfair competition", what are "substandard" food and drug products, what licenses for communications media are in the "public interest", or which community action programs are "broadly representative of the interests of the community" are all examples of the decisions high and medium-range civil servants must make to give meaning to broad statutory mandates on a case by case basis. There is no way that decisions can be made without values entering into these decisions. From these, significant political consequences flow which, in turn, clearly affect private centers of power as well as the quality of life in society at large.[7]

Conflicts, therefore, can and do arise between what a supervisor, manager or agent believes is effective for a program or applicable in terms of guidelines and what a higher superior thinks is feasible or desirable. Public groups or organizations affected by interpretations of civil servants in executive positions can also exert influence at higher levels of government to neutralize, water down or overturn such administrative decisions. They can also exercise subtle but effective pressure on the executive himself or herself by offering unsolicited advice, information or favors.

A lawyer working in the Antitrust Division of the Justice Department explained in one of our seminars that large corporations invite his colleagues to lunch regularly to discuss cases involving other companies or to share information on business practices. While not attempting to influence decisions affecting themselves directly, these firms hope to establish good rapport with anti-trust lawyers who someday may be prosecuting them for violations. They also seek to obtain valuable information on current trends in the division and how far they might go before being prosecuted. Such "free lunches" clearly influence the objectivity of Justice Department lawyers as well as business decisions, although they do not technically violate professional codes of conduct for lawyers.

A thorough knowledge of laws and regulations, along with a well-run and open process and resistance to undue outside influences, can help protect an executive from interest groups or political pressures. If an atmosphere of impartiality pervades one's activities and discretionary functions, the performance of a director, manager, supervisor or agent can be easier and more effective.

Problems, however, can also arise from below when career personnel serving under an executive are not in agreement with his or her perspective, or when they drag their feet or do not meet minimum efficiency standards. Acting with a sense of fairness towards one's subordinates, encouraging constructive criticism, fighting for programs with higher levels of authority or with other agencies, and focusing on the delivery of good services to the public all are part of the responsibilities of executives as well, and can go a long way in stimulating a spirit of commitment and dedication among those under a supervisor or manager.

(B) Collegial Decision-Making

(Staff interaction, team work)

Some influences in the decision-making process in government are exercised by groups of people acting together as a team rather than as individuals. No one person makes the final choice (or recommendation to a higher official), but several have an input at the same level. Advisory staffs (in both the executive and congressional branches of government), as well as agencies requiring a considerable amount of team effort and horizontal give and take (e.g., Antitrust Division, Arms Control and Disarmament Agency, Legal Services Corporation) are examples of this type of collegial process. The viewpoints of several working together are molded into a consistent whole, since the outcome usually requires a consensus statement or recommendation. Some of the most crucial influences to which each participant must relate are the judgments and perspectives of other members of the team, and not merely the positions of a higher executive or pressures from outside of government.

The effectiveness of this type of decision-making depends upon the degree of harmony and respect among peers. Choices emerge out of a simmering process in which several persons are involved simultaneously. Each must listen to the recommendations of others and be willing to modify his or her own judgments accordingly. In such a situation, emotion and passion can be dysfunctional to the outcome, especially when these are manifestations of personal insecurity or ambition. Persons on ego trips or who are unable to bend can be a threat to reaching an effective consensus for action. On the other hand, there is a danger of too much acquiescence in or loyalty to the dominant attitude prevailing on the staff or in the agency. When participants are too willing to compromise in order to reach a consensus, there is the likelihood that the group as a whole accepts a position that is less effective or rigorous than is possible or desirable.

The literature on the Watergate episode provides us with clear evidence that staff persons can get so caught up with loyalty to the team that they lose a sense of what is right and wrong, as well as the ability to provide a diversity of opposing perspectives for consideration. A self-critical attitude and the possibility for the effective expression of dissenting views was not kept alive among Nixon's closest advisors and the outcome was disastrous. Without specific efforts to preserve such an atmosphere conducive to the discussion and debate of wide-ranging alternatives, a staff or agency can become too insulated and overlook some of the consequences of its choices or recommendations.

A sense of routine or feeling that one's efforts are insignificant by themselves can also be an obstacle to effective collegial decision-making. Such occupational hazards built into consensus-building can dull the awareness of team members as to the important implications of their work for overall policy outputs. It is important not to lose a sensitivity for the people whose lives eventually will be effected by the collegial choices in which one contributes only in part.

The essay in Chapter 3 emphasizes the necessity of keeping one eye focused on the day-to-day functions of one's office, and one eye cast in the direction of the broad goals which government serves to correct any narrowing that can take place in one's focus and loyalties. The final four essays in this volume highlight the motivational resources and vision which religious faith can provide in offsetting the problem of routine or sense or meaninglessness in one's daily public service.

(C) Information Gathering and Evaluation

(Technical experts, scientists)
Due to the complexity of problems and highly technical aspect of many issues, a crucial factor for good choices by policy-

makers is having adequate and pertinent information from specialists or those with scientific expertise. These persons sometimes
function in collegial situations, but frequently act alone in inves-
tigating a question or problem. They collect and sift empirical
data, evaluate information in terms of its impact on program objectives, and lay out the consequences of alternative strategies of
action.

Their input into decisions is primarily in the quality and extent of the information they provide which shape the framework
in which options at a higher level are made. Integrity depends
more upon one's objectivity and completeness rather than on
one's administrative behavior or horizontal relationships. Leaving something out can mislead the person or persons responsible
for the final choice.

Truthtelling therefore is the most important contribution a
specialist can make. For this reason it is crucial that such an
individual sort out his or her biases on objective reality. One's
preferences—even in the most scientific or technical of
issues—can color the information that one gathers or the description of consequences of alternative courses of action one gives to
policymakers.

Conversely, institutional self-deception can reduce a specialist's objectivity as well. Subtle pressures from superiors to hear
what they want to hear can skew the completeness or accuracy of
what is included in a technical report. Data experts can be asked
to justify with facts the validity of a policy or alternative already
selected for other reasons. While such pressure need not always
lead to undesirable consequences, encouragement to falsify data
or leave out information damaging to official policy can seriously
hamper institutional self-criticism as well as reduce the
policymaker's awareness of the range of consequences of certain
choices.

Reporting information up the chain of command during the
Vietnam conflict was a classic example of how self-deception can
be built into the whole data collection and analysis process. Top
civilian policymakers and military strategists in Washington
wanted favorable reports from the Saigon embassy on the progress of the war. In turn, field leaders were subtly pressured by

diplomatic and military personnel in the embassy to provide empirical data on body-counts and areas cleared of enemy control that favored our own cause. As a result, in one instance a division commander upon receiving unfavorable information from a district advisor about continued Viet Cong operations in a "pacified" area is reported to have said: "Son, you are writing our own report card. Why are you failing us?" Such distorted information was then used to deceive both top policymakers and the U.S. public as to the real facts of the war and our chances of winning it on our own predetermined conditions.[8]

No one person alone can prevent institutional self-deception once it has become ingrained into a policymaking process. Each specialist, however, has the responsibility of communicating information and exploring the costs of alternatives as accurately as possible and in a clear but nonthreatening manner. A person in such a role must be able to keep his or her own personal bias from distorting what is reported, but also has to be willing to risk disagreement or disapproval from superiors in order to provide them and others with the widest possible range of choices in their work. Various methods for doing this effectively, and for marshalling information and support against ill-conceived policies, will be discussed in my other essay on strategies for influencing bad policies.

(D) Housekeeping and Maintenance Functions

(Secretaries, receptionists, stenographers, clerks, general office personnel)

Many government workers have no formal relationship to the decision-making process as such. These include secretarial and other office personnel engaged primarily in the housekeeping tasks of day to day maintenance.

These people, however, provide the necessary infrastructure for decisions by taking care of important functional details. They can contribute to an atmosphere of effective communication and collaboration in an office, and can also speak with plain common sense when practical issues are at stake.

They also are frequently the first point of contact that the public has with the government, and often are the ones who perform many services requested by taxpayers from elected officials or civil servants. As a result, they shape the immediate impressions that people have of a Congressperson or department or agency, and thereby can contribute to maintaining public confidence in and respect for government.

All of these contributions are very important for the smooth running of an office, for the promotion of morale and for the creation of a positive atmosphere in which good decisions can be made and effective assistance offered to the public. A realization that such work is a vocation to service and not merely a job or slot to be filled, can go a long way in helping persons in these positions make invaluable contributions to the decision-making process as a whole. The final essay in the volume on various types of attitudes about one's work will elaborate upon the ingredients that enhance such a wider consciousness.

IV
CONCLUSIONS

The foregoing descriptive framework of the types of input into governmental decision-making and the pressures or conflicts that persons experience at different stages of the process no doubt overlooks many complexities and nuances that characterize the life of a public servant. Some of these refinements will be treated in the other essays and in the subsequent discussions with government personnel following each chapter.

Hopefully this initial topography, however, has clarified some of the major differences in responsibility and influence that characterize the various stages of policymaking as a whole. All of the roles analyzed in this chapter require far more than political efficacy, technical expertise, obedience to rules or administrative competence to be performed well. They involve value-laden judgments and attitudes regarding the meaning and consequences of public service even in its seemingly most insignificant aspects.

For these reasons, it is clear that pure rationality and efficiency (understood in a narrow sense) are insufficient to evaluate performance at any level of public decision-making. Nor can an official's responsibilities be fulfilled merely by not breaking federal regulations or professional codes of ethics. Without some deeper commitment, some overall sense of purpose, an ability to think beyond one's own interests, and an awareness of how one's actions affect people whom one never will meet, the choices that a government official makes will lack the vital ingredients necessary to enhance the public weal. Max Weber's classic distinction between policymakers who must take a stand on issues involving value choices and civil servants who merely execute orders with no judgmental input of their own no longer adequately describes the responsibility divisions in public service.[9]

All political and administrative judgments which involve discretion also involve the judger's values whether they are aware of these or not. Without a consciousness of this aspect of public service choices, an understanding of the decision-making process would be reduced merely to who gets what, from whom, when and how. It is the purpose of subsequent essays and discussions in this book to go beyond the parameters of such a reduction. Becoming more reflective of the implicit value choices that underly one's input into decision-making makes one more responsible for the consequences of one's daily work and the quality of life in our society as a whole.

NOTES

1. A presentation of various models useful for analyzing decision-making in government and a summary of organizational theory literature on the subject can be found in: Graham T. Allison, *Essence of Decision: Explaining the Cuban Missile Crisis* (Boston: Little, Brown, 1971).

2. For an excellent analysis of how the role and power of Congress in policymaking has changed in this century, cf. Samuel P. Huntington, "Congressional Responses to the Twentieth Century," *Congress and America's Future*, ed. David B. Truman (Englewood Cliffs: Prentice-Hall, 1965), pp. 5-31.

3. For a recent treatment of the tensions that develop between political appointees and high-level bureaucrats in the Federal government, cf. Hugh Heclo, *A Government of Strangers: Executive Politics in Washington* (Washington, D.C.: The Brookings Institution, 1977).

4. For a description of the development of this administrative discretionary role of career civil servants that carries with it significant political consequences, cf.: Herbert J. Storing, "Political Parties and the Bureaucracy," *Political Parties, U.S.A.*, ed. Robert A. Goldwin (Chicago: Rand McNally, 1964), pp. 37-58. John A. Rohr, "Ethics for Bureaucrats," *America*, Vol. 128, No. 20 (May 26, 1973), pp. 488-91. John A. Rohr, *Ethics, Values and Administrative Responsibility: A Training Manual for Government Managers* (Washington, D.C.: U.S. Civil Service Commission, 1976), pp. 22-56.

5. Storing, *op. cit.*, p. 152. Rohr, *Ethics, Values and Administrative Responsibility*, p. 40.

Since the New Deal in the 1930's and the growth of government programs the Congress has delegated considerable discretionary authority to federal agencies in interpreting and applying broad regulations. This has led to an increase in the political power of the bureaucracy and to greater interaction between bureaucrats and groups affected by their decisions in society at large. For a critical assessment of this growth in the politicization of the federal bureaucracy cf., Theodore J. Lowi, *The End of Liberalism: Ideology, Policy and the Crisis of Public Authority* (New York: W.W. Norton and Company, 1969).

6. Rohr, *Ethics, Values and Administrative Responsibility*, p. 55.

7. Rohr, "Ethics for Bureaucrats," p. 490.

8. Daniel Ellsberg, *Papers on the War* (New York: Simon and Schuster, 1972), p. 121.

9. Max Weber, *Politics As a Vocation*, trans. H. H. Gerth and C. Wright Mills (Philadelphia: Fortress, 1965).

Topography Conversation

Brian Smith: My assumption is that the decision-making process is a continuum, and at all points there are different ways of making inputs. At each stage there are particular resources that people have because of different skills or positions. The purpose of laying out this topography is to provide a kind of map so we can trace the point at which values are likely to be a factor in the decision-making processes.

Margulies: I thought it was a remarkably good description from my point of view. There were some things that I thought justified a little further attention in my own experience and some that were not as clearly delineated as they might have been. Where I sit in HEW involves me in looking at health resources nationally. Are there enough people to provide the medical care needed? Are they located in the right places? I look at such questions as these. The power I have to influence the development of appropriations, the characteristics of those appropriations, where money goes and for what purposes is much greater than what's reflected in this paper. At the beginning of the appropriations process we have considerable influence on how and where appropriations extend since we write the initial words. Secondly, an important factor that's not explicit in this study is that we bureaucrats are usually responsible for the development of basic data and the assumptions on which data are based and the analyses of the data. All of these factors can skew things in widely different directions. Finally, we have considerable influence in the way in which money is spent and the way in which our large grants activity is implemented. In part, this is because we write the rules of the law by which legislation is administered. The language is filled with the Secretary's "shall" or the Surgeon General's "shall", giving us enormous discretion and latitude as to how things are carried out. I never cease to be amazed at the hierarchical strength there is in our kind of system. When you get to a certain level of authority, the degree of one's authority is surprising.

Gessert: Besides being a topography of decision-making, this is a demography also. You have identified the key people but there are some omissions that one must take very seriously. One is the legislative staffs who have little or no public visibility or accountability but I think play an increasingly important role. I know in the defense area with which I am associated that certainly is true. Legislative aides and key staffs of the Senate and the House play a tremendously powerful role but do so with very little public visibility or public accountability. Not even the news media apparently know very much about many of these people or subject them to very much critical analysis comparable to what their principals or people in the executive branch are subjected to. This element of decision-making in the government needs more attention. Furthermore we all must consider the increasingly crucial role of outside bodies that aren't exactly pressure groups or lobbying groups but are established consultant commissions that are engaged on contract. There's a major business of going to agencies outside the government; a practice that is once again very largely obscured from public gaze and as a result has little or no accountability to the public. Finally, and once again I speak with more certainty in the Defense area, decision-making is not distributed in any sense evenly or even by protocol but can be traced to individuals or networks of highly influential people who talk to one another constantly but largely outside the formal channels.

Lowell: I think the 2,000 appointed officials in the executive branch get kind of short shrift in this study in comparison to their importance. They get lumped with the elected officials in a way that probably does not do justice to either. The pressures on appointed officials seem to me to be of quite a different kind than those on elected officials. The principal pressure that I, a career civil servant, have observed on the appointed officials in my agency is the pressure to respond quickly and dramatically. The average tenure of appointed officials is two years. That's the time in which they have to make a mark or to do what the President had in mind when he appointed them. Career executives, on the other hand, can think of themselves as seeing the long-range good of the mission that they have to carry out. They often see the short-range immediate accomplishment orientation of the politically appointed official as really being detrimental to the overall goal in the long run. Just a quick example from my own area of responsibility which is the Government's Equal Employment Opportunity Program. It's apparent to me that I'm thinking in terms of lasting improvements over an extended period. But my bosses want to see improved statistics this year, and substantially improved next year. I just throw that out as a kind of conflict that can arise when career executives and political executives, working toward a similar overall objective, find that their subgoals really don't mesh very well. Of course, it is just possible that very conflict works toward the best outcome!

Margulies: I can confirm your point from my vantage point. In the health area we have two personnel systems: the Civil Service and the traditional commissioned corps made up of people who in the past could rise to the rank of Surgeon General. Now political appointments can come in at all the top levels. The sense of loyalty between the two is strikingly different. They both serve the political administration which is in, but the corps people identify with the permanent corps and the people who come in from outside identify much more with where they came from and will be returning. Both of them can be politically sensitive and responsive but the loyalties are quite different with the two.

Lowell: The appointees are often brought in with the idea of reform in mind. So they need to move in quickly and take reform measures sometimes even before they are fully knowledgeable about what it is they are reforming. Change for its own sake can become very important. Few stay long enough to live with the results of their changes. I'm in a very interesting and unusual agency from that standpoint. I've been with the Civil Service

Commission for 16 years and, up until last January, two of our three commissioners had been there longer than I had. They really were no longer viewed as Democratic or Republican political appointees; rather they had become identified with the Civil Service Commission. They'd been there through 3 or 4 administrations. In January, 1977, President Carter appointed three new Commissioners. They came in as representatives of political parties and, even more significant, as representatives of a President who specified in his political campaign that he wants to reform the bureaucracy which has been so unresponsive. So they are really more identified with him than they are with the agency. I would say that's probably still true after a year and a half. They are still seen probably by the majority of people as outsiders who have come in to do a one-time job.

Haughey: Any other comments on decision-making in general or on this essay's adequacy in introducing the subject matter of our volume?

Dungan: This is an excellent topography, but like all descriptions, in dissecting the processes, one loses something of the actual dynamics. It tends to understate the complexity of the relationships and also takes something of an excessively negative view about what individuals can and should be doing. It places more strictures on personal freedom to take risks than I believe is desirable. For example, the reference to the lawyer in the Antitrust Division being worried about meeting with people who hold a client's viewpoint and reluctant to deal with them on a professional level to discuss the matters of mutual concern. Also, the elected official worrying about whether the anti-war people are going to support his efforts in non-war, peace-related matters. I would say that it's his responsibility not simply to follow but also to lead. You describe him as a person who's being pushed around by the forces out there. I think what is overlooked there is the role of politician as educator as well as representative. To my mind, that's a very important facet of the elected representative's role. And beyond the elected officials to the bureaucrats—I have a terrible sense of people not standing up and saying, "That's foolish, that's wrong, that's incorrect, or that's inappropriate.'' There is too much sitting back and second-guessing somebody up the line. "The Secretary won't like this," or "the Congressman won't think that's right." They've never tried! They've never engaged him in a human dialogue or even tried to approach him in many cases. They usually are restraining themselves for fear of pushing, I think, too far, and being themselves, right or wrong.

Margulies: I agree. I see too many employing a no-risk approach for their own security or convenience. They presume what the next level of decision will be and don't care to challenge it even if they think it's wrong. People are much too frightened, really frightened for their careers. The head of my department, whom people fear, will fire people without hesitation. But even before him, when we had a specialist in academic history who, instead of making too many decisions, never made any, there was still the desire too frequently to say what was expected of one rather than what one thought. The freedom to challenge decisions in our agencies is far greater than is suspected or used.

Dungan: There are risks. Let me give you an example. The other day we were up on the hill testifying before the Oversight Committee on Human Rights, and getting a lot of grief from a group of so-called moderate Human Righters who were complaining that the Administration was applying standards unequally. At one point, to the consternation of my colleagues, I said, "Well, Congressman, with all due respect, don't you think that perhaps the Congress is somewhat responsible for this because of the way they wrote the legislation which provided insufficient guidelines to the Executive Branch for applying these standards?" Immediately, they are all beating their breasts and accusing themselves of not being wholly responsible in drafting the legislation. I'm not trying to pose as a brave fellow—but if that intervention had not occurred, the record would have shown . . . "The Executive Branch is irresponsible, inconsistent, stupid, insensitive, etc." Furthermore, I think the result of the ensuing dialogue may advance both the legislative and the executive understanding of the "rights" issue in all its complexities.

Silverstone: You raised the issue of risk-taking. This is a very serious problem, but for the most part, people in the bureaucracy may appear faceless and complaisant because that is what the political leadership wants. Early in my government career, I was a lawyer dealing with contracts, among other matters. One of the staff people in the contract office, who did his best to avoid making decisions on his own responsibility, used to busy himself writing messages to his file cabinet. His perception of every conversation and every event in which he was involved would be duly recorded and put into the cabinet. I was dumbfounded and disturbed by this behavior. When I inquired, he patiently explained that it was necessary to be prepared for whatever might come, and a brash youth like me should not be so quick to condemn those more experienced than I. Well, the day came when there was an investigation of the contract operation. It was all over the newspapers. There was nothing really wrong, except for inefficiency and ineffective contract policy, but other groundless allegations were implied, as frequently happens when people look for administrative rationality in government operations. My friend had this massive documentation to cover himself in a situation where it was pretty much everyone for himself at the lower echelons. Outrageous as his behavior had been in terms of good administration, it turned out to be quite rational in an environment where those who take risks, and (as in this case) those who don't, may be left to fend for themselves.

Gessert: John Silverstone's remarks reminded me of something I wanted to mention. A lot of decision-making takes place in government as adversary or advocacy proceedings rather than on the basis of values or moral judgments. In the Defense area, there are adversary proceedings, if you will, between the Arms Control Agency and the Defense Department; between the Defense Department and the State Department; between them and the White House, etc. In some sense we have tried to make these serve as normative procedures. Maybe it's because we have so many lawyers in government but we seem to reduce many key decisions within the government to an adversary or advocacy proceeding where you make the best argument that you can possibly make as a lawyer would make it in litigating a case for his client—quite independent of whether or not you think that's the right thing to do. I'm uneasy about that development within the government. It is not critiqued by academicians and ethicists. One final point: in this paper, on the whole, you regard the special interests, the lobbying activities, as something that should be resisted rather than caved into and I think you need some normative judgment about that. There are some special pleadings that are in fact worthy. I would suppose that you and I could judge them to be taken on notably moral grounds. Just because they're special pleadings doesn't necessarily mean they are less moral or less insightful or wrong.

Breslin: I have been trying to give some thought to the issue of power and what kind of decision-making power those of us on Congressional staffs actually have. We have a self-limiting power, as I now see it. I can't think of anybody on the staffs I've studied and been involved with who has ever made a suggestion to a Senator that doesn't take into account two factors. One is: Will it kill or help him politically? The second is: If it kills or helps him politically, it's going to affect my career. I won't stay in politics if he isn't re-elected. That's a very powerful and conservative factor. Staff members make continual decisions on what to allow their Member to be confronted with and what to filter out. What a Senator sees or doesn't see is often determined by these on-going judgments. And, I have found that many staff members use their position to protect their Senators from "controversial" issues.

Salzberg: There was an earlier comment suggesting that legislative staffs have little public visibility and accountability. I accept the visibility part, but I'm not sure one could say we're not publicly accountable. We are accountable for everything we do in the sense that our members are made accountable to the public.

Silverstone: Brian, I think that you will find that those you lump into Housekeeping and Maintenance have a far stronger role in and access to and control over decisions than you indicate in your paper.

Dungan: I agree. It's an extremely important element in this whole process. Such elementary things as whose call gets through, how she treats clients, how sharp she is in making judgments, the amount of time other people can spend, etc.

Lowell: Have you ever sat in your office when your secretary really didn't know you were there and heard decisions being made for you? Substantive ones at that! I've found myself in one or two positions—either marvelling "How come I'm getting paid this much and she's making a better decision than I would have?" or "How am I going to amend the damage she's done, not to mention let her know that I overheard this without ending our entire relationship?"

Silverstone: I have spent over twenty years in government service, and I'm still trying to find out where decisions are made. Certainly in the Congressional/Executive relationship, it is often hard to pinpoint where an idea began. Who makes policy? Before I joined the Air Force Secretary's office in the 1950's I was taught some people make policy and some people carry it out. I had been on military duty before coming to Washington, and some of my old associates said it must be nice to be in the Secretary's office because that is where policy is made. It was nice, but I did not see much policy made there. A lot of papers were signed, but their substance was pretty well set before they reached the office. And when they came in, there was no time to identify and study all the issues and implications. I went to my friends in Charlie Wilson's office, and said: "It must be nice to be in the Secretary of Defense's office because that is where policy is made." Well, their answer was pretty much like my own. And, believe it or not, that is what the folks in the White House said, too. Well, so far as the White House is concerned, maybe there were some really big decisions that were made by Ike, such as the decision not to undertake active military operations in Indochina. But the everyday decisions, the things that affected most people's lives, weren't actually decided; they happened. Of course, in those times there were those who said that the decisions were being made by George Humphrey, over in the Treasury Department.

But I didn't know anyone there to ask. On the basis of the evidence I could collect then and from my experience since, it became clear to me that no one makes policy. You cannot pinpoint responsibility for decisions and you cannot identify where they start. I have overstated the case, perhaps, and if pressed I might admit exceptions to this blanket principle. But they are exceptions.

2
Values, Rules and Decisions

John Langan

I
MORAL UNCERTAINTY

There are times in our lives when we know that being moral or upright is very difficult, and other times when we think that it is an ordinary and everyday quality which we expect to find in most of the people around us. Much the same thing holds true for our ordinary views about moral knowledge. Sometimes we think that everyone knows what is morally right, that moral knowledge, unlike scientific or historical knowledge, is universally available to everyone who looks into his soul or hears the voice of her conscience. At other times we think of moral knowledge as something very difficult or even impossible of attainment. These are times when we are caught up in seemingly endless controversies about whether abortion is right or wrong or when we reflect on the inconclusiveness of most ethical theories. We are especially likely to think this way when we feel a deep perplexity about what we ought to do in a situation that has been thrust upon us.

A classic example of the uncertainty that we sometimes find in our practical lives is found in the following passage where a famous philosopher considers the principle that "goods held in trust are to be returned to their owners." This principle has been examined by philosophers since the time of Plato.[1] On the one hand, it seems to be a direct consequence of such attractive general principles as "The rights of others are to be respected" and "Agreements are to be kept," while on the other hand it seems to lead to such unacceptable conclusions as holding that it is right to return a weapon to its owner if he is insane or dangerous. Now our famous philosopher in considering this principle and the problems to which it gave rise, makes the following observations, which illustrate the difficulty of applying general principles to cases. He says:

> "This [the principle] is true in the majority of cases, yet a case can crop up when to return the deposit would be injurious, and consequently unreasonable, as for instance, were it to be required in order to attack one's country. The more you descend into the detail the more it appears how the general rule admits of exceptions, so that you have to hedge it with cautions and qualifications. The greater the number of conditions accumulated the greater the number of ways in which the principle is seen to fall short, so that all by itself it cannot tell you whether it be right to return a deposit or not."[2]

The famous philosopher who takes this somewhat sceptical and permissive line is a writer who is normally not noted for either scepticism or permissiveness. He is Thomas Aquinas. The difficulty of arriving at a specific judgment about just what action ought to be done, which Thomas here points out in rather general terms, is something that we are already familiar with from our work and our personal lives. It is a difficulty that should not be evaded but that should be regarded as indicating a limit to what even the most sophisticated system of moral casuistry can do in forming our moral judgment. It is vitally important, as Aristotle pointed out long ago, that we ask no more of ethical theory than it can give us:

> "We must be content, then, in speaking of such subjects and with such premisses to indicate the truth roughly and in outline, and in speaking about things which are only for the most part true and with premisses of the same kind to reach conclusions that are no better."[3]

Now the purpose of this essay is not to present nor to argue for a particular moral theory nor to persuade people that they ought to adopt a moral point of view or to undergo a moral conversion. Rather, it aims to suggest some ways of thinking about our lives as moral and rational agents that may clarify the experiences of conflict and uncertainty that are characteristic of our efforts to do the right thing and to lead morally upright lives.

II
A STRATEGY FOR THINKING ABOUT MORALITY

In thinking about morality, it is worth bearing in mind that, while morality has or should have a place of special importance in our lives, it is only one of many concerns that engage our practical energies and that it competes for our attention and commitment with these other concerns, that is, with the desires, the hopes, the anxieties, the inclinations that we have for ourselves, for those dear to us, for groups that we belong to, for humanity and the world at large. We are interested in survival and security, in sustenance and shelter, in sport and spectacle, in sex and science, in sociability and salvation. Even though not all of us are interested in all of these things, it is true that all of us have interests and desires outside of our concern for morality that are important to us, and that are at least potentially in conflict with it. The plurality of desires and interests that we have as individuals is important not merely for us in our personal lives but also for the larger society in which we participate. For social policy has to be shaped in ways that are sensitive to the different weights that different groups attach to different interests. The plurality of our desires and interests, though it presents problems for moral theory and practice and for social policy, is also a sign of the complexity and potential richness of our lives; and it is a source of the variety and fascination of the human condition.

But we cannot accept this plurality of desires simply as a given; we have to organize it into some coherent plan of life for ourselves as individuals and into a coherent set of policies for our society. This is a task which the mainstream of moral philosophy from Plato[4] and Aristotle[5] down to John Rawls[6] and Robert Nozick[7] in our own time has assigned to reason. A key part of this task is to relate our desire for the morally good, our desire to be upright and virtuous, our desire to follow the guidance of conscience, to our other desires and interests in a way that is both theoretically intelligible and practically helpful. We could attempt to work out those relationships primarily on the subjective side, that is, within the moral psychology of the individual; and we would then focus on the order and relation of our desires to each other. An obvious risk in this strategy would be that we would be approaching the ordering of our desires within an implicitly individualistic framework with the goal of achieving a harmony of desires within the individual and of producing tranquility of soul; the claims of goods that challenged this tranquility might well be ignored, and social life and social goods might well be reduced to mere means to individual fulfillment.

Alternatively, we could work mainly on the objective side, on the side of the goods that are to be desired. The risk of this strategy would be that we would end up with an ordering of goods whose relationship to the actual desires of persons would be obscure and problematic and that might contain unacknowledged elements of subjective preference and cultural bias. An example of this would be the contention of Aristotle[8] and Aquinas[9] that the highest good for human beings consists in the contemplative activity of theoretical reason directed to the noblest objects. This is a view that may well be true, but it cannot be denied that it leaves many people somewhat cold and inclined to say, "That may be a philosopher's idea of happiness, but it certainly isn't mine."

An intermediate strategy that may avoid some of these risks is to consider the notion of value, a notion which has both objective and subjective aspects. Once we clarify this notion to some extent, we can then make some suggestions on the relation of moral values to values more generally considered and also consider some of the features of an approach to morality via the notion of values as compared with an approach to morality by way of the notion of rules. The effort here will be to provide instruments for understanding experience and not to propose a particular moral theory or set of standards for right action.

III
VALUES

We can begin with the thesis that values are common characteristics of things to which we have an affirmative relationship. This rather abstract point can be clarified in three ways: First, values are both objective and subjective. It has been fashionable in some intellectual and popular circles to think of values as simply private, subjective attitudes that we adopt to things. "After all," we say to someone with whom we disagree, "that's just your value judgment." Also, we do know that people have disagreements about what things are valuable and that they usually don't make much headway in settling these disagreements. We sometimes speak as if different people made up their own values, more or less arbitrarily, and we give up the project of looking for a common standard or norm of values. We get used to thinking about values as mushy and ill-defined in contrast to facts and figures, or as something like a perfume, attractive but hard to label or to locate. Now I want to argue against this way of thinking about values and to propose that we think of values as real features of things to which we respond. When I experience the majesty of the Rocky Mountains, I don't simply see some jagged peaks about which I decide to have a favorable reaction. No, when I experience them, I am overwhelmed—the value in them in some way lays hold on me. Similarly, when I am sick in the hospital and I experience the friendly presence of a nurse or a doctor or a visitor, this can be a therapeutic and valuable experience and it can stir a response of hope and gratitude, of renewed strength and trust. It is part of my whole response to things and persons in the world, that I find them valuable. I don't *make* them valuable. They *are* valuable, and I respond to their value. Now things can be valuable in many different ways, because they meet my physical, or my emotional needs, because they produce emotional states in me, because they give aesthetic pleasure, because they are morally good, because they are religiously inspiring, because they are associated with other good things and remind me of them. This means that we all live with a plurality of values, to which we are not equally sensitive and to which in fact some of us may be rather insensitive. Thus we probably all know people whose awareness of aesthetic values is almost nonexistent, just as there are people who are color-blind. Everyone finds food valuable because it meets a basic and universal human need, but some people don't care about its look, or its taste or its aroma. Since values also have a subjective element, they have to be experienced. Many values have to be learned and taught as well, for instance, because they involve response to complex wholes that are not readily understood or reactions to the feelings and thoughts of other persons or the use of skills that we have to learn. If I don't learn some language, there is nothing I will find witty. If you don't tell me how you feel, how can I learn the value of sympathy? Subjectively, we respond to values in many different ways, which Aristotle lumped together under the general heading of appetite and which William James spoke of as pro-attitudes. We can esteem, be moved by, preserve, buy, consume, remember, praise, wear, laugh at, grieve for, venerate, adore the things that we value. What is common to all of these responses and reactions is first, that they move from me back to the valued things and thus take me out of myself in some way and, second, that they are affirmative and thus welcome the connection that exists between me and the object. Neither the variety of our responses nor the fact that some of them are learned nor the fact that some of them are not universally shared requires us to think that values are purely subjective. We encounter values as given in our experience of the world and the things in it.

The richness and interest of our lives depends to a crucial extent on the variety and character of the values that we respond to. Here the extent and the character of our education is tremendously important as well as our willingness to share the experience of persons different from ourselves who can broaden and deepen our experience of new values.

A second clarification for our original thesis about values has to do with what may have seemed to be the most puzzling and abstract feature of it, namely, the claim that values are common characteristics of things and not things themselves. The reason for this is that we need to distinguish between values and the things that embody and carry value. Individual things or persons are not identical with values, though they are valued or valuable.

The extent to which values can be separated from the things that embody or incarnate them varies quite a bit depending on the nature of the values involved. Thus one loaf of bread is as good as another in satisfying my hunger. But the aesthetic value of a Rembrandt is different from that of a good copy. The love that I experience from one person is not simply replaced by the love of another person, though some limited substitution is possible. Also, a particular thing or person can embody several different values. A loaf of bread satisfies my hunger; but if it has been baked by my mother or my wife or my son I may experience it as a manifestation of love and care. Also, values are not incompletely realized in things. No one act of love captures once and for all the value of love, no one painting or landscape exhausts the value of beauty.

In summary, individual things and persons and activities are not to be identified with values, but are instances of embodiments or realizations of values. This is, I think, one reason why we so often speak of values themselves in abstract language—e.g. truth, beauty, honesty, efficiency.

Third, the way in which I have been speaking may be misleading if it suggests that we have, or should have, a merely passive, receptive attitude toward values. While the account of values that I am proposing avoids the pop existentialist notion that we somehow create our own values, we should recognize that we often have to make or bring about the things and situations and actions that are embodiments or realizations of value. This is clearly true with regard to machines that are efficient and histories that are truthful and paintings that are beautiful. It is also true with regard to actions that are loving or generous or courageous. But we also bring moral values into being by the things that we suffer when we are patient and by the things that we refrain from doing when we are tempted.

The two principal spurs to our activity in making values real are imitation and correction. We see or experience something valuable, and we want to do something similar, to carve a beautiful sculpture or to give a generous gift or to make a hole in one. Or else we experience disvalue in a situation: pain or need or fear or discomfort, or guilt, or anger, or insecurity and we want to do something about it. We feel the urgency of bringing about something valuable in the situation. We want to correct injustice, to feed the hungry (including ourselves), to eliminate pain, to replace a slum with decent housing, to clean up our rooms, to confess our sins. In imitation, the value pulls us to action; in correction, the disvalue pushes us to action. Values and disvalues are motives, that is, they move us to action. In short, we feel the necessity of action to bring about value; and normally in our lives as human agents this involves our having an idea or plan of what we want to do. This idea or plan is really a more or less specific form of the value we want to realize or embody—an idea of health or justice or beauty or honor. The more specific this idea is, the more likely it is to be personal and unique and the more likely it is to provoke disagreement and criticism from other people, who may also want to bring about instances of justice or goodness but who have their own ideas of what constitutes justice or goodness and of what things and situations embody it. Here also we find that values are influenced by the beliefs that people have, common-sense beliefs, scientific beliefs, religious beliefs, all of which shape the plans we form to realize our preferred values.

Now, if you reflect on the general account of values that I have been proposing, you can see that values, however abstractly we talk about them and even if we give them big capital letters, are among the most common and ordinary things in our lives. In Molière's *Le Bourgeois Gentilhomme*, M. Jourdain makes the remarkable discovery that he has been speaking prose all his life without knowing it. Similarly, we have been experiencing and embodying and realizing and aiming at values all our lives. This doesn't make us remarkable or exceptional in any way—just normal human beings. We may be more or less successful in realizing the values that we aim at, and that will say a lot about how happy we are. Of course, our actions will say most about what we commonly call "our values," that is, the values that attract us to activity and the disvalues that impel us to do something. A person's sense of values shapes the way she organizes her life, the kinds of choices she makes. As you can see from your own experience, there are many values and different kinds of values that we can respond to and attempt to realize. But, especially as we grow older, we build up habits of response, or non-response to certain kinds of values, which turn us on or turn us off. We assign, usually in an informal way, priority to some values over others; and this shows up in our patterns of choice and action. Thus we find that certain values are dominant in our lives or are characteristic of ourselves and other persons. We become careful, compassionate or brave or skillful in a sport or a craft. We change things around us so that they are orderly or beautiful or efficient. We also learn to put up with the absence of certain values that we cannot realize either because they exceed our powers or because attaining them will conflict with other values that we prize more highly. Thus I realize that I will never attain the speed of a four-minute miler or show the heroic solicitude for the needs of the poorest that marks Mother Theresa of Calcutta.

As we go on in life, we discover new values or new forms of old values; when this is a matter of fundamental values, we have a process of conversion that sometimes surprises us and even the people closest to us. Sometimes the attractiveness of old values fades. As St. Paul says, "When I became a man, I gave up childish ways" (1 Cor. 13, 11). Sometimes, this change is a matter of growth, sometimes it is a matter of loss and defeat. We also discover the ways certain values are connected to each other or are in tension with each other. Thus we find that seeking power and having trusting relations with all our neighbors are efforts to realize different values and that we cannot sustain both these efforts, even though there is no strict logical incompatibility between these values in the abstract. There is for each of us a limit to the values we can attempt to actualize in our lives; and there is a certain sadness in recognizing this. There is even greater sadness when, because of fear and distrust, we come nowhere near this limit. And there is sometimes disaster and even tragedy when we overstep this limit. When we get near the limit, whether as individuals or as members of social institutions, there are usually difficult decisions to be made. As we grow older, we should, I think, get wiser and firmer about our values and also more tolerant of different values and the alien forms these often take.

Now a lot of our thinking and our talking about values has been focused on values in the life of the individual person. We might look in the world as a collection of passengers in ship, each in his or her own cabin with a personal set of values which he or she is trying to realize. But this would be a sadly incomplete picture. For one thing, it overlooks the importance of social contacts and social context in teaching us values and in providing us with the conditions that make the pursuit of personal values possible. Most of our values, the values that are operative in our lives, we have learned from others; and we depend on others in our efforts to realize them. Also, a dialogue with other persons is the principal means of extending our own sense of values, and of grasping new ways of realizing values. Furthermore, a shared community of values is especially important in sustaining our awareness of values that we sometime lose sight of and in sustaining our commitment to values that are hard to make real. It is vitally important to us that other people value us and value our efforts to realize our central values. Also, some of the most important values in our lives are not to be realized by us individually, but in our collective life. Peace, order, social justice, charity, liberty, sense of community all require that people live together in certain ways. The ship we are on has common rooms as well as personal cabins and also rooms where people join together in small groups. The values to be realized by society at large, by churches, hospitals, clubs, corporations, labor unions, schools and families, all require social cooperation and social values.

Working out the activities and the situations that will realize these social values is a process that requires an enormous amount of dialogue and interaction. It's what a free society is all about. This process requires vast social experience and patience, and it is, I think, getting more difficult all the time as people make more and more demands on the social system, in order to realize more values. Carrying this process on to a conclusion requires that we have certain ground rules, that there be certain moral and legal norms for weighing the values and rights of different persons in society. The massive book by the Harvard political philosopher, John Rawls, *A Theory of Justice*, is one effort to do this. Educating and encouraging people to respond to more and different values may make for richer lives for some people, but it also makes for a more difficult task for society and its managers. As I've indicated, responding to values and trying to realize them in our lives is something that we all do all the time. We should recognize that response to values does not of itself bring about a moral transformation and is compatible with a high level of selfishness and aggressiveness. Some values such as power can be very dangerous in their embodiments. The pursuit of values can involve a great deal of social conflict, especially when there are rival claims to one thing which is an embodiment of values for different people.

The point of these observations is that values alone are not enough. We need decisions about what values to pursue and moral and legal *rules* to guide these decisions and regulate the whole process. Here we find the lively areas of disagreement that make people feel sceptical about values and value judgments. But here also we find the strongest need for dialogue and decision in a democratic society and the greatest contribution of intelligent and sensitive leadership. We can also see the reason for the special place that moral values, both individual and social, have because they enable us to hold together in our personalities and in our social institutions the various drives and desires that we have to realize and enjoy the values that attract us. So we need courage in aiming at important values that are difficult to attain, temperance and moderation so that some values do not monopolize our attention and distort the structure of our personalities, prudence and honesty in weighing and knowing our values, and justice in acknowledging the claims of others to their values.

As you can see, these moral values presuppose the existence of other values that attract and motivate us, and so we can think of them as second-order values or values about other values.

IV
SACRED VALUES

As an anticipation of some of the specifically religious issues to be treated later in this volume, I would like to offer some comments about a category of values that have special importance, namely, sacred values.

Each of us could begin by asking himself or herself: what are your sacred values? This is a question that can be asked and at least partially answered by each of us, even those who do not have strong religious beliefs. For sacred values have certain characteristics that can be considered independently of religious belief. They are not found only in churches or in theological treatises, but in our lives. First, they have priority. No value can really be sacred for us unless we give it a high priority in our set of values, unless we are prepared to sacrifice other, lesser values for it. We may sometimes fail to make these sacrifices, but then we are doing just that—we are failing. Second, sacred values are ultimate; that is, they are connected with the ultimate mysteries of understanding the world and the meaning of our life in it, of our individual personalities and destinies, of suffering and death. They are values that we relate to ultimate questions and that we do not understand as momentary satisfactions. For instance, when St. John tells us that God is love, he tells us that the ultimate source of our being and of the world's being shows the characteristics of concern and benevolence and generosity and that love is a sacred value. Third, sacred values are given. That is, they are not made or manipulated by us. In our religious awareness, in our spiritual lives, in our peak experiences, we are aware that some values are supremely good and real. They are, as we say, what life is all about; and they help us to say who we really are regardless of the success or failure of the particular projects we are engaged in. Fourthly, sacred values are transcendent. That is, they take us out of ourselves, our schemes and our plans. Though our experience of these values is profoundly fulfilling, our fulfillment, even our attainment of these values is less important to us than the values themselves. As Isaiah said when he saw Yahweh enthroned in the temple and heard the seraphim proclaiming his holiness, "Woe is me: For I am lost; for I am a man of unclean lips, and I dwell in the midst of a people of unclean lips; for my eyes have seen the King, the Lord of hosts" (Is. 6, 5). Fifthly, sacred values are in the long run unitive. We know that religion has been a sadly divisive factor in the history of humanity, but I think that such divisions are the result of the entanglement of sacred values with other values, notably the desire for power. A good case can be made that, at least in the higher religions, sacred values are open to all persons, regardless of race or class or national origin and that since these values are spiritual, they are not divided when they are shared but are rather enriched and multiplied. In this respect, they are like knowledge and unlike money and material goods. Also, the attainment of sacred values is not marked in any important or interesting way by quantitative rankings or measurements. Thus it is a mistake for one person to want to experience these values more than another person does; there is no point in wanting to be holier than anyone else. This is a consequence of the unitive character of these values (my having more doesn't depend on your having less) and on their transcendent character (they take me out of myself). Sixthly, sacred values call us to a responsive way of life. While they are manifest to us as gift and grace and not as something that we make or accomplish, they do not leave us inert or passive spectators, but call us to enter into a new way of life in which they will influence and transform our desires for other values. In the Christian tradition, God graciously gives faith and justification and calls on us to do works of love. These works, the actions that are our response to sacred values, are embodiments or realizations of these sacred values (love, peace, knowledge) or of values that are thought to be akin to them. But it is important for all of us to see that people of other religious traditions can share in this work of embodying and realizing sacred values, which they understand in their own way. The work of realization is itself a meeting ground for those who enter into it.

Now its shared commitment to the embodiment and realization of God's love involves the religious community very deeply in the world and its values, which are precisely what we mean by secular values. For Christians and for Jews as well, the effort to realize values in response to the sacred value of God's love involves a turning back to the problems and values of the world.

There are two sources for this turn to the world that I would like to point out. One is the nature of love, which, in the classic definition of Aquinas, wills good for the other.[10] That is, in the terms we have been using, love desires the realization of value for others. Now, since God is perfect, we realize his love in us not by doing good or realizing value for him, but by sharing in love which he offers to our brothers and sisters. Love, like some of the

other virtues we mentioned, is a second-order value; it presupposes other values and directs itself to the realization of them
for others. So love in the religious communities of church and
synagogue has especially directed itself to realize those values
that are most closely akin to their sacred values—the sharing of
knowledge in education, aid to the poor and the needy, the healing work of hospitals, and the establishment of a just social order.
The precise institutional forms that these special ministries of
love take vary from age to age; but what is characteristic of all of
them is that they involve the religious community very deeply in
fundamental human concerns and values. Jewish and Christian
attempts to respond to sacred values and to realize values in
response do not take the form of creating a separate sacred world
but of working to make a more valuable common world. This is in
accordance with the Hebrew doctrine of creation, which affirms
the goodness of the world and its values and which is the second
main source of the Jewish and Christian turn to the world. In the
Biblical perspective, the realization of values, the opportunity to
lead a happy and fulfilling life is a sign of God's blessing and a
manifestation of his love. A ministry which meets the needs that
others feel is a sharing in God's own love. Jewish and Christian
theology have continually resisted every effort to separate the
God who created the world and its values from the God who
brings salvation. So the turn back to realizing human values in the
world does not represent a fall from grace to sin, but rather a
trusting response to God's love.

V

VALUES AND MORALITY

One basic reason why we have been thinking about our lives
as subjects of desire and as moral agents in terms of values is that
we needed a category that would be broad enough for us to see
the connections that are present and effective in our practical
lives. We did not want to adopt categories that would take as
fundamental the usual distinctions between sacred and secular, or
between ethics and politics or between individual and society or

even between self and others. This is not to deny that such distinctions can and should be made; for they are obviously important in a great deal of our thinking and activity. But it is an inherent part of the project that we have entered into that we need wider frameworks for understanding some of the connections that are often obscured by our more ordinary categories.

We also wanted a fundamental category that would be flexible enough to contain the divergent experiences and judgments of people who come from varied backgrounds, who hold beliefs that are often contradictory, who belong to different levels of society, and who go through different stages of life. The category of value can be applied to a wide range of phenomena in our lives in a tolerant and comprehensive way. Unlike those old favorites of moral philosophy, "the right" and "the good," it permits us to describe this range of phenomena in a reflective way without forcing us to take substantive or controversial positions in moral theory. For this reason it can also be a useful instrument in our efforts to understand the proposals and activities of those who hold moral and religious views that are at variance with our own. It is also an important instrument in thinking about changes in individuals and in society over time. Thus we are more comfortable with the claim that a person's or a society's values have changed than we would be with the thesis that what is right (as contrasted with what is thought to be right) had changed. (These may be two reasons why the notion of value is more commonly employed in the literature of the social sciences than in strictly philosophical or theological argument.) Of course, we should not be misled by the descriptive usefulness of the notion of value into thinking that we can avoid the hard questions of what things are really right or obligatory or into drawing illegitimate inferences from "X is ultimate value for Y" to "X is an ultimate value" or to "X is good."

More directly to our purposes, we can use the notion of value as the framework within which to make positive connections among ethics, religion, and the general direction of our practical lives. Thus, we have already indicated some ways in which sacred values in the Jewish and Christian religious traditions lead us back to service in the world. There are also in the Jewish and

Christian traditions close connections between moral values and sacred values, which are the bases for characterizing these traditions as forms of ethical monotheism. In these traditions God himself is morally good and loving as well as holy; and he requires morally good action from those who are his worshippers (cf. Jn. 9, 31).

VI
MORAL RULES

Adverting to the notion of values, and more particularly to moral values can also serve to broaden our understanding of morality or of what Bishop Butler in the eighteenth century spoke of as "the moral institution of life." Very often we think of morality as largely or even exclusively a matter of rules drawn up in a code. The religious origin of this way of thinking about morality is, of course, the Ten Commandments. The ultimate model is a legal one, and restricting our understanding of morality to this model produces legalism.[12] Debates about whether or not there are exceptionless norms of moral conduct, especially in the area of human sexuality, arose within a highly legalistic conception of morality. Legalism is also manifest in regarding a code of professional ethics as giving adequate or sufficient direction for the moral life of persons in a profession.

The central importance of moral rules, however, is not to be denied. Without some agreement on moral rules, no society could endure. The contemporary English philosopher, P.F. Strawson, has put the matter in the following terms:

"Now it is a condition of the existence of any form of social organization, of any human community, that certain expectations of behaviour on the part of its members should be pretty regularly fulfilled: that some duties, one might say, should be performed, some obligations acknowledged, some rules observed. We might begin by locating the sphere of morality here. It is the sphere of the observance of rules . . . This is a minimal interpretation of morality."[13]

It is important that we acknowledge the social basis and the social function of morality without taking a purely instrumental view of morality as merely, to use Strawson's term, "a public convenience." The function of certain elements of morality in preserving such social values as order, security, mutual trust, solidarity, and fraternity also enables us to see the basis for giving legal status to some moral rules. Strawson maintains that the content of this minimal level of morality has to include "the abstract virtue of justice, some form of obligation to mutual aid and to mutual abstention from injury and, in some form and to some degree, the virtue of honesty."[14] He rightly points out that recognizing the necessity for principles on this minimal level of moral rules serves to correct "the idea of unbounded freedom of choice of such principles on the part of the individual." This is, however, an idea that is more likely to appeal to romantic anarchists and to some existentialist and analytic philosophers than it is to either the general public or the shapers of social policy.

The minimal conception of morality and the functional view of moral rules that goes with it has been invoked to explain how morality can arise even in a collection of egoistic individuals, since even they would need it in order to attain certain social values that are required in order for them to pursue their own values.[15] But the minimal conception of morality, when combined with an egoistic theory of human motivation, is bound to be unstable and incomplete. It is unstable because it relies on the individual's pursuit of his own interests and values to keep him within the boundaries set by the minimal moral system. But while the existence of the system may be to the individual's advantage because it provides security and order, it is not always to the individual's advantage to obey its norms in particular cases. So it should not be surprising to find individualistic defenders of a "law and order" conception of morality engaging in various kinds of sharp practice, particularly when they think these are likely to go undetected and so will do little damage to the order of society. For minimal moral rules will come to be seen as merely barriers to the fulfillment of one's desires, unless the person develops a positive regard for moral values as such. When morality is seen as little more than a series of negative prescriptions, then, in moments when strong desires conflict with these prescriptions, the attraction of various non-moral values is likely to overwhelm an attraction to minimal moral values. This attraction is bound to be weak and ambivalent because these minimal moral values are conceived in largely negative terms. The point is not that proponents of a law and order conception of morality are insincere or hypocritical, but rather that their impoverished conception of the moral life is bound to leave them motivationally weak and divided. Something of the vulnerability of this minimal conception of morality, especially when it is applied to political life, lies behind the conclusion of Jeb Magruder's *An American Life*:

> "No one forced me or the others to break the law. Instead, as I have tried to show, we ignored our better judgment out of a combination of ambition, loyalty, and partisan passion. . . . If we consider how many people broke the law in the Watergate affair, men who were usually model citizens in their private lives, we must ask if our failures do not somehow reflect larger failures in the values of our society. . . . I and many members of my generation placed far too much emphasis on our personal ambitions, on achieving success, as measured in materialistic terms, and far too little emphasis on moral and humanistic values. . . . We had private morality but not a sense of public morality."[16]

VII
MORALITY OF RULES AND MORALITY OF VALUES

The minimal conception of morality is also incomplete because, by focusing so much on rules and principles, it neglects those states of character which we call virtues. These are habits of acting which enable us to do what is right in a way that is normally easy and congenial, so that virtue serves as a kind of second nature. In the words of Aristotle, "The virtue of man will be the state of character which makes a man good and which makes him do his own work well."[17] Understood in this way, virtues serve as means to doing what is right, and to conforming to the demands of moral rules. But virtues are also at the same time qualities of character which we find admirable and attractive in themselves. In fact, in the eighteenth century, David Hume took this attractiveness or tendency to elicit approval as the defining feature of virtue.[18] Virtues are, I would suggest, the prime exemplifications or embodiments of individual moral values. The positive attraction of a virtue such as honesty or fairness or justice or courage and the resulting desire to be a person exemplifying that virtue together contribute positively to the fulfilling of the demands of moral rules. But at the same time they provide goals to be pursued and challenges to growth in the moral life, since they can be possessed in greater or lesser measure and also can be exercised in different ways in different situations. Also, virtues stand in a complementary relationship to each other and are mutually reinforcing parts of the full moral development of the person.[19] It is, of course, clear that some virtues are easier than others for a given person to practice and that some figure more prominently in the character of a given individual than others. It is also true that moral and non-moral aspects of character are joined together in traits that attract us or evoke our approval. For instance, the courage of Churchill was accompanied by a certain bulldog style (as well as by an artful use of cigars). Usually our response to moral virtues and values is not to these in some pure state but as an embodiment by a particular individual. It is important to remember that moral values are carried primarily by persons. For this reason, one of the standard ways of passing on moral values is by telling stories about the actions of persons with suitable comments expressing approval and disapproval. We can here think of the kinds of attitudes and actions commended in political gossip, in lives of the saints and biblical stories, in feminist biographies, in Westerns and sports stories. We recall what was said earlier about the importance of imitation in our active response to values. Encouraging people to be attracted to virtue may sound both abstract and priggish; on the contrary, it is simply one aspect of something that we are doing all the time and that has an important influence on the kind of community we live in. This telling of stories is a central type of the praising and blaming which Aristotle took as indicative of our moral attitudes,[20] and it encourages the building up of certain habitual ways of acting. On the other hand, it does not offer much in the way of clear and specific guidance for the handling of new and difficult situations. For even in a coherent moral community, which contemporary America is not, different stories point in different directions; and appeals to different virtues or qualities of character can have contradictory consequences. For instance, loyalty and honesty conflict when it is a matter of telling a damaging truth about an old friend. We have been arguing that the minimal conception of morality is incomplete because it focuses on rules to the neglect of virtues, but it is also true that an approach that focuses on virtue to the neglect of principles, such as a morality of sincerity or of sympathy, is also incomplete.

The more serious difficulty with the minimal conception of morality as the imposition of rules on the appetites of individuals for the sake of order is that it fails to take seriously the fundamentally social character of morality. Strawson speaks of "a situation which everyone would agree to regard as characteristically moral, the situation in which there is reciprocal acknowledgement of rights and duties."[21] There is something profoundly misleading about the idea of a purely individual or personal morality, that is, a set of principles which I alone would acknowledge. A satisfactory account of morality clearly has to accord an important place to the conscience of the individual and to respect the privacy of personal decision. But the activity of conscience which is our power for making moral judgments about particular problems, normally involves weighing the conflicting values in a particular situation, applying principles to cases, and discerning the relevance of ideals or moral virtues to the situation. It would be an inappropriate extension of the functions of the individual conscience to regard it as the origin of moral principles and values. This would make the development of a moral community a matter of happy coincidence and would effectively reduce the scope of moral principles to claims about what I as an individual ought to do.

Now the minimal conception of morality as social restraints on the individual pursuit of self-interest goes beyond this purely individualistic conception of a morality of conscience, for in the minimal conception of morality principles or rules are intended to hold universally. The moral principles of the minimal conception meet the requirement of Kant's categorical imperative that "I can also will that my maxim should become a universal law."[22] This formal requirement of universality enables us to separate claims that are more or less disguised ways of advancing my self-interest from principles that by applying universally to all (myself included) make possible a mutual recognition of rights and duties. It also catches something of what is involved in the Golden Rule and in the New Testament story of the servant in debt who refused to forgive the debts owed to him. (Mt. 18. 23-35)[23] The formal requirement of universalizability, which most philosophers today regard as essential to any principles or norms that would claim to be moral, ensures that we conceive moral principles as applying equally to all. Contemporary moral philosophers also regard two other features as necessary for moral principles: 1) that they be prescriptive, that is, they require or prescribe certain kinds of actions, and 2) that they have a special status variously characterized as definitive or overriding or authoritative or supremely important.[24] In this last feature, moral principles, of course, come very close to sacred values as we characterized them earlier. It is clear that moral principles have a special urgency and seriousness. If a person regularly subordinates what he calls his moral principles to the pursuit of non-moral values such as power or prestige or convenience, we will conclude that he is being hypocritical in his profession of moral principles.

These two features together remind us that the affirmative response appropriate to moral principles and values is not one of contemplative admiration or of enjoyment, but one of commitment. As William James saw, the living of the moral life is a strenuous matter, made even more so for those who believe in God. As he puts the matter in his own vivid prose:

"In a merely human world without God, the appeal to our moral energy falls short of its maximal stimulating power. . . . When, however, we believe that a God is there, and that he is one of the claimants, the infinite perspective opens out. . . . The more imperative ideals now begin to

speak with an altogether new objectivity and significance,
and to utter the penetrating, shattering, tragically challenging
note of appeal."[25]

VIII

MORALITY AND LOVE

But a number of philosophers have felt that a purely formal
definition of morality in terms of universalizability, prescriptive-
ness, and authoritativeness leaves out a fundamental aspect of the
point of view that we take in making our moral judgments.[26] This
omitted feature, which I mentioned earlier as absent from the
minimal conception of morality is the other-regarding aspect of
morality. It can be found in utilitarianism, which requires that in
determining what the right action in a situation is, we take account of the consequences in pleasure and pain for all other persons.[27] It can be found earlier in Hume's observation that "sympathy is the chief source of moral distinctions."[28] Much earlier it
is present in one of the classic stories of moral instruction, the
parable of the ewe lamb which the rich man took from his poor
neighbor (2 Sam. 12, 1-15). This is a story which Nathan told to
David as a means of getting him to see what he had done in
arranging for the death of Uriah so that he might take his wife,
Bathsheba. As this story illustrates, sympathy in its moral aspect
calls us to go beyond our present perception of our interests, and
is not merely a matter of feelings that we happen to experience
with regard to those near us. Sympathy relies on imagination to
make this move beyond our immediate experience. Adam Smith,
who was a distinguished moral philosopher as well as a great
economist, stated this point clearly:

"Though our brother is upon the rack, as long as we
ourselves are at our ease, our senses will never inform us of
what he suffers. They never did, and never can, carry us
beyond our own person, and it is by our imagination only that
we can form any conception of what are his sensations. . . .
By the imagination we place ourselves in his situation, we

conceive ourselves enduring all the same torments, we enter
as it were into his body, and become in some measure the
same person with him, and thence form some idea of his
sensations, and even feel something which, though weaker in
degree, is not altogether unlike them."[29]

Without endorsing Smith's views on analogy as the unique way in
which we know the feelings of others, we can see that he has hold
of a very important point about the basis of our moral response to
the needs and claims of others. Our living of the moral life requires not merely the rational application of universal principles
to cases but also the exercise of sympathy and imagination for
understanding the consequences of our actions on the lives of
others, and the nature of their reactions to what we do.

A more prosaic and naive example of what is involved in
seeing things from the moral point of view is provided in a revealing confession by Jeb Magruder:

"I must admit that I did not fully consider just how
wrong our act of wire tapping was until I learned that Haldeman, Dean, and Ehrlichman—my *friends*—had secretly
taped their talks with me. I went into a rage. Those were
private talks. They had no *right* to do that. Finally I realized,
not just intellectually, but in my gut, that we had no right to
wire tap Larry O'Brien's phone, either."[30]

Here we can see the move to recognizing that principles (in this
case, both legal and moral) apply universally and to feeling the
hold, the obligatoriness of principles across the divisions created
by partisan and personal interests. We see also how, because of
the reversal involved in his friends' tapping of his own phone,
Magruder is brought to see matters from a perspective beyond
that provided by his own interest. This was a situation where
events taught what imagination and sympathy had failed to perceive. This episode may also suggest the dangers of relying on
sympathy alone in our approach to moral issues. For in our lives
the actual occurrence of sympathy with others is limited by the
interests and biases we have accumulated over the years.

Sympathy needs to be enlightened and extended by the principles and values that reason discovers in its moral activity. To be fully moral, sympathy needs to be made the basis for principles governing our treatment of all persons without losing the sensitivity to the needs of individuals that it can give us. To paraphrase a famous dictum of Kant's, sympathy without principles is blind; principles without sympathy are empty. We should recognize as a defining feature of the moral point of view and of moral judgments that they "involve or call for a consideration of the effects of his actions on others . . . not from the point of view of his own interests or aesthetic enjoyments, but from their own point of view."[31] The moral point of view understood in this way is a manifestation of regard for others; carrying out the demands of morality and responding to moral values is radically a work of love. In religious terms, it is a response to the sacred value of love that we believe to be at the root of all things.

NOTES

1. Plato, *Republic*, I, 331e-332a.
2. Thomas Aquinas, *Summa Theologiae*, I-II, 94, 4c, tr. Thomas Gilby, O.P. (New York: McGraw-Hill, 1966), v. 28, p. 89.
3. Aristotle, *Nicomachean Ethics*, I, 3, 1094a 19-23, tr. W. D. Ross.
4. Plato, *Republic*, IV, 439c-440b, 442c.
5. Aristotle, *Politics*, I, 5, 1254 64-5.
6. Cf. John Rawls, *A Theory of Justice* (Cambridge, Mass.: Harvard University Press, 1971), pp. 407-424.
7. Cf. Robert Nozick, *Anarchy, State, and Utopia* (New York: Basic Books, 1974), pp. 48-51.
8. Aristotle, *Nicomachean Ethics*, X, 7-8.
9. Thomas Aquinas, *Summa Theologiae*, I-II, 3, 8c.
10. *Ibid.*, I-II, 26, 4c.
11. Cf. Joseph Butler, Bishop of Durham, *Fifteen Sermons*; in *British Moralists 1650-1800*, ed. D. D. Raphael (Oxford: Clarendon, 1969).
12. For a criticism of the effects of legalism on the moral awareness of Catholics, cf. Louis Monden, *Sin, Liberty and Law*, tr. Joseph Donceel (New York: Sheed and Ward, 1965).
13. P. F. Strawson, "Social Morality and Individual Ideal," in

Readings in Contemporary Ethical Theory, ed. Kenneth Pahel and Marvin Schiller (Englewood Cliffs, N.J.: Prentice-Hall, 1970), p. 348.

14. *Ibid.*, p. 354.

15. Cf. Thomas Hobbes, *Leviathan*, Part I, ch. 14.

16. Jeb Stuart Magruder, *An American Life: One Man's Road to Watergate* (New York: Atheneum, 1974), pp. 317-318.

17. Aristotle, *Nicomachean Ethics*, II, 6, 1106a 22-23.

18. David Hume, *Enquiry Concerning the Principles of Morals*, Appendix I "Concerning Moral Sentiment," in *Hume's Moral and Political Philosophy*, ed. H. D. Aiken (Darien, Conn.: Hafner Publishing, 1970), p. 265.

19. Cf. Thomas Aquinas, *Summa Theologiae*, I-II, 65, 1 for a discussion of the interconnection of the virtues, a notion that derives from both Aristotle and the Stoics.

20. Cf. Aristotle, *Nicomachean Ethics*, II, 9, 1109b 17-24; III, 1, 1109b 30-34.

21. Strawson, p. 352.

22. Immanuel Kant, *Groundwork of the Metaphysic of Morals*, tr. H. J. Paton (New York: Harper & Row, 1964), p. 70.

23. The English moral philosopher, R. M. Hare, has interpreted his parable as suggesting the universalizability of moral principles and attitudes in his book *Freedom and Reason* (Oxford: Clarendon, 1963), pp. 90-111.

24. For an introduction to the issues involved in recent controversies over how morality is to be defined, cf. W. K. Frankena, "The Concept of Morality," in *The Definition of Morality*, ed. G. Wallace and A. D. M. Walker (London: Methuen, 1970), pp. 146-173.

25. Cf. William James, "The Moral Philosopher and the Moral Life," in *Essays on Faith and Morals*, ed. Ralph Barton Perry (Cleveland: World, 1962), pp. 212-213.

26. Cf. Frankena's writings, especially the essay cited above and *Ethics*, 2nd ed. (Englewood Cliffs, N.J.: Prentice-Hall, 1973), pp. 113-116. Also, Kurt Baier, *The Moral Point of View* (New York: Random House, 1965), ch. 5.

27. Cf. John Stuart Mill, *Utilitarianism*, ch. 2.

28. David Hume, *A Treatise of Human Nature*, Book III, Part III, Section VI, in *Hume's Moral and Political Philosophy*, p. 167.

29. Adam Smith, *The Theory of Moral Sentiments*, Part I, Section I, ch. 1; in *British Moralists 1650-1800*, ed. D. D. Raphael (Oxford: Clarendon Press, 1969), II, 201-202.

30. Magruder, p. 317.

31. Frankena, "The Concept of Morality," p. 156.

Values Conversation

Haughey: One of the unknowns in the interaction between personally appropriated and perceived values and public policies is the meaning of values. John's paper lights up a number of the obscurities in that terrain, not the least of which is our overall cultural assumption that values are somehow or other totally subjective. In clarifying this and a number of points, he proceeds to the subject of whether values are sufficient for public order. Finding they are not brings up the subject of rules and the need for some regulation of values. If I were to lead off with a question, I'd like to start from your own experience of the conflicts or the tension between personally held or perceived values and the public policies for which you are responsible in one way or another.

Dungan: I think you're forcing an emphasis on conflict which, speaking for myself, I don't often perceive. I do not personally experience tremendous value conflicts going on; at least conflict in a terribly burdensome moral or ethical sense. Therefore I find, to some extent, some of this rather artificial. In trying to delineate this thing are we perhaps in danger of dessicating it? I don't like setting this tone of values-in-conflict. Government work is like ordinary human life, you take things a step at a time and don't often find this conflict of which you speak.

Salzberg: As a U.S. representative on the Inter-American Development Bank, you obviously can forego making loans to some governments that don't have the best records in our eyes. I assume that some of these loans are not only important economically for the country concerned but are maybe critical for the resilience or the staying power of the government in office. In some of these cases, don't you find yourself weighing economic justifications for the loans as opposed to moral considerations for not supporting the loan?

Dungan: I think there are a whole range of moral considerations involved in the kind of situation you pose. But even before getting to those, I have to figure how good my information is. Will the loan indeed have the beneficial economic benefit that you, for example, have imputed to it? If I granted the loan that's going to have good effects on the people, will it at the same time have an assist-effect on a government which we consider to be bad? That's a political decision, not really a moral judgment, an ethical judgment.

Margulies: Well, does that reduce the moral issue to a political issue or merely disguise it from your observation?

Dungan: I'm saying it's a judgment in the practical order which may or may not be as sharply a moral question as we sometimes like to think it is. We can pose the question as a clear-cut moral issue when we may not even have enough information to make it that clear.

Margulies: Supposing it's just a fuzzy moral issue, as most of them are?

Breslin: What is your responsibility to get the information before you make your decision?

Dungan: I'm suggesting it's a possibility that we are constructing something that appears to be clearly good or bad, moral or immoral, when, as a matter of fact, I would say it's usually indifferent. It doesn't partake of some ethical value but what one is basically doing is making a prudential judgment in which you are saying that with all the information I have, I lean this way.

Breslin: I don't think the paper was saying "Here's the right answer or the right value" or "Here's a bad value". At least part of the argument was that there are many values that you can hold and therefore our responsibility in the decision-making process is to at least realize or take into account the conflicting values that there are.

Lowell: I agree with the fact that many government decisions are made in the absence of perfect knowledge. We just don't have the time, or the resources. They're just not available!

Salzberg: Or the insights, sensitivity or whatever.

Lowell: But it's that very absence of perfect knowledge that leaves both the room and the imperative for good judgment, moral judgment, value judgment. If I had perfect knowledge— if I knew I had all the facts and could line them up—I would almost feel compelled at the end of that to accept what came out of the facts. I would have no personal judgment to play. But it's the absence of this kind of condition that makes it necessary for me to bring to bear whatever values I've got because I know that ultimately I'm making a decision in the absence of perfect knowledge. If it's going to be a good decision it's only going to be good if my values are good and if I put those values to work on that decision.

Dungan: What I am terribly anxious about frankly is a kind of an assumption that we can be very close to sure that something is morally right or morally wrong. The very distance between oneself and those one is making decisions about in most government decisions makes it difficult to say anything more than "I've done my best". This is particularly true in the human rights area.

Salzberg: Let's take a situation where there's serious deprivation of human rights and the loan is not for a basic human need. I think there's a conflicting value situation. If the loan goes forward, it has a number of effects. There was, for instance, a loan to El Salvador, a $90 million hydro-electric power loan. I assume that must have been quite a significant loan to a country of that size.

Initially the administration told the Salvadorian government that we would oppose the loan so consequently they withdrew their application temporarily. Then there were some fairly marginal improvements in the situation in El Salvador but as far as I can determine, the situation today is as bad as it was then. Because there were seen to be some improvements, some commitments by the El Salvadorian government to lift some restrictions on human rights, we went ahead and voted for the loan. The situation is still as bad as it was. I'm not very happy with the way that was done.

Dungan: It's a very good case since it's small enough and discrete enough and I was heavily involved in the process. I did go through the ethical judgment question. The factors are essentially as you related them, John. The only one I would add was there was a change of government somewhat after the point where we held the loan back. Then some months later we came around and changed. I would say you were generous in saying there were marginal improvements in the human rights or civil rights area.

Salzberg: You might explain how there was a change in government.

Dungan: Yes, there was an illicit election loaded with fraud. It's a crowded country with a birth-rate over 3%. There was a situation as long as I've known that country where you've had an oligarchical situation—the famous fourteen families. It's a country with a very low consumption of electric power. The position of the U.S. government is to presumably keep pressures on the Salvadorian government not only to improve the rights of persons, but also to my mind a more important one, to develop economically. It's impoverished and from all signs it's going down not up. What is the long run economic answer to El Salvador leaving aside the human rights situation and the situation of the government? It is to go into some kind of light industry. What do you need for light industry? You're weighing here the interests of a group of people in a geographic entity whose long run vi-ability, no matter who's in power, depends on the ability to have energy at reasonable prices. This is my thinking but you take a gamble.

Margulies: It sounds to me like you were resolving this around the thesis presented in the paper, namely around a series of conflicting values.

Dungan: It's true, but I don't believe that either my decision or the U.S. government's decisions that I delivered were moral in the nice, clean sense.

Margulies: That's the point Janet was making, that they are not nice clean decisions but they're rather values in balance against other values which it sounds to me you were weighing in the case you just summarized.

Dungan: Sure, there are conflicts. I guess I have a tough time seeing them as nice clean, moral issues—issues of conscience.

Breslin: Why do issues of conscience have to be clear?

Dungan: Maybe I am a victim of my early education!

Margulies: It would be nice if they were but it would knock hell out of literature!

Dungan: If I might press this a little bit more. The oligarchy really didn't care about the electric generators. They get as much water as they need. If they don't get more water to raise crops, it really is no big thing to them.

Salzberg: You're saying that people who have influence in the Salvadorian society would not be hurt.

Dungan: Precisely. They are quite indifferent or they couldn't have gone on for the 20 years that I've known El Salvador with as much indifference to the needs of the poor.

Salzberg: Well, then I suppose for the masses of people their plight would have remained the same or worsened and I suppose the people would have no other recourse than revolution.

Dungan: That is a very likely outcome that you think is possible from inaction. Then that sets in train a whole bunch of other questions like: What is likely to happen in such a revolution? Are the revolutionary forces going to be capable of, you know, performing normal government functions?

Salzberg: You had mentioned that the hydro-electric power was important to develop the light industry. Is the presumption that, given your loan, the economic social structure will remain the same?

Dungan: No, it isn't my presumption. I would say that I don't think the Bank as an institution is very heavily involved in even having an idea, much less pressing its ideas about what the development priorities should be in El Salvador.

Breslin: I don't see how you can help but . . . I feel we underestimate our influence, both as a country and as an economic influence overseas. Whatever we do, even the fact that we are thinking about action, has an immense effect on another nation.

Gessert: I think we also tend to overmoralize it in this administration. I feel great empathy for Ralph's moral humility combined with moral sensitivity and I wonder if there's a distinction to be made between the extent to which values enter into our own judgments and the extent to which we try to use our values to pressure somebody else. This is very counter-productive. Among other things it imputes an immorality to the opposition and it imputes a morality to your own position. That's one of the more disturbing things to me about moralizing public policy. Carter's announcement of the Arms Restraint policy for example, puts us in a very embarrassing, very hypocritical, very vulnerable position, and puts our opposition into equally polarized positions. There's a distinction to be made between how much we use values to inform our own judgments and projecting that morality and proclaiming it.

Smith: A central part of morality is what is actually going to result from our actions if we do something. If we give a loan what are going to be the consequences? How much do you evaluate past performance? Unless there's some sort of evaluation as an individual and as a corporate institution there's something lacking in the moral decisions. What has happened in a comparable situation when we have done this before, in situations under different regimes?

Dungan: Your point is very well taken. We certainly don't do it as much as we should in the Bank.

Breslin: What I believe you are talking about, Ralph, are morals. These have an absolute tone to them, for example, *the* moral thing to do in Africa, *the* moral answer, *the* right thing to do. But values are something else. As a country I think we have always taken action on the basis of some value or another. So, you and our country value stability. We don't like revolutionary changes; our party system and our economic system to some extent support that value of stability.

Dungan: Let me tell you why I was reacting. I think, particularly since the Vietnam War, we are elevating what indeed are values into moral judgments.

Breslin: But haven't we always been doing that? Haven't we always seen stability to be a value and on the basis of this and other values proceeded on to make moral judgments?

Silverstone: Unless it's the stability of a communist system. We have always had a variety of values. There's a variety of values which conflict and there are hierarchies of value, and hierarchies within hierarchies, and exceptions.

Dungan: But we don't hesitate to destabilize.

Breslin: Obviously what we're talking about in El Salvador is a question of destabilizing.

Dungan: You're bloody well right it is! That's anti-stability, so there, you have a kind of moot value.

Breslin: Yes, but you made the decision based on the value that it was better for El Salvador to pretty much stay like it is with a greater chance of economic development versus what you might have decided, namely, not to issue the loan which could increase the likelihood of some kind of instability.

Silverstone: Well, it might with equal conviction be argued that bringing that "big" $90 million dam into "little old El Salvador" and promoting a big electric generator development is one of the best techniques possible to destabilize a situation because it could undermine the status quo.

Gessert: The question in an earlier part of our discussion had to do with the relationship between the sufficiency of our information and the moral rightness of our decisions. Sure, we need to know as much as possible but in the final analysis, I think, the key, the tough decisions we are asked to make are almost always decisions based fundamentally on values rather than being predetermined by what the facts of the case are. Often it's not true that more facts will give you more wisdom about how a case has to be resolved. I don't think information is the central issue at stake here. What is, I think, is the sense and depth of our own values and whether they are operative. We can be using them too in a banal or clichéd or politically rhetorical way. We tend very much, when we promote our foreign or domestic policies, to promote them as if they were value judgments and frequently make our value rhetoric a substitute for facts or knowledge. In fact we're not beyond suppressing some facts and knowledge in order to win our point on moralized grounds.

McCormick: I think a very careful distinction has to be made between the terms "moral", "morality" and "moralizing". I think what your objections are substantially aimed at is the term "moralizing" in political discourse, not an introduction of the term "moral" into it.

Gessert: I am, in brief, coming down on both sides of our conversation. I am with that part of the conversation that says there are conflicts of value and that moral sensitivities and moral judgments have to be brought to bear on them. On the other hand, I'm very much with Ralph in feeling that there is always a tentativeness in the public arena, it's always a judgment call, it's always a proximate solution. Virtually, all key decisions are made on a marginal call. What I'm saying, I guess, is that there ought to be two levels to this question of values, morals and decisions. One has to do with making the decision, the other with defending our our judgments or proclaiming them against our opposition or trying to explain what we are doing in the world. I think that at the exterior level to look for the best common denominator to explain our decisions has a distinctive moral quality to it rather than attempting to justify ourselves to the world on moral grounds. In part because they have to be explained and accounted for and debated in terms of a common denominator, so that we retain the flexibility to be proven wrong if that's the case and we grant to those we have defeated in the political decision-making process the benefit of having equal moral stature.

Dungan: I'd just like to underscore what you've just said. The intrinsic nature of most of the decisions I face involves choosing the less bad, if you will. There's something intrinsic in the decisions I'm involved in which precludes saying "That's right or that's wrong." It's terribly presumptuous, in this day and age, to be terribly sure. I was struck in John's paper where he observes that educating and encouraging people to respond to more and different values makes for a difficult task for society and its managers.

Silverstone: I think that the introduction of the word "moral" and the phrase "moral approach" into public discourse is unfortunate. I immediately reach for my wallet every time I hear the word "moral" in a politician's or a bureaucrat's defense of a political position. In the human rights area, I am uncomfortable with statements which appear to identify our policy with American or Western morality. They ignore the fact of the universal struggle for human rights that is going on throughout the world, and that is not the patented property of one tradition or people. Belief in the value of human integrity and dignity is widely shared, and there are many approaches to it. The implication of the American moral tradition argument is that human rights values are something which other people don't really have. Clearly, we've got to be sensitive to values, we've got to be moral, but we oughtn't ever imply in public discourse that morality is on one side or the other. Another observation I had: the real value questions don't surface in deciding policy. As you remember, my thesis in our earlier discussion was that policy is never really decided. The art of government is to structure the making of decisions in a way that the value issues are buried or are impossible to consider. We set up a process where the most frequent reactions are: "That's not what this committee does" or "It's not under our jurisdiction" or "It's the wrong forum". To keep the peace and to keep the system from being torn apart or overloaded, we structure ways of dealing with everyday events that avoid a direct confrontation of the value issues. Under normal pressures, the place where the value question is really vital is in fact-finding. There's Ralph over there at the IDB Executive Board wanting to do the right thing. What he decides is a relevant question to ask and investigate is influenced by his values. Facts just don't exist. They have to be perceived, found, and arranged; and that is done on the basis of what you think is important. Every actor along the line decides "What do I perceive is of value in what is coming before me?" Values are the basis for the decision as to what is relevant. And that is the most important decision that gets made—or happens.

3
Plural Loyalties and Moral Agency in Government
David Hollenbach

An important aspect of dilemmas of conscience for the public official is the experience of conflicting and overlapping loyalties to the different groups or communities to which the decision-maker belongs.[1] This essay will focus on the decision-making process from this point of view.

An agency staff member or bureau director has commitments not simply to general values and ideals but also (perhaps primarily) to concrete people. In the concrete process of decision-making, value judgments are heavily dependent on the persons and groups which claim one's loyalty. Public officials are bound to other persons by the ties of friendship. Their relationships to peers, subordinates and superior officers shape their value judgments in important ways. Most also have commitments to a political party. Elected officials are bound by commitments to their constituencies. Loyalties to the people and beliefs of a religious community, to all the other citizens of the nation and to the human community as a whole also enter the decision-making process, sometimes in crucially important ways. All these loyalties can be the result of interest group pressures or self-interested decisions about how to stay on top of the heap. But they can also represent the public official's genuine convictions about where moral commitment and loyalty should be placed. They express the moral values of an official in a most concrete way. Consequently, moral conflicts in public life can be fruitfully looked at as conflicts between these concrete commitments to various persons and groups.

In what follows, several theses will be set forth in hope of clarifying how this plurality of loyalties is an important clue in the effort to understand the moral life of government officials. I hope to show that a politician or bureaucrat can remain a genuine moral agent only to the extent that he or she both maintains and is conscious of this plurality of loyalties. It is precisely this overlapping of loyalties that keeps the bureaucrat from becoming a political opportunist. It is the continued effort to balance the claims of these different groups that makes the task of government more than simply a job.

Several well-known examples will illustrate how decisions about one's principle group loyalty are often of central importance in public action. When Eugenio Martinez was on trial for the Watergate break-in, Judge John Sirica asked him what motivated his action. Martinez responded by describing his loyalty to Cuba and his opposition to "Communist conspiracies." It pertained, he said, "to the Cuban situation. When it comes to Cuba and when it comes to Communist conspiracies involving the United States, I will do anything to protect this country against any Communist conspiracy."[2] In other words, Martinez' loyalty to the anti-Communist Cuban group in this country had undergone a process that Robert J. Lifton calls: "totalization"—an "all or nothing psychological plunge into a pseudo-religious ideology."[3] Such an ideology is pseudo-religious, for it serves the same identity-forming function as does religious belief. It engages the whole of one's personhood in a deep, overriding commitment. The dangers of such total and singular commitment are evident. Misplaced commitments of this sort have the effect, in Hannah Arendt's words, of "shielding men from the impact of reality and . . . ruining the mind's capacity for judgment and for learning."[4]

Commitment to a group and loyalty to one's role within the political process, however, can play an extraordinarily positive function in public morality. When Attorney General Elliot Richardson was ordered to fire Watergate special prosecutor Archibald Cox, he resigned rather than violate the pledge of political impartiality he had made to the Senate. His overriding loyalties were to his oath of office and to "the very integrity of the governmental process." Richardson's loyalties were apparently no

less firmly established than were Martinez's. But precisely because these loyalties were plural—to his oath of office, to the
President, to the Senate and to his fellow citizens represented
through the American governmental process, and perhaps to
friends and a public whose respect he desired—Richardson re-
tained his "capacity for judgment." Though his commitments
were real, they were not collapsed into that all-or-none psychological plunge of a totalistic ideology.

Reflection on these two cases raises an important issue
which needs clarification if we are to understand the responsibilities of government decision-makers from the moral point of
view. Martinez's actions point to the danger of overcommitment
to a cause or faction. Richardson's decisions show the value of
independence of judgment and multiple loyalties. We must ask,
however, how the government official can retain this independence of judgment and still function in a way that influences
governmental action. If we were to conclude that "exit" or resignation from office is the only option when loyalties conflict, government service would be deprived of the influence of groups
whose voices must be heard if totalization is to be avoided within
the bureaucracy itself. In a perceptive study, Albert O.
Hirschman has observed that the exit option seems a characteristic of the American spirit, rooted in our historical experience:

> Even though the opportunity to "go West" may have been
> more myth than reality for large population groups in the
> Eastern section of the country, the myth itself was of the
> greatest importance for it provided everyone with a paradigm
> of problem-solving. Even after the closing of the frontier, the
> very vastness of the country, combined with easy transporta-
> tion, makes it far more possible for Americans than for most
> other people to think about solving their problems through
> "physical flight" than . . . through ameliorating and fighting
> *in situ* the particular conditions into which one has been
> thrown.[5]

As Hirschman points out, this tendency to emphasize "exit" as
the appropriate response to conflicts of loyalty is a costly one. It

reinforces the need to conform on the part of those unwilling or unable to pay the price of exit. It also removes those with more broad-based loyalties from participation in the task of governing. In other words, the American acknowledgement of the validity of a pluralism of loyalties tends to be operative more in private life than in the decision-making of government officials while they are actually on the job. If this tendency is to be counteracted, we need to understand better how loyalty to one's office and to its job description can be actively combined with loyalty to other groups (e.g., family, friends, church, or even the nation or humanity as a whole).

ROLE-SPECIFIC MORAL OBLIGATIONS

As a first step toward understanding this interrelation of loyalties, the obligations that arise from assuming responsibility within government must be recognized. This can be stated in my first thesis: *One's role in government carries moral obligations with it which are role-specific*. In accepting a position within the government a person makes a commitment to fulfill the role assumed. This obligation is not simply a functional or mechanical one. It is a genuine claim on one's energy, time and personal creativity channeled through the job description of the role. The obligation is not a general one such as concern for the well-being of the nation or the world. One's role in government specifies particular responsibilities, sometimes in great detail. Such role-specific obligations as responsibility to superiors in an agency, faithful execution of assigned tasks, careful gathering of information and analysis of data, respect for "standard operating procedure", the use of one's intelligence and creativity—all these are genuine moral responsibilities and not simply practical "rules of the game." This is so because of the way human responsibility and agency is organized in any modern complex organization such as the government.

Modern organizations function through a division of labor. Action is facilitated by a diversification of roles. When it is properly structured, such differentiation of roles leads to a more effective processing of information, to better informed social decision and to a generally more effective pursuit of the task for which the organization or agency exists. As Kenneth Arrow has pointed out, the functioning of any bureaucracy depends on a *distribution* of both information and responsibility within the organization.[6] If all persons within an organization had to know everything about the task at hand, and if all persons were seen as equally responsible for everything done by the agency, the total amount of knowledge and responsibility of the group would be limited to what one person can know and do. Bureaucracy, organization and the differentiation of roles has the increasing of knowledge, responsibility and action as its primary purpose. Thus, from a social point of view, role differentiations within a bureaucracy can increase moral agency and responsibility. The various roles and positions within the organizational structure create role-specific obligations for those who occupy them because of this social purpose of bureaucracy. The responsibility to do one's job well, to analyze and communicate information accurately and to recognize both the scope and the limits of one's role is not simply a bureaucratic duty. It is an important part of the moral task of the government official. Loyal execution of these responsibilities is a genuinely moral enterprise.

Nevertheless, it is not without reason that "bureaucrat" has become an unsavory epithet in our society. Bureaucracies frequently fall far short of the goal of increasing knowledge, responsibility and socially effective action. They can and do become obstacles to achievement of these important social goals. Role-specific obligations and loyalties, therefore, are not exhaustive of the moral responsibilities of public officials. The genuine value of a job well done or a role well played can tend to obscure the weaknesses or breakdowns that are present within the organizational structure. Exclusive loyalty to role-specific obligations in one's agency or bureau can blind a civil servant to these weaknesses and breakdowns. This is so precisely because role-specific loyalties are morally significant. Were the tasks of government less important than they are, the psychological possibility of confusing moral responsibility with not rocking the boat would be considerably less than it is in fact.

In other words, the virtues of bureaucracy can also be its vices. The danger of "totalization" of one's loyalties is not limited to Cuban anti-Communists, Maoist revolutionaries or Red Brigade terrorists. A subtler but nonetheless dangerous form of totalization can occur in the Executive Office building, the regulatory agencies, the Pentagon or on Capitol Hill. This subtler form of totalization might be called white-collar ideology. It represents a loss of the sense that one's role-specific obligations have moral weight *only because* of the larger moral purpose of government and its bureaucracies. Complex organizations have an inherent tendency to deaden this sense of larger purpose because of the necessary specialization and focusing of vision which they call for from those who staff them.

At their worst, bureaucratically and hierarchically structured organizations have important similarities to what Lewis Coser has called "greedy institutions." These institutions, among which Coser includes the military and religious orders, "seek exclusive and undivided loyalty and they attempt to reduce the claims of competing roles and status positions on those they wish to encompass within their boundaries. Their demands on the person are omnivorous."[7] It would be a mistake to see all complex organizations as "greedy" in this sense. Nevertheless the demand to be a "team player" and to follow "the rules of the game" can be great indeed, especially for those who are upwardly mobile within the bureaucratic hierarchy.

The omnivorous demands of the institution are perhaps most notable in the military. This is so because of the extremely great importance of predictable action and accurate information in an area where human lives are so obviously at stake. The stakes are similarly, though less dramatically, high in many government agencies. Health care administration, law enforcement, regulation of the economy and many other government functions call for high levels of commitment to the task at hand. Men and women moving up the ladder within these agencies are not under pressure to make large investments of their loyalties for entirely bad reasons. But the danger is ever present that this commitment will become totalistic and *simultaneously* directed to something other than the genuine moral purpose of the role-specific loyalty.

Such displacement of loyalty was dramatically exemplified by some of the "overzealous" participants in the Watergate affair. It touched even those not directly involved. For example, in the midst of the "Saturday night massacre," Alexander Haig is reported to have responded to William Ruckelshaus's refusal to fire Archibald Cox by stating bluntly: "Your Commander-in-Chief has given you an order."[8] Such appeal to duty is not in itself wrongheaded. In this situation it was misplaced and wrongly focused because it was an attempt to co-opt the totality of Ruckelshaus's loyalty precisely when his plurality of loyalties was so important for the purposes of good government itself.

Max Weber, one of the founders of modern sociology, thought that the modern bureaucratic state necessarily makes this kind of total claim on the moral commitments of those who staff it. Weber distinguished the responsibilities of the politician or political leader from those of the civil servant or bureaucrat. In Weber's view, modern organizational structure makes it necessary that the balancing of loyalties to the many communities of the nation be the exclusive prerogative of the politician or political leader. The task of the civil servant, on the other hand, is that of facilitating and implementing choices made on the higher level of politics. As Weber put it in his well known essay "Politics as a Vocation":

> To take a stand, to be passionate . . . is the politician's element and above all the element of the political leader. His conduct is subject to a quite different, indeed, exactly opposite, principle of responsibility from that of the civil servant. The honor of the civil servant is vested in his ability to execute conscientiously the order of superior authorities, exactly as if the order agreed with his own conviction. This holds even if the order appears wrong to him and if despite the civil servant's remonstrance the authority insists on the order. Without this moral discipline the whole apparatus would fall to pieces. The honor of the political leader, of the leading statesman, however, lies precisely in an exclusive, personal responsibility for what he does, a responsibility he cannot and must not reject or transfer.[9]

In my view, this analysis is both inaccurate from a factual point of view and unjustified from a moral point of view. Weber was right in pointing out that complex bureaucracies exert powerful pressure on civil servants to functionalize and totalize their responsibilities according to role-specific obligations. He was also correct in noting the amount of personal authority such bureaucracies appear to bestow on those at the top. This latter point is perhaps part of the explanation for the emergence of the "imperial presidency." Weber's analysis, however, does not take sufficient account of the fact that civil servants make many decisions of moral significance other than decisions to obey orders and execute decisions made by others. There are many opportunities to shape policy through the way reports are prepared, the way issues are shaped, and the way overlooked values are interjected into an agency's internal discussions which have little or nothing to do with following orders and much to do with wider loyalties. Also, from a factual standpoint, Weber's description of the "exclusive personal responsibility" of the political leader is one-sided. It fails to take into account the genuine limits and constraints on the action of those at the top. In large measure, these constraints are due to the extra-bureaucratic loyalties of those down the line.

From a moral perspective Weber's description is also inadequate. If the functionalization of bureaucratic responsibility is carried to this extreme it will lead to the effective denial of the moral and personal agency of the civil servant. It achieves this effect by neutralizing the impact of the loyalties of the official to all groups except the agency or bureau. Commitments to family, to a community of friends, to a religious community, and to the citizens of both one's own and other nations become private affairs. Decisions and action on the job become purely technical. This is unacceptable from a normative point of view, because it amounts to a kind of moral schizophrenia, a splitting of private and public life in a way that is both psychologically and morally destructive.

If this split were to become firmly fixed in our national ethos we could rightly ask whether work in government itself has moral meaning. Such work, some might conclude, has no *moral* significance or value at all. To be a moral agent, however, is to weigh competing loyalties and competing goods and to act in a way which attends to their rightful claims. The human task of decision-making is a response to the call which arises from these goods and loyalties. To experience oneself as a moral agent, in other words, is to sense that one is called to serve values, persons and communities that are not merely functional or subordinate to the dynamics of the bureaucratic process. This experience of the depth and dignity of one's work can be called an experience of vocation. The tasks at hand are not simply part of a job one does in order to enjoy the benefits of human interaction when one is on holiday. These tasks are themselves part of the overall venture of living one's life in interaction, friendship and love with others.

THE SCOPE OF LOYALTY

To conclude otherwise would represent the full alienation of work from those loyalties and values which create a meaningful existence. It would make it impossible to experience work in government in any sense as a moral task and a human vocation rather than simply as a job. James Bresnahan has described what it means to experience life in the legal profession as a vocation in a way that clarifies what I mean by speaking of government in these terms:

> There are two poles in this . . . awareness of calling in one's life work. On the one hand there is a posture of hope and trust, of courage and hardiness in adversity, of ambition to use well one's special skills in critical analysis and persuasive speech. There is the hope we had in law school to do great things for others, to be recognized for this and be rewarded for this by others, to be champions in the adversary system of justice. There is also our memory of ever growing realization that one cannot live by the needs and the responses of others alone. The forward reaching effort has to be grounded within, too, and finally justified because one is convinced that one has done one's best, however others measure it, and

that one has satisfied one's own sense of consistency and found one's own fulfillment. This experience of vocation, then, includes a constant tension between one's sense of personal "autonomy" and the powerful "heteronomy" of concrete conscious life lived, both in the area of work and in the realm of intimacy, *with and for* others.[10]

A vocation, in other words, is a sense of being called by good and of having loyalties which are larger than those codified in the "rules of the game." Furthermore, some of these goods and loyalties must be seen as in some sense ultimate, i.e. as the fundamental reason why one is involved in the work at all. As Bresnahan puts it, "every experience of vocation has implicit within it *something* of this peculiar element of ultimacy, this confrontation with the challenge which death and love puts to our striving for consistency."[11] At the same time, a vocational life means living out these personal loyalties under the concrete conditions of a socially structured role. If either these ultimate personal loyalties or the daily commitment to one's governmental role is lacking, work in government cannot be said to be a vocation or even a form of vocation. It will be simply a job, useful no doubt, but finally not humanly meaningful in itself. On this basis a second thesis can be proposed: *A governmental role can be considered both an exercise of moral agency and a vocation only in the context of loyalties which are broader, more inclusive and more fundamental than role-specific obligations*.

The broader loyalties to family, friends, church, party, the nation and all humankind, each in different ways, give government decision-making a significance that a simply functional job can never have. For the work of a government official—both civil servant and political leader—touches the lives of the members of all those other communities in extremely important ways. To experience one's work in government as a vocation and an act of moral agency is to realize that it cannot in fact be divorced from one's other loyalties, even if one should want it to be so divorced.

One basis for such a vocational experience of one's work as a politician or civil servant is the purpose of government itself. A civil servant or politician can rightfully claim that the responsibilities of his or her role make moral sense in light of the overall purposes of the task of governing. On the basis of personal experience one can accurately and legitimately claim in most cases that in being loyal to the responsibilities of office one is being loyal to the Constitution, to the cause of justice, to the liberty and welfare of one's family and fellow-citizens and to the task of preserving peace and security in the world. Loyalty to the government itself can be experienced as a truly worthy commitment. Nevertheless, if this kind of loyalty is taken for granted and left totally unquestioned, it begins to resemble the kind of loyalty demanded by totalitarian governments of their citizens. A totalitarian government is one which presumes that it is so fully serving the interests and good of the people that it has the right to co-opt unquestioning acquiescence by citizens to all its actions and decisions. If unquestioning "team play" is demanded of government officials—whether they be senators or GS-14's—a process of totalization has begun, even if it is not the tyrannical and fanatical totalization of a totalitarian regime.

The principle of limited government is the core of the American governmental system. This principle is relevant not only to the way we interpret the relation between our government and our citizens. It is also very significant in the effort to understand the public responsibilities of those who work in and for the government itself. American constitutional government rests on the principle that the state is not an end in itself. The end of government is the service of the rightful interests of very diverse communities of people. This diversity is considerably greater than is the flexibility allowed by the demands of bureaucratic efficiency and effectiveness. The linchpin of American political thought is the claim that the state cannot and must not attempt to define the total existence of persons. Citizens have a value and dignity transcending that defined by law. Citizens have moral claims on and against the government. Similarly, therefore, government officials cannot define the moral meaning of their work simply with reference to the obligations which are specific to their roles. The notion of limited government applies not only to the government-citizen relationship. It also applies to the relation between the loyalties which government figures have to their roles and the loyalties of these same people to other communities. Therefore, an official or politician cannot define the moral meaning of his or her work solely by referring to the overall purposes of government in an abstract way. This kind of appeal will only make sense experientially, psychologically and morally if the official can at the same time affirm that fulfillment of role-specific obligations will in fact serve the purposes for which government exists, namely the just promotion of the liberty and welfare of the many communities of society as a whole. In most cases, such an experiential, psychological and moral justification for "playing by the rules of the game" will be present. Cases where such justification is lacking are unfortunately more common than we would like to admit.

An analogy between physical sight and moral vision may help make this point clear. Human sight is capable of depth perception because it looks at the world from a variety of viewpoints. If looked at from a single perspective the world would be flat. Nothing would stand out in relief. An infant gradually learns to perceive three dimensions by its shifting perspectives. Moral vision depends on the same kind of plurality of viewpoints. The perception of the moral depth of one's work arises when it is looked at simultaneously from several different moral perspectives. One of these perspectives is that of the obligations of role or job description. The other regards the work from the viewpoint of the larger values which make claims on the total governmental process—values such as the liberty and welfare of those the government is to serve.

LOYALTY IN A BROADER CONTEXT

In the concrete experience of the public official this plurality of perspectives and its resulting moral depth perception is sustained by membership in more than one community of loyalty. A congressperson or agency director or bureau staff member is not totally defined as a human being by a job description or decision-making flow chart. A public official is both official and citizen, official and family member, official and friend. He or she is official and Democrat or Republican, official and member of a religious community, official and part of the interdependent community of the human race. Loyalties to these many communities keep moral vision from going flat. Maintaining such loyalties is thus an indispensable condition for retaining both the moral perspective and the genuine moral agency necessary if the task of governing is to be truly a vocation. The American principle of limited government is a guarantee of the legitimacy of this pluralism of loyalties. Thus we can formulate a third thesis: *The limited nature of American government is relevant not only to the relation between state and citizen but also to the way officials should interpret their professional responsibilities. Government work can be considered an act of moral agency to the extent that it provides scope for loyalty to broader communities and values.*

The principal point of this thesis is that role-specific obligations and the moral meaning of government work are not self-contained. These obligations are ultimately rooted in loyalty to a moral community which cannot be exhaustively defined by law or in terms of governmental structure. The nature of this larger community and the kinds of loyalties to which it rightfully lays claim is, of course, subject to diverse interpretations. The moral pluralism of American society makes a full agreement about what deeper loyalties are the true foundations of government activity highly unlikely. It is not my purpose to settle this profound issue, or even to sketch its many facets. In my view, and the view of the Judeo-Christian religious community, the most fundamental loyalty of government officials ought to be the same as that of all citizens: loyalty to the community of all persons, each of which is seen to have a transcendent worth and preciousness, and each of which is worthy of genuine respect and love in a community of solidarity. There are other possible interpretations of what this fundamental loyalty ought to be, for example, those proposed by Marxist, libertarian, Freudian or Skinnerian thought. There are also important variations within the Christian and Jewish interpretations of this fundamental loyalty. Each of these approaches to fundamental loyalty has important political consequences. Pluralism also reigns in the way people interpret the causal roots and effective consequences of government policies.

My chief purpose in raising the question of the pluralism of moral visions in American life is not to presume to resolve it. Rather, it is to argue that it is both impossible and undesirable to leave one's basic loyalties behind when deciding what one's responsibilities are within government itself. It is evident, of course, that the basic loyalties of other persons can help clarify the strengths and weaknesses of one's own commitments. For this reason, moral righteousness or priggishness is certainly not called for by this perspective. Indeed, genuine debate and dialogue about these larger loyalties is at least as much in place among government officials as it is anywhere in our society. Nor does the perspective advanced here imply that loyalty to one's superiors or to the standard procedures of government is somehow unimportant. Role-specific obligations are real, and both the oath of office and its less formal analogues make clear that they are a central part of the loyalty of any public official.

LOYALTY AND PLURALISM

Despite these facts, however, the pluralism of American social visions shows why it is so important that politicians and civil servants retain and develop loyalties to communities broader than the government itself. If they do not, they will be in danger of altogether surrendering their moral agency while on the job, surrendering themselves to a strictly functional mode of acting and decision-making. Such a functional approach defines all governmental issues as problems to be solved by technical skill. This will make for bad government, for, to quote from Hannah Arendt once again: "it shields men from the impact of reality and ruins the mind's capacity for judgment and learning." The kind of judgment and learning she has in mind is not that derived from either the methods of scientific management or from a nose sensitive to where the political winds are blowing. It is moral judgment and learning that is called for. Extra-governmental loyalties are an indispensable source for this. Therefore, a final thesis can be formulated: *The identification and development of one's extra-governmental loyalties is essential for responsible government service. In a pluralistic society respectful attention to the loyalties of others is an important part of responsible service. So is loyalty to one's role-specific obligations. But neither of these provisos means that a functionally defined role becomes one's sole loyalty in office.*

It is clear that the perspective adopted in this essay opens up the possibility of conflict between broader, extra-governmental loyalties and the wishes of one's superiors or one's constituency. If this perspective is put into action, occasions for "rocking the boat", "blowing the whistle" or "breaking the rules of the game" will likely arise.

Compromise and cooperation are clearly values essential to good government. Moral righteousness can undermine genuine governmental effectiveness as surely as can moral blindness. But we have learned from experience that there are occasions when dissent or intervention is called for.

Western moral and political tradition has not been completely silent on when such dissent or intervention is justifiable. Political and moral reflection has led to the formulation of a set of norms for the use of military force as a means of resistance to or intervention in the activity of others. Dissent or intervention in the operation of the bureaucratic process will not involve the use of military force. They may, however, be in some measure disruptive of the peaceful life of a bureau or, in the extreme, of the psychological or social tranquility of many citizens. Public dissent by officials can also be harmful to an agency or to the process of government as a whole. So, though it is sometimes necessary, it always needs to be justified. Adapting the norms developed in the context of military resistance and intervention, the following criteria for action based on an appeal to one's broader loyalties over against those which are role-specific seem apposite:

1) the action serves public rather than private purposes;
2) it seeks to right a grave wrong;
3) its harmful effects are outweighed by the expected good consequences;
4) the action has a reasonable chance of success;
5) non-disruptive alternatives have been exhausted;

6) the action is sustained only so long as is necessary to attain the good sought;

7) the means used do not render impossible the attainment of the good sought;

8) the means used are not themselves morally unjustifiable.[12]

The use of these criteria in the concrete involves both one's loyalties to extra-governmental communities and one's commitment to role-specific obligations. That there will be disagreement on how they are to be applied in particular cases is evident. The effort to use them responsibly is part of what it means to see work in government as an exercise of moral agency and as a vocation. These disagreements will be explored in greater detail in later essays in this volume. It is hoped that this discussion has at least partially shown why the dilemmas of government decision-making are part of its dignity.

NOTES

1. This approach to the question has been stimulated by Michael Walzer's provocative book *Obligations: Essays on Disobedience, War and Citizenship* (New York: Simon & Schuster, 1970). Though I am not in agreement with Walzer's fundamental theory of obligation, his approach to "pluralistic citizenship" has been most helpful.

2. Carl Bernstein and Bob Woodward, *All The President's Men* (New York: Simon and Schuster, 1974), p. 234. Frank Sturgis, another of the Watergate conspirators, is reported to have used identical language in his guilty plea before Judge Sirica: "When it comes to Cuba and the communist conspiracy involving the United States, I will do anything to protect this country." See William B. Dickenson, ed., *Watergate: Chronology of a Crisis*, vol. I, (Washington, D.C.: Congressional Quarterly, Inc., 1973), p. 10.

3. *History and Human Survival* (New York: Random House, 1970), p. 71.

4. Hannah Arendt, "Lying in Politics" in *Crises of the Republic* (New York: Harcourt, Brace, Jovanovich, 1972), p. 40.

5. Albert O. Hirschman, *Exit, Voice and Loyalty: Responses to*

Decline in Firms, Organizations and States (Cambridge: Harvard U. Press, 1970), p. 107.

6. See Kenneth J. Arrow, *The Limits of Organization* (New York: W.W. Norton, 1974), esp. p. 68.

7. Lewis Coser, *Greedy Institutions* (New York: Free Press, 1974), p. 4. I am grateful to John Haughey for calling Coser's work to my attention both in his book *Should Anyone Say Forever?–On Making, Keeping and Breaking Commitments*, and also in personal conversation.

8. See Elizabeth Drew, *Washington Journal: The Events of 1973-1974* (New York: Random House, 1975), p. 54.

9. "Politics as a Vocation," in H. Gerth and C.W. Mills, *From Max Weber: Essays in Sociology* (New York: Oxford U. Press, 1958), p. 95.

10. James F. Bresnahan, S.J., "Theology and Law: A Deeper Understanding of Vocation," in *Capitol University Law Review* 7 (1977), p. 29.

11. *Ibid.*, p. 32.

12. For a discussion of these criteria as they arose in the just war theory, see William V. O'Brien, *Nuclear War, Deterrence and Morality*, (New York: Newman Press, 1967), pp. 17-44.

Loyalty Conversation

Haughey: Could you start us off, Dave?

Hollenbach: Yes. My main concern is to try to place the moral dimensions of peoples' work in government within the context of their entire moral lives. I am trying to show that multiple loyalties, or in some sense being a pluralistic person, is at the heart of this. My contention is that in adjudicating competing claims on one's loyalties, one becomes a moral actor.

Haughey: Is this multiple loyalties issue a real one for all of you?

Margulies: Let me just share with you an experience I had which begins to answer your question. It had to do with a program I was directing; a big program involving regional medical organization. As a program, it had come from a shabby situation to a high level of acceptance in the administration. I had a budget, consequently, of about $150 million and a nationwide program, and a good many people committed to it. It was something I really believed in, and testified about because I felt it was really very important. No sooner was it expanded than it ran into budget difficulties and the decision was made to do away with it in the very same year. At the beginning, the President budgeted it at the highest point it had ever been and in the rectification of the budget it was wiped out. The program would have created a lot of primary care. It was getting to poor people and to rural areas and getting the professions together to act as they never had before. So, the question I was confronted with was: "What do I do when the time comes for me to testify before the legislative committee?" I did a lot of soul-searching in the course of the whole process, both in the beginning when I was pushing the program and later when I was

91

asked to defend the administration's position. It was a very an-
guished period of time and I have never felt that that decision was
a clean one—that I necessarily did the right thing or the wrong
thing. I decided to defend the curtailment because by doing so I
was serving the people who had given me that position—the
administration.

Breslin: Couldn't you have communicated your negative
sentiments in some other way?

Margulies: No. I work for the administration as a civil servant. I
feel my responsibilities are to those people who employ me. Previously, I had had my innings. I was given my chance to state my
position within the administration and was overruled. They said
"you're wrong", having heard me.

Lowell: But in an appropriations hearing you testify as an extension of your Secretary or your Chairman or the top official; you
know you are there not to give the opinions that you may have
had at the beginning of the process. Your own views having been
overruled, you're there to be a resource that your leader needs.
You are called on not to give your opinion but to give his answer.
That is what is expected of executive branch officials by the
Congressmen who are sitting behind the desk. They're not looking for disputes among the resource people.

Margulies: Well, that may be, but they might have said, "Now, in
your personal professional opinion, what do you think?"

Dungan: If it were a moral question, a serious moral question,
one in which indisputably it's right or it's wrong, in the public
interest or not in the public interest, I think the answer is very
clear. But if it's a question you can look at one way or another,
then since you're hired by the administration, the way I think one
handles that with perfect fidelity and with perfect communication, given what you described is: "Senator, the administration's
position is thus—I support it—I don't have a personal position."

Hollenbach: What about the broader sense of how the other loyalties work in your whole day by day task, not just in the moment of the crunch? Do you experience the sorting out of your loyalties as a kind of daily moral task? What strategies do you employ to be consistent about your loyalties?

Margulies: You may delay your strategy up to the point of retirement so you never really do what ought to have been done.

Gessert: Let me make a general comment of some uneasiness about this paper and that is that there's a tendency to suggest that if I am in government service I am measurable morally by the number of conflicting loyalties I have. I think there is practically an identification of loyalties to extra-governmental communities as essential to performing one's governmental tasks morally. To be sure I think there's obvious educational value to be exposed to a lot of communities and so on, but the paper almost elevates that educational value to somehow an ethical system or a moral system. Are you suggesting that the degree of ethical sensitivity or responsiveness one has is primarily a function of a number of loyalties or the conflicting loyalties one has? It seems to me that the kind of case described by Dr. Margulies is in essence a searching out of the truth and the justice called for rather than being torn by what you describe as loyalties. Here's the way ethical dilemmas are perceived or really ought to be perceived—"What is the truthful or just thing to do in this case?" not "What is the balancing of loyalties?"

Hollenbach: But is it either/or? Can't the search for the objective truth include the process of weighing these other loyalties? It's a balancing of these loyalties that helps you to arrive at the ultimate decision that is morally best.

Haughey: It seems to me that loyalty is one of the aspects in the ethical sorting-out process but it's not the only one. Maybe it is being given too comprehensive a role here.

Gessert: Let me be more specific. I think that loyalties to allies or commitment to allies is a substantive moral issue. Judgments as to what we should do in NATO I think are legitimately made in terms of what kind of commitment we have made to our allies, what kinds of expectations we created for them or what kind of expectations they have with respect to us, and so on. And I would tend to preserve commitment as a moral category to instances in which you have made fairly specific commitments, have created expectations that need to be fulfilled, or re-examined or re-evaluated etc. I don't deny that there's a good educational value in your loyalties to your family, your friends, your church, etc. and getting other points of view. But when it finally comes to a decision I have to make, I ask: "Is it right or is it not right?" That decision needs to be made in terms which are much more substantively specific than how does my family feel or what's the relationship of my commitment to my family or to my church or whatever. I may be informed about my decisions by associations that I have which affect my heart and my loyalties, but still it's a question of searching for what is the justice in a given case. For example, the decision to deploy enhanced radiation weapons. I wouldn't want public officials to make that decision in terms of some complex set of conflicting loyalties. I want them to resolve that issue in terms of what is a sensible defense deterrent posture and does this fit into it?

Dungan: I, too, Dave, was concerned by the thrust of this paper which placed more emphasis on interest-group loyalty conflicts which are extrinsic rather than intrinsic to substantive considerations about a particular decision. The further one gets away from the intrinsic substantive considerations around issues and moves in the direction of pressure groups or group loyalties or whatever, the further one gets away from truly ethical decision-making. All of those contacts can inform that decision, but they ought not to be dominant elements in it.

Langan: There's a difference, a basic difference about two ways of conceiving the resolution of moral conflicts. When one thinks mainly in terms of loyalties, that suggests links to particular persons and groups. Another more abstract approach tends to conceive matters on the basis of principles. Some people try to settle issues in terms of their awareness of persons and their ties with persons. Other people spontaneously move to a principles approach. You can work these two approaches back and forth in support of each other or in illumination of each other, though they can also be in conflict. What we need is a kind of reflection on where we think loyalty is the appropriate model and where an approach in terms of rational substantive principles is the appropriate model. I think that we all live on both of these approaches and that it is a mistake to regard either one as the unique way to being a moral agent.

Silverstone: American civil servants have serious loyalty questions. I do not mean loyalty in terms of support for the Constitution, the country, and the government. But there is always the question: "Who am I working for?" I am a lawyer. Whose lawyer? This is a terrible dilemma for lawyers in the government. All law students are taught that you serve a client. Well, who's the client? I think that's where the real loyalty question lies. If you're talking about loyalty to groups or institutions outside government, that's one thing. But if you're addressing loyalties, at least loyalties in terms of people within the government structure, that's another thing. For example, "Am I serving my Division Chief or my Secretary or my President?" An official, with good motive, suggests that a subordinate represent the facts or information in such a way that will be useful for his organization's mission or mandate but may mislead the Secretary or may mislead the President. The official feels it will be easier for the President to make a decision if he doesn't know certain things. Where does the subordinate's loyalty lie? And what does that loyalty demand of you?

Hollenbach: That's really the issue I'm trying to get at. I'm not so much interested in the interest-group—people manipulating me or pulling me or pushing me on the grounds that are essentially non-moral, but on this question: "Where are my final moral loyalties, so to speak? Who are the people I am most interested in?"

Lowell: I am very sympathetic with your paper, Dave. I don't think that when you're talking about loyalty and your government position you can talk about it only as cold, clean, objective decision-making. Loyalties that are pulling on you, on your emotions, on your heart and your affective kinds of leanings ought to enter into the decision-making process. It's not a sign of weakness—it may be a sign of weakness to ignore these. Not that the ultimate decision hinges on these, but that kind of input helps you ultimately to make the decision that is probably the best. You are making a decision as a person, not just as a mind.

Breslin: I think this loyalty issue is very interesting, in part because it's one thing that politicians demand of their staffs but seldom give to their staffs. I did my doctoral dissertation on the relationship between eight senators and their staffs. One thing I found in my dissertation that intrigued me was the number of times the staff members referred to the senator as a father and that they see the staff as living a family situation. The father image is a very strong one and the Senators usually are old enough to be our fathers as most of the staff is young. That gets into the issue of loyalty because you're hitting a whole variety of psychological motivations for why we do things. We have a different way of being gratified and satisfied by our work than the rest of you in government. So much depends on how the Senator reacts to what you do—if he approves. Yet, most Senators that I've studied were not what you would call warm men. For a variety of reasons the personal staff gets very little feedback from them on how they're doing and on those few occasions when there is—those little scratches of paper saying "good work!"— they're saved. We are all working for one man's career. Loyalty here has a very special meaning because you put such significance on how the Senator reacts to what you do.

Salzberg: But doesn't that bring up the problem of totalization mentioned in the paper?

Breslin: It does. But I see it this way. Part of my job is to hire and fire people. And when we're talking about loyalty, my first question is: "Could you be or are you loyal to the Senator?" It's a very different situation to work immediately for a personality.

Everything I do is in his name. I sign his name. I write a statement that goes under his name. We pass a piece of legislation that's his bill. The staff must have his interests at heart.

Margulies: Sure, there's no institutional support for him. He's not a party. In a way everyone's his enemy. It's always him against the world. It's him against the world back in his district; it's him against the world in Congress.

Haughey: I wonder how far you can go with this father paradigm for loyalty. Doesn't it seem that part of the sickness of the Nixon White House was that just such an image of loyalty was being nutured?

Silverstone: The father became the godfather, you might say.

Haughey: And you seem to be ignoring the power factor and the gratification that comes from being with or in or alongside the powerful.

Hollenbach: Let us move on to another aspect of the paper. Does it make some sense to you to talk about working in government as a vocation, and not simply as a job? I use this whole loyalty thing in my essay to surface that. Do you think of your work as a vocation and if you do, could you flesh that out a bit?

Silverstone: I was troubled by the word "vocation", especially in relation to government work. I originally came into a department that, as an outsider, I had not held in high regard, yet in the process found things I enjoyed doing, and I was doing "good", too. But I didn't come into government as a vocation. Maybe I thought of law as a vocation. I came here only as a desparate temporary measure—to eat for a little while. But I found that there were various things I could do that were good and got great satisfaction out of it, but vocation? What's that?

Lowell: I think I carry my vocation with me. Right now I'm in a job that I find quite satisfying, that enables me to use my talents.

That has not always been the case. I have been in government jobs where I wasn't really quite sure as to the job's contribution to the overall public good. When in that kind of position I found it necessary to find other avenues to satisfy the need I had to do what I perceived as being good. There have been times in my life, for example, when I have been much more involved in civic affairs or in local church affairs than I am right now. That was because at that time the vocation that I had to use my talents to serve greater goods than my own was not being satisfied in the job which I was performing in government.

Gessert: I'm very much of a split mind on this. Self-consciousness about work in government as a vocation carries with it all the dangers of pretension and arrogance and crusade, etc. I like to think that government is some kind of calling to serve the public interest or the public service, and in fact I think we have probably done something to our government by making it too much like everything else, a career that somebody simply enters into and stays in and satisfies his own relatively private needs for livelihood, etc.

Salzberg: If I understand the concept I would think my role as being more of a vocation than a job. I chose to work for Congressman Fraser because I believed in much of what he was pursuing and found his views similar to mine. In addition I feel in my position that I am encouraged to express my views.

Hollenbach: What would your work have to be like in order for it to be a way to realize your vocation? If you can subscribe to the idea of seeing your work as a vocation, what conditions have to be there for you not to have to find a realization of your basic commitments elsewhere?

Lowell: You have to be fortuitous enough to be working at the level of your competence—neither above it nor below it. And that's not everybody's good fortune, or not everybody's good fortune at every point in his or her career. You can be in a job that's way over your head—there really is a contribution to make but you're not able to do it. Or you can be in a job so long that you've exhausted the contribution you can make there, yet you need to remain employed. Not everyone has the option of saying "Well, I've finished doing this, now I'll go find something else that gives me the same kinds of satisfaction and where I can perceive myself making contributions." Another question is: Can you shape the job? In the Congress where you have some personal relationships with your leader, and even in the larger bureaucracies, each of us winds up with one supervisor. You have to be able to perform in the context of a superior who provides an environment in which you can operate with some freedom and independence.

*Crahan: Much of what I hear here describes contentment with one's job rather than a vocation. It would seem to me that a vocation would have to involve more directly the objectives and morality of the specific work that one was going to do or was doing—the consequences of that work in a broader sense, not only with respect to one's own particular life. This is also related to the other topics we are discussing—the loyalties to family, church, and others. Those loyalties are subsumed under such rubrics as loyalty to class and within class to special interest groups. These not only can affect your work within the government but help determine the type of life that you want for your families.

Gessert: On listening to this conversation I can't help thinking about my own Reformation background and Lutheran vs. Calvinist concepts of vocation. For Luther the fundamental impact of the concept of vocation was to accept your situation in life and its place in God's order of things. A static concept. Anybody who's doing anything, is somehow enriched in being able to see the place of his work in the order of things. It doesn't set government apart in a distinctive way. A Calvinist conception of voca-

---

* Dr. Margaret Crahan is the current holder of the John Courtney Murray Fellowship at the Woodstock Theological Center. She is an Associate Professor of History at Lehman College, C.U.N.Y.

tion was much more dynamic. It called you to the maximum use of talents, not just for job satisfaction or whatever but in order to transform the world after the image of God's law and God's redemption of mankind and so on. In that scheme of things there are certain vocations that in some sense are more worthy than other vocations—at least distinctive in some important sense. We have lost something in our notion of what government is about if we reduce it to just like any other job where it's primarily a matter of saying that you have some role and you reach a level of competence and have gotten all your job satisfactions and so on and so forth.

4
Should Decisions Be
the Product of Reason?

John Langan

One straightforward answer to the question of how personal values should influence decision-making in government is to maintain that while personal values should be shaped by each person's religious faith, government decision-making in a pluralistic society should be the work of reason alone. In this way the natural and the supernatural, the kingdom of God and the city of man would be kept apart in a way that respects the distinctions made by earlier theologians and statesmen and that reflects the reality of the society in which we live. Faith and reason, nature and grace, church and state, personal values and government decisions would then come together only in an accidental way in the lives of individual decision-makers in government who happen to be religious men and women.

This line of thought undoubtedly responds to certain real aspects of the Washington situation, in which persons of many different religious persuasions or none work together in alliance and in competition to shape the decisions of our government. We have probably found in our experience a great diversity in the motives and attitudes of those working in government. People of selfless wisdom share the same offices with grasping careerists, hard-nosed technicians ride the same elevators with bleeding-heart idealists, callow and tactless reformers sit at conference tables with seasoned manipulators of the levers of powers. We all know that there are moments in Washington life when votes count for more than values, when influence outweighs altruism. In the diversity of values and the conflict of faiths that is characteristic of our culture, it seems that we should aim at a purely rational approach to policy that strives as much as possible to keep religious divisions and differences in ultimate values in the background. In this view we should regard appeals to personal values as pointing in contradictory directions and as falling short of the standards of rational objectivity that should inform public decisions. This rationalizing approach is not without attractions; few of us would want government decisions to be irrational or to involve the imposition of minority theological views on a recalcitrant public. On the other hand, we are likely to find that the effort to be purely rational in the inherently political process of making decisions is frustrating and paradoxical and that this effort leads us back to many nonrational factors that are inescapably present in our lives and our society. We are driven to ask what reason can do and what its limits are. We need to sort out our attitudes to reason and our expectations of what guidance it can give us.

In doing this, we will not be examining in a scientific way the various factors that can influence decisions, nor in testing hypotheses about the causes of decisions. Instead, we will be looking at a kind of philosophical map of our capacities as human agents in societies. This reflective mapping can be confirmed or criticized on the basis of one's experience and one's understanding of one's own activity; but it cannot be proved or disproved by a simple argument or by an empirical test. It will be tentative and incomplete. It will be normative as well as descriptive; that is, it will make certain claims about how people ought to behave as well as how they do behave in fact.[1]

REFLECTIONS ON REASON

"Reason's last step is the recognition that there are an infinite number of things which are beyond it; it is merely feeble if it does not go so far as to grasp that."[2]

"The heart has its reasons which are unknown to reason; we are aware of it in a thousand ways."[3]

This paper is largely a reflection on these texts, from the *Pensées* of Blaise Pascal, the famous mathematician and theological writer. This reflection will look at these texts not in their original context of theological argument in seventeenth-century France but in the philosophical and political climate of twentieth-century America. Our aim is to suggest how it is possible and appropriate for personal commitments to ultimate values to shape the making of decisions and the formation of policy in a pluralistic society like our own.

On a first reading of our chosen texts, we may think that Pascal is being suspicious of or even hostile to reason, that he means to protect religious faith by decrying reason, that in effect he wants to blindfold the eyes of reason and to urge us to leap by faith into the unknown and unfathomed abyss. This is likely to make us suspicious and uncomfortable, for we probably share the general Western esteem for reason. We have little desire to be more unreasonable than is necessary, especially in areas of our lives where we feel vulnerable to public scrutiny and criticism. But a closer reading of what Pascal is saying reveals something that is more interesting and more complex than mere theological depreciation of reason. For we should remember that Pascal also affirms that the Christian religion "alone has reason for its ally."[4] Rather, what Pascal is pointing to here is reason's discovery of its own limitations and its awareness of inner factors and processes which are somehow beyond it and yet are akin to it, which are, in his words, "the reasons of the heart." Now these are paradoxical discoveries for reason to make, for how can reason come to know its limits except by going beyond them? As Wittgenstein observes, how can we think a limit unless we can think both sides of it?[5] How can we know what we don't know unless we know it? Furthermore, what sense does it make to talk of "reasons of the heart"? If these really belong to the heart, how can they really be reasons? Would not accepting them and acting on them put us outside the guiding light of reason and under the blind sway of emotion and desire?

These questions leave us uncomfortable, and yet I would suggest that for most of us these texts have a promise of truth to them, even if we are not sure of how to read that promise. We may strive, as Plato and Thomas Aquinas urged that we should, to follow the dictates of reason. We may think of ourselves in the terms of Aristotle's definition as rational animals, and we may feel the attraction of Hamlet's great cry:

> "What a piece of work is a man! how noble in reason! how infinite in faculty! in form and moving how express and admirable! in action how like an angel! in apprehension how like a god! the beauty of the world! the paragon of animals!"[6]

We can take pride in the fusion of reason and power that produces the marvels of modern technology from BART to NASA. But we also run up against the limits of our thought and knowledge more often than we like, and we feel movements within us that make us both more and less than rational agents. We may not feel confident that we can find adequate words for these experiences, but we cannot doubt that we have them. They point to deep perplexities in our understanding of ourselves as human persons, perplexities that confront us, whatever may be our place in society or our religious orientation. These perplexities do not affect bureaucrats and politicians alone, for they are universally human. They are invisibly present beneath all the papers to be shuffled, silently present in all the meetings to be held. They are in the background whenever human beings attempt to decide important questions of value and when they try to fashion a more fully human manner of life for themselves and the other persons to whom and for them they are responsible. In our work and in our reflection the question emerges: "What can reason do?" And this question is not merely a private existential question bearing on the awareness and destiny of each individual. It is also a question that bears on our life together in an organized society, on our expectations of each other, and on our ways of dealing with each other.

DIFFERING USES OF "REASON"

Before we attempt an answer to the question, "What can reason do?" there are two important points that we should reflect on. The first has already been mentioned: it is the generally favorable evaluative connotation of such words as "reason", "rational" and "reasonable". Thus we endorse an action when we say, "It was the only reasonable thing to do." Correspondingly, the evaluative connotations of "unreasonable", "irrational", and "irrationality" are generally unfavorable. "He's been acting irrationally over the last few weeks" is not the kind of thing one wants to have in a report about oneself. We expect other people to have reasons for many, if not most, of their beliefs and actions, particularly those that are done consciously or deliberately or those that affect the interests of other persons in important ways. We are often inclined to feel guilty or threatened or deficient if we are unable, when challenged, to provide some reasons for our principal beliefs and actions. We don't normally expect these reasons to be conclusive or to be acceptable to all questioners; but we do want them to be intelligible, to provide at least the beginnings of an account of why we think and act as we do. We often have to deal with conflicting reasons, reasons for and against a particular belief or course of action; and we recognize our need to weigh reasons carefully, at least on some occasions. But, unless we are deeply involved in an issue or are being harassed by some amateur Socrates, we do not usually feel the need to trace the reasons we offer to ourselves and to others back to ultimate principles. Nor do we normally feel a need to put our reasons in apple-pie order so that they form conclusive arguments. Normal patterns of forming beliefs and of acting are shot through with reasons, but our lives do not achieve the rational order of a geometrical demonstration. You will notice, by the way, that I have shifted from talking about "reason" as a human characteristic and ability to talking about "reasons" for belief and action, reasons that are to be expressed in statements. This is one illustration of what will be our second preliminary observation, namely, that "reason" is a term used in different ways and different contents, and that some of our perplexities about reason can be worked out by adverting to these different uses and contexts.

But before we consider the varieties of reason and reasons we should mention that reason is not always favorably regarded. There is a long Christian tradition of distrusting human reason and the wisdom which it professes to attain. Thus St. Paul asked the Corinthians: "Has not God made foolish the wisdom of the world?" (1 Cor. 1, 20) Luther spoke of reason as a whore corrupting the Gospel. If Pascal saw reason as the ally of faith, other Christians have regarded it as a potentially subversive ally and have insisted on the word of the Lord in Second Isaiah: "For my thoughts are not your thoughts, neither are your ways my ways" (Is. 55, 8). In addition to the Christian distrust of reason, there has been present in our culture at least since the end of the eighteenth century a countercultural tradition which sees reason as contrasting with nature, life, feeling, spontaneity, poetry, ecstatic fulfillment, and the individuality and originality of genius. Thus Goethe's Werther cries out:

> "Oh, you rationalists . . . You abhor the drunken man and detest the eccentric . . . I have learned in my own way that all extraordinary men who have done great and improbable things have ever been derided by the world as drunk or insane."[7]

This countercultural tradition, which marks romanticism and existentialism and which has been influential in both the student revolts of the sixties and the religious revivals of the seventies, questions both the special prestige of the activity of reason in such disciplines as logic, science, and philosophy and the function of reason in regulating and planning the other activities of life. It sometimes makes common cause with traditional Christian views on the limits of reason and sometimes champions the ecstasy of Dionysius against the obedience of Christ. It is worth bearing in mind as a counterweight to the esteem for reason that is shared by the shapers of advanced industrial society, by the philosophers of the classical tradition and those Christians (largely, but not exclusively, in the Roman Catholic tradition) whom they have influenced, and by the non-Christian thinkers of the Enlightenment (the "Age of Reason"), and their contemporary followers who call themselves liberals, rationalists, empiricists or positivists. It is likely that most of us, because of our education, our temperament, and the kind of work we do have a deep-seated esteem for reason and rationality, even though we might hesitate to call ourselves rationalists. Reason occupies a central place in the network of values in our culture, even though its place is not free from challenge or attack.

REASON, KNOWLEDGE AND BELIEF

We have to some extent anticipated our second preliminary point about reason, namely, that the term is used in a variety of different contexts and so differs in its meaning and reference. The most satisfactory way to indicate some of these differences in context and meaning and at the same time to develop a sense of the complexity of the concept of reason is to consider some of the contrasts we commonly make between reason and other aspects of human life. Each of these contrasts could itself be the subject of a philosophical or historical treatise, so our presentation will have to be a summary of a few main points. But this series of contrasts will enable us to get a firmer hold on what is meant by talk about reason, a notion which figures in our thinking about ourselves, our work, and our society in many different ways. We will see that we are rarely confronted with a stark and simple choice between irrationality and reason.

In the first place, reason is contrasted with experience. Aristotle in the first chapter of the *Metaphysics* makes a distinction between experience which is knowledge of particulars, and the knowledge of universals which is present in the arts and sciences and in theoretical knowledge generally.[8] But this is not merely a contrast between two kinds of objects that we can know: it is a contrast between two ways of knowing. To discover something by reasoning is to learn by sitting back and thinking about a problem or an issue; it is, we may say, white-collar knowledge. To discover something by experience is to learn by encountering particular things in one's world in some direct way, e.g., by seeing or touching, by testing or by suffering. Both the British empiricists and the American pragmatists made experience the te of reason and distrusted abstract reasoning. It should be reme bered that, with the exception of pure mathematics, logic, some branches of philosophy, there is always a complex weaving of reason and experience in our intellectual projects. Aristotle himself, though he valued reason very highly, held that experience was particularly important for action and observed that "men of experience succeed even better than those who have theory without experience."[9] As we shall see when we consider the contrast between reason and memory, experience is not merely my contact with those external realities that affect me here and now; it can also be the accumulation of my previous contacts with these realities along with my awareness and interpretation of them.

Reason can also be contrasted with intuition as a manner of knowing. Here the difference is between intuition as an immediate intellectual grasp of some idea or truth and reason as the movement of the mind from premises or evidence to a conclusion. It is in this contrast that we see what is distinctive and most attractive in reason, the possibility that it offers of arriving at truth with certainty in a way that overcomes doubts and contrary assertions by clear rational argument. From the time that Greeks first developed geometry as an axiomatic science, philosophers and others have felt the attraction of exhibiting human knowledge as a deductive system in which conclusions could be proven. Thus Descartes speaks admiringly of the "long chains of simple and easy reasoning by means of which geometers are accustomed to reach the conclusions of their most difficult demonstrations."[10] As early as Plato, however, it was seen that the first principles of a deductive system could not themselves be proven, and so both Plato and Aristotle relied on intuition to provide knowledge of these first principles. Intuition has, as Bertrand Russell once observed, "all the advantages of theft over honest [toil]" and seems to make things too easy. It also has serious difficulty in handling disagreement, for the intuitionist cannot prove [his] case by offering reasons. If he could, he would not need to [appeal] to intuition in the first place. All that he can do, when [confronted] by fundamental disagreement, is to urge his critics to [consider] the matter again. In the theory of knowledge, the in[tuitionist] has the same vulnerability that affects the person in other areas of inquiry who relies on hunches for which he is unable to offer proofs or clear rational justifications.

I suspect that your own experience shows that reliance on hunches is often unavoidable and is sometimes very fruitful but that in very controversial situations one wants something more publicly persuasive than personal hunches. In practical life, it should be pointed out, we usually appeal to intuitions and hunches not to ground the first principles of our knowledge, but to get to conclusions when some of the steps on the way are obscure. We normally want clear, rational justifications for the positions we take, especially if we think that we are going to be asked to justify them to others, but we may find that we often have to settle for less. Constraints of time and the limits of our knowledge may, when combined with the need to solve an urgent problem, require us to recommend policies or to take decisions that go beyond what we can know or prove or reasonably foresee. But we can take some comfort in Godel's Theorem, which proves that even in mathematics there are true propositions that cannot be proven in an axiomatic system.[11]

A third contrast is one that is often overlooked, but is particularly important for the way in which human beings understand themselves and their actions. It is the contrast between reason and memory. We are familiar with the contrast commonly drawn between learning by rote and learning by reason, between memorizing a rule or a formula or a pattern of words or actions so that we can merely repeat it and understanding it so that we grasp the reasons for it and can use it creatively in new situations and perhaps even revise and improve it. This way of making the contrast between memory and reason makes an important point about the way in which we should do most of our learning and teaching, but it can easily lead us to ignore the fundamental role that memory has in our conception of ourselves. For it is memory that provides an essential element of continuity in the development of our lives. Reason in its purely deductive form has commonly been thought to give us knowledge of what is timelessly true, of truths that hold for all possible worlds. It gives us access to universal norms and principles that interpret and regulate our experience. Memory, on the other hand, gives us access to our own past experience and is an essential constituent in our knowledge of ourselves as individuals living at this time and as agents who are what we have been as well as what we are. Memory provides for history and for the continuing identity of the self as agent, and so it serves both individual and social functions. It brings us into a living relationship with past experiences of success and failure, of virtue and vice, of perplexity and aspiration and accomplishment, from which we grow as persons capable of understanding ourselves and entering into the experiences of others. As we all know, memory is selective and not simply reproductive. This has led some philosophers and historians to regard it with scepticism as an unreliable guide to truth. The fact that memory is affected by our experiences of value and the loss of value should prepare us to look at it critically as a source of information; but this same fact should also alert us to its richness as a source for understanding our character and the ways in which we react to our experience. Hence we can see the importance of memory in many forms of psychotherapy and of spiritual growth. For we have to understand ourselves not simply as instances of a universal set of human characteristics and capacities, but also as concrete individuals who have come to be what we are by moving along a particular path of experience. If we disregard this path of experience, we run the risk of misunderstanding ourselves in a radical way which can be tragic or absurd. None of us, as Kierkegaard argued against Hegel, is simply the Idea or universal Mind; the thinker who forgets his own existence is ultimately absurd, no matter how noble or profound he may seem.[12]

On a more prosaic and specific level, memory provides the basis for the importance of experience in practical matters. Without the activity of memory in recalling past achievements and failures and thus contributing to the creative reassessment of actions and strategies, experience would simply be a dead weight and could not be a positive factor in selecting personnel and deciding policy. The judgments of a person of experience may fall short of certain ideals of rational clarity, for they may include elements which have not been isolated and analyzed in a systematic fashion. But precisely for this reason these elements are likely to be overlooked in a purely rationalistic account of policy formation. The appeal to experience, which involves a selective remembering of the past, is a means of uncovering some of the complexities and uncertainties that can thwart the rational application of means to an end, and can make rational planning ineffective. It is particularly important when a policy is to be applied across class or cultural lines, that is, when factors that can influence the outcome of a policy are especially liable to be overlooked (e.g. designing high-rise apartments for low-income families). Pointing out the importance of experience and thus of memory in the complexities of practical life does not deny the possibility that relying on past experience can be misleading or that it can distort one's interpretation of a new experience in confusing and damaging ways (e.g. the parallel often drawn between stopping aggression in central Europe and defeating the Viet Cong). Memory alone cannot be a reliable guide to action in a changing society; but rational analysis without memory misreads the nature of human agents in society.

A fourth important contrast that should be mentioned is that between reason on the one hand and faith and revelation on the other. When we talk about faith, we are talking about an attitude and a personal relationship to One who communicates knowledge to us; and when we talk about revelation we are talking about the knowledge that is communicated, which is both knowledge of the Person who reveals or communicates and of the truths which are being communicated. In this contrast, reason is not merely logical, deductive thought but includes the whole range of human experience and intuition as well. For these are all modes of knowing which form part of our standard operating equipment as autonomous human beings, whereas in faith we are in a relation of dependence on another. What is known by faith, what is revealed by a personal being with authority is not fundamentally dependent on our control and criticism and revision. Faith commits us to an attitude of obedience, which is voluntary on our part and which may or may not be shared by others. Thus what we know in faith may not serve as a basis for policy decisions and laws in a democratic, pluralistic society; the justification for this is not that reason must be independent of faith, but that the obedience of faith has to be free if it is to be authentic. Reasons for action can be drawn from the affirmations of faith, but they can serve as reasons only for those who make the loving commitment of faith.

REASON AND GUIDES TO ACTION

So far these contrasts have been between reason on the one hand and various alternative sources of knowledge or belief on the other. The next four contrasts will deal with reason not so much as source of knowledge, but rather with reason as guide to action.

The fifth contrast is between reason on the one hand and tradition, custom, and law on the other. This is a contrast that we are familiar with from efforts to achieve the rational reform of social institutions and practices. Here reason usually serves as a standard for judging an institution or a practice or for comparing several institutions and practices. Thus we would judge it irrational for a state to have a law allowing only two years imprisonment for murder and, say, twenty years of possession of narcotics. The characteristic danger of rational reform is the imposition of abstract universal norms in a way that ignores the rationality inherent in given social institutions or that rides roughshod over the diversity of particular cases.[13] We then wind up with reforms that look good or reasonable on paper, but that are disastrous in practice; and by setting reason too sharply and neatly in opposition to tradition and custom we produce a culture that is unable to come to terms with the values of its past and that ignores the positive contribution of tradition.

The sixth contrast is between reason and force as means of settling disputes and of effecting change in society. Thus John Locke in arguing for a person's right of self-defense against those who have a settled design upon his life observes that "such men are not under the ties of the common law of reason, have no other rule but that of force and violence, and so may be treated as beasts of prey."[14] The contrast between reason and force should not be understood in such a way that there can be no rational use of force; but it has to be admitted that the use of reason and the use of force to resolve disputes are two fundamentally different ways of achieving one's ends and of dealing with other persons. For in replacing the instruments of rational persuasion with those of force, one threatens the free self-determination of the other and treats the other as standing outside the boundaries of rational community. The successful application of force takes away the freedom and voluntariness of the other person's activity.[15] The standard justification for the use of force is that the person or community against whom it is to be used has already broken the bonds of rational community by threatening the life or liberty of those who resort to force in self-defense. Under certain circumstances resort to force can be justified and rational; but force does not thereby become a normal means for the rational attainment of personal or political ends. Rather, it serves as an extraordinary means for dealing with certain kinds of evil in the world; it is brought within the realm of legal and rational order in civilized communities by virtue of the state's monopoly of the deliberate use of this means. The possibility of the rational use of force reminds us that the world in which we try to live as rational agents contains persons and social groups that refuse to acknowledge the equal dignity of other persons as rational agents. The rational use of force is only possible in a world that conforms only imperfectly to rational norms of order and justice. For those who think that a fully rational world is readily attainable, any use of force will appear to be simply irrational. From the standpoint of the observer of history, the necessity for the use of force reminds us of difficult (and sometimes appalling) truths about human conduct; and both the recognition of these truths and a realistic response to them are rational. As Hamilton wryly observed in Number 28 of *The Federalist*:

"The idea of governing at all times by the simple force of law (which we have been told is the only admissible principle of republican government) has no place but in the reveries of those political doctors whose sagacity disdains the admonitions of experimental instruction."[16]

A seventh contrast is that between reason and emotion as sources of activity. This is one of the most familiar contrasts in our culture. Each of us has probably said at some time or other to

someone who vehemently disagreed with us, "Stop being emotional, and think about the matter reasonably." The primacy of
head over heart has been urged by philosophical moralists since
the time of Plato and has been commonly regarded as a necessary
condition for human progress in virtue and for observance of the
moral law. The rule of emotion and nonrational desire has been
generally thought to be dangerous both for the health and happiness of the individual and for the security and order of society at
large. Since Freud, we have also come to see more clearly the
dangers of an overly rigid rule of reason and the super-ego over
the emotions; but this is a point that was made by Aristotle himself when he ordered that "intellect rules the appetites with a
constitutional and royal rule,"[17] and not despotically. The function of reason in the classical tradition was not to efface or eliminate the emotions, but rather to regulate them in the light of its
knowledge of the good for the person and of our society as a
whole.[18] In these tasks, however, reason is not alone but works
together with will.

Here we come to the last of the contrasts that we are to
consider, that between reason and will. There are many philosophical problems connected with the notion of will, but here we
will take will to be human appetite or desire precisely as this is
informed by reason and is capable of freely choosing to act or not
to act, to act in one way or another. The primary activity of will is
choice.[19] When I commit myself in love to another person, when I
decide to tell an unpleasant truth to my boss, when I refuse a third
serving of dessert, when I opt to go to *Star Wars* rather than
watch *Kojak*, when I actually adopt a certain plan of life for
myself, in all these cases I am not merely reaching certain conclusions or thinking certain thoughts; no, I am also willing or deciding to do certain things. I may not actually do the thing that I
decide; circumstances may intervene, I may change my mind.
But I am set to do the thing; and normally, unless I am the victim
of some pathological condition, I do it. But the activity of the will
is a distinct aspect of human activity, not reducible to either the
intellectual activity of reason or to external activity. As Thomas
Aquinas observed, "The will enters between the mind and the
external action, for the mind proposes the object to the will, and

the will causes the external action."[20] Decision is a step beyond mere thinking and reasoning about good things that attract us and beyond a judgment that something should be done. There is in it an energy, a commitment, a readiness to put forth effort to overcome difficulties that stand in our way. Hence we speak of "will-power," and we connect closely the ideas of willing and trying; for our efforts are a more reliable indication of what we will than our accomplishments.

Will is active after reason and is dependent on reason to present alternatives. But it does not always choose in accordance with reason. For in a familiar but mysterious way, we can will not to do what we think is right, we can reject what we believe to be the best thing for us. How it is possible for us to choose against our conscience and even against our sense of our own good is a problem both for a theory of human activity and for the actual conduct of our lives. But it is part of our experience that we can choose lesser goods or even what we know to be wrong. Our whole experience goes against the claim of Socrates that no one does evil willingly. The goods that we encounter in this life do not compel the decision of our will but leave us free. But it is indicative of the close links that there are between will and reason, that we find the deliberate choice of evil or the rejection of good irrational.

More positively we believe that the activity of will that finds expression in commitment should be open to rational criticism and should be informed by the rational virtues of fairness and honesty, even though the activity of will is not reducible to the activity of the intellect or reason. The importance of subjecting commitment to rational scrutiny has been eloquently underlined by Senator Thomas McIntyre of New Hampshire, who recently said on the Senate floor:

"I believe in firm and outspoken commitment to principles and convictions. I would readily agree, as someone once said, 'that there are times when compromise offers little more than an easy refuge for the irresolute spirit.' But I would make a distinction between commitment that is rooted in reality—commitment, for example, that recognizes the linkage between problems and the consequences of ignoring that linkage when applying solutions—and commitment that denies reality and is in truth but the blind and obsessive pursuit of illusion."[21]

In this overview of the contrasts between reason and various nonrational factors in human activity and of some of the meanings that reason can have in relation to human activity, we can see that we are not confronted with simple alternatives of being rational or irrational in our understanding of human conduct and in our own activity. There is no question of having reason without experience or tradition or emotion or will. Nonrational factors are inescapably present in human activity and not merely as obstacles to be overcome by reason but as sources of and partners with reason. This holds true whether we are speaking from a religious perspective or not. In the decisions that we take as individuals and as a society there are and must be factors at work that stand in a living and creative tension with reason. There are, as Pascal saw, "an infinite number of things" that are beyond reason, and yet of which we are in some way aware.

An important caution should be added at this point: recognition of how important and indispensable nonrational factors are in the shaping of our lives should not be taken as a blanket endorsement of irrational beliefs and courses of action. The limitations of reason that we have seen in this series of contrasts do not justify actions taken against reason or the rejection of reason in our search for the true and the good.

REASON AND RATIONALITY

A further reflection on this series of contrasts has to do with the paradoxical character of what we have been doing; for we have been offering a reasoned and orderly though sketchy account of factors that stand over against and limit reason; and we have been suggesting that it is reasonable to give proper weight to these factors in human life and activity. We have been using reason to think both sides of the limits of reason. This might suggest that we have now overturned the contrasts that we set up or that there is something fishy about our entire enterprise. The root of this paradox is that in addition to the various specific notions of reason (e.g. as deductive system, as source of abstract social norms, as thought independent of emotion), there is a further concept of reason as the general human search to make sense of our world and our lives and the human ability to do this at least to some extent. We are rationalizing animals through and through. As a contemporary English philosopher, Roger Trigg, has observed in his book on *Reason and Commitment*: "Rationality cannot be an optional extra, if it is possible at all."[22] Reason as our general need and capacity to understand ourselves and our world does move across the contrasts that we have proposed. So some believers set out to understand the revelation that they accept by faith and in the process of doing this become theologians. Apologists for faith attempt to show why it is reasonable for us to assent to conclusions that we cannot reason to. Psychologists classify and attempt to give a rational explanation of our emotions, and historians and social scientists do the same for our institutions and traditions. Reflective persons try to discern how much weight it is reasonable to give to our emotions and our intuitions in the management of our lives.

It is reasonable to respect the limits of reason, and reason in this general sense enables us to probe the limits of reason in its more specific aspects and to make judgments about the scope of particular modes of reason. As rationalizing animals, we attempt to achieve at least a rough coherence among our various sets of beliefs and to impart a general direction to our lives; and we form judgments about the reasonableness of fitting specifically rational and nonrational elements in this general project even though we recognize that neither our lives nor our beliefs can be made into one rational system. Thus we can apply to reason what Aristotle said about the soul and the mind:

"Mind as we have described it is what it is by virtue of becoming all things."[23]
"The soul is analogous to the hand; for as the hand is the tool of tools, so the mind is the form of forms."[24]

The point here is that reason is not limited to understanding the formal deductive systems of mathematics and philosophy but that reason is our common instrument for comprehending and ordering the world in which we live and act. In fulfilling this task, reason is called to understand and affirm many things outside itself.

If we accept this comprehensive notion of reason, we allow for the possibility of making judgments about the reasonableness of our beliefs and decisions and of accepting rational criticisms of them at the same time that we avoid committing ourselves to a narrow concept of rationality which would relegate such nonrational factors as experience, intuition, faith, tradition, emotion, and will to the sidelines. Rationality in this wider sense requires that we devote appropriate care to understanding all of these factors as they are relevant to the particular decisions that we are called on to make.

Rationality in this wider sense also leads us beyond ourselves as individuals and requires us to take seriously the experience, the intuitions, the faiths, the traditions, the emotions, and the decisions of other persons. At certain times in the past, rationalism has been closely associated with individualism, partly because it was thought that only by consulting one's own awareness could an individual achieve rational certainty, partly because it was argued that the rational individual alone could be free of the irrational influences of society and history. But once we reflect on the necessarily social character of language and on the way in which our ability to give reasons to one another depends on our ability to use language, we can maintain that rationality is a social enterprise. In our work we live through conflicts which we are likely to perceive as conflicts between reason (which *we* understand and formulate) and prejudice, self-interest, and irrationality (which others use for their own ends). No one would deny that such situations can occur, but they have to be set within the larger task of discovering and elaborating shared norms of rationality which bridge over the struggle of interests and wills that we are all familiar with in our social life. For when I appeal to reason in a policy dispute, I do not merely assert my own views on what reason requires, but I appeal to norms and values and ways of thinking about experience which I may misread and may misuse. Furthermore, these norms and ways of thinking do not belong to me as an individual but are open to all, though in a manner which allows different people to appropriate these norms and ways of thinking in different ways and to different degrees. Part of the wider task of reason in society is to find ways for people to work together in a community of argument and mutual correction, and these ways may not exactly coincide with the dictates of reason when this is taken in one of the narrower senses that we mentioned earlier in our series of contrasts or with the conclusions of reason that any individual may reach. "A decent respect for the opinions of mankind"—and not merely for their opinions but also for their entire situation—is an important part of rationality in the wider sense that we have been reflecting on. *The* rational policy or *the* reasonable thing to do is not simply the conclusion of an argument, but has to be determined by consideration of all the relevant nonrational factors that are present in the persons who are making the decision and in the persons who are affected by it. Our judgments of what is reasonable in a particular case are not abstract or universal but have to be particular and concrete. Recognition of relevant nonrational factors is not simply a lapse into irrationality or a concession forced on us by external necessity: it is an integral part of what it is to be a rational human being in community with other independent human beings.

Commitment to rationality in this wider sense is a kind of political charity, a way of loving one's neighbor as oneself, of respecting real differences among persons, and of treating other persons as ends and not as means. Rationality in this wider sense is marked by its reliance on mutual understanding and persuasion rather than propaganda, force, and manipulation of others. It is a value which calls forth commitment and requires the exercise of virtue. To be rational in this sense involves not merely a passionless exercise of a purely cognitive faculty but requires positive attitudes of esteem and concern for other persons and a strong desire to be fair and impartial in one's decisions and to stand fast against the temptations and distortions of perception that any effort to shape policy brings with it.

Rationality in this wider sense is not to be identified with religious faith, but is complementary to it. It can be found in wise and competent public servants of all religious persuasions and none. Rationality in the wide sense that we have been describing can serve as a common secular faith, an ideal calling forth virtue in those who respond to it and benefiting the society to which they belong.[25] But I would suggest that it can be strengthened and enlightened by the resources of Christian faith and commitment. It can be strengthened because of the motivating power of religious belief and symbols, especially by the concrete symbol of Jesus as the example of a sacrificial love that is free from worldly ambition and false respect for persons, a love that liberates others. It can also be strengthened by the sharing of values and hopes that is characteristic of the believing community when it is responding to the grace of the Lord. Rationality can be enlightened by the vision of faith, which stands as a corrective to the persistent tendency in human culture to settle for a restricted view of human dignity which makes reason merely a technique for the satisfaction of desire and which interprets our social life as merely the resolution of conflicts of interests. The ideal of a genuine social union[26] of persons expressing their nature as free and equal rational agents and living together in mutual respect and concern is not to be identified with the kingdom of God but is a prefiguration of it. For the fullness of human rationality is to be made perfect in Christ Jesus, "whom God made our wisdom, our righteousness and sanctification and redemption" (1 Cor. 1, 30).

This article has attempted both to sketch out certain contrasts between reason and other factors in our lives that bear on our beliefs and decisions and to argue for a sense of reason that goes beyond these contrasts and includes them in the human subject's effort to understand and shape the world. Like a great deal of analytic philosophy, this paper aims at providing a map of our experience. As an aid to the formation of one's judgment and the clarification of one's views on the issues that this paper considers, I am proposing the following questions for reflection.

1) Is there, or can there be, a unique rational method, e.g., systems analysis, for arriving at policy decisions?
2) Should reason be regarded as merely a technical instru-

ment incapable of solving the real moral problems of government?

3) Are there cases in which too narrow a conception of reason has produced bad policy results? Cases in which neglect of reason has produced bad policy results?

4) Where do you think the factors that we have contrasted with reason should play a part in the forming of decisions? Are there any points at which they should not be allowed? Or at which they pose a special danger?

NOTES

1. A comprehensive account of current work in empirical psychology on decision making is Irving Janis and Leon Mann, *Decision Making: A Psychological Analysis of Conflict, Choice and Commitment* (New York: Free Press, 1977).

2. Blaise Pascal, *Pensees*, tr. Martin Turnell (New York: Harper, 1962), p. 209.

3. *Ibid.*, p. 163.

4. *Ibid.*, p. 222.

5. Ludwig Wittgenstein, *Tractatus Logico-Philosophicus* (London: Routledge and Kegan Paul, 1922), 5.61, p. 149.

6. William Shakespeare, *Hamlet*, Act II, Scene II, 11. 318-323.

7. Johann Wolfgang von Goethe, *The Sorrows of Young Werther*, tr. Victor Lange (New York: Rinehart, 1949).

8. Aristotle, *Metaphysics*, I, 1. 980a22-982 a1.

9. *Ibid.*, 981a 14-15.

10. Rene Descartes, *Discourse on Method*, tr. John Veitch, Part II in *The Rationalists* (Garden City, N.Y.: Doubleday, n.d.), p. 52.

11. Cf. Ernest Nagel and James R. Newman, *Godel's Proof* (New York: New York University Press, 1958).

12. Cf. Soren Kierkegaard, *Concluding Unscientific Postscript*, tr. David Swenson (Princeton, N.J.: Princeton University Press, 1941), pp. 107-113.

13. For an important discussion of the descendence of rational conduct on tradition and of the limits of abstract rationalism, cf. Michael Oakeshott, "Rational Conduct," in *Rationalism in Politics* (London: Methuen, 1962), esp. pp. 104–110.

14. John Locke, *An Essay Concerning the True Original, Extent and End of Civil Government*, ch. 3, par. 16, in *Social Contract*, ed. Sir Ernest Barker (New York: Oxford, 1962), p. 12.

15. Cf. Thomas Aquinas, *Summa Theologiae*, I-II, 6, 4.

16. Alexander Hamilton, James Madison, John Jay, *The Federalist Papers*, ed. Clinton Rossiter (New York: New American Library, 1961), p. 178.

17. Aristotle, *Politics*, I, 5, 1254b4-5.

18. Cf. Plato, *Republic*, IV, 441e-442c.

19. Cf. John Rawls, *A Theory of Justice* (Cambridge, Mass.: Harvard University Press, 1971), pp. 411-415, for a discussion of principles of rational choice.

20. St. Thomas Aquinas, *Summa Theologiae*, I-II, 13, 5, ad 1.

21. Thomas J. McIntyre, "The Canal Treaties and the New Right," Washington *Post*, Friday, March 3, 1978, p. A23.

22. Roger Trigg, *Reason and Commitment* (Cambridge: Cambridge University Press, 1973), p. 151.

23. Aristotle, *De Anima*, III, 5. 430a15.

24. *Ibid.*, III, 8, 432a 1-2.

25. Cf. John Dewey, *A Common Faith* (New Haven, Conn.: Yale University Press, 1934), for the presentation of service to the common values of humanity as a "realization of distinctively religious values inherent in natural experience" (p. 78).

26. Cf. Rawls, pp. 520-529, for a discussion of the notion of social union.

Reason Conversation

Haughey: This paper is inviting us to sort out our attitudes toward reason's capacities and our expectations about what reason can deliver in this whole world of decision-making. Are our decisions the product of our reason or reasoning or arrived at by reasons? The last part of the paper widens the concept of reason to reasonableness, and invites us to do the same.

Langan: The idea both in this paper on reason and the other paper on values is to sketch out categories that are comprehensive, that can be mulled over by people from different traditions, religious or nonreligious, as an aid to understanding themselves and their work.

Margulies: I liked this paper very much. I saw high school and college friends there. But there's a solitary character to it which bothered me. The socialization process in governmental decision-making makes the way we handle issues more anthropological than philosophical. I had the feeling of solitary observation or isolation in these sets of views. I saw one person standing alone doing things which one person standing alone never does in government.

Langan: Yes, I suspect that like most philosophers I fall back on an individualistic pattern, even though I try to correct that later on. Philosophers usually work by going off and thinking, rather than going down to the office for a meeting. But I think it's implicit in the position that I am trying to describe that reason is not a purely individual thing.

Margulies: I see that the kinds of negotiations that we are in represent the whole range of the processes you describe—the rational, the emotional, the psychological. For example: We have the Health Planning Act to administer and our concern with the Health Planning Act is of two kinds. It is to be used to lower the costs of medical care and it is to be used to improve access to medical care. We set out a bunch of guidelines and those guidelines were interpreted correctly by the Secretary to mean that we wanted to close hospitals. When we published guidelines it was a bombshell—over 55,000 protesting letters. What struck me was the kind of letter that came in. There is an 82 year old man 100 miles west of Bozeman, Montana who has always lived in a small town and gone to the closest hospital which is probably considered inefficient. If he breaks his hip and they take him 200 miles away to a strange town, he'd probably die. If he stays at home and looks down on Main Street and sees a place he knows, he'll probably get up and walk out of there. So you see, reason and efficiency aren't the only things. The little old man from Montana has challenged our initial assumption. What are we saving money for? Is there something we're missing in our great desire to save money?

Dungan: Let me add a slight demur. If one thinks of the 82 year old man in Bozeman, Montana, that's one case. But think of the two hospitals five blocks away from each other, each operating at 60% occupancy, then think of the public good including the patients who inhabit those hospitals and pay large charges. What's reasonable about that decision?

Margulies: I am left with the question: Is there or can there be a unique rational method, for example, systems analysis for our decisions in government? For some of us there are values to be inserted which perhaps you could get into in systems analysis but I rather doubt it. It would be such a clumsy system it would never be perfected. What that hospital that has always been there means to people—who knows how to decide how much it is worth? I am confident it is worth something and I doubt any rational method could be devised that would include this kind of factor in its calculations.

Lowell: I agree and would take the point one step further. You have to make decisions in the absence of full knowledge and I don't think that's irrational. We make most of our decisions in some kind of time constraint and so we act on the basis of the reasons we know plus the memories we have and intuitions that come forth and the emotions that are expressed and the attachments that we have and I suppose they are all called loyalties. Loyalty to that man in Bozeman is a reason, even if it's not rational, or maybe it's rational even if it's not a reason, and it's got to enter into the final decision-making.

Margulies: Just for a point of accuracy, the man is not in Bozeman—if he were there, there would be no problem!

Gessert: What's that slogan we always use around Washington? "There's no reason for it, it's just policy." What you said, Joe, is true, that no decision that one ever makes in government is made on the basis of certainty. It's always made on the basis of uncertainty and with a lack of knowledge of what the exact consequences will be. Whether one decides to deploy the neutron bomb, whether one decides to transfer cruise missile technology to allies, whether one decides to save this man 100 miles from Bozeman, finally has to be a judgment call and it's a judgment call that is informed by reason and by as much reason as you can bear. With respect to systems analysis, as a practitioner of that black art I would not want it to be ever believed that one could make a decision in government on the basis of systems analysis. What it can provide is as much as you can find out about the means available to get to some of your objectives. But recognize the limitations of that analysis. That information is invaluable but it's not a sufficient basis for making a decision. The basis for making a decision is probably all the other things that you weren't able to get into that fairly reductionist tool. You don't have an independent basis within systems analysis for judging the ends.

McCormick: But when you talk about means and choices of means, to what extent might part of the problem be in the ends themselves? That is, sorting out amongst many pursuable, desirable goods, which ones deserve a preference at this particular time and in this particular society under these particular circumstances?

Gessert: Yes, that's what I was intending to say. The fundamental decisions in government tend to be much more decisions about ends and not merely technical decisions about means to ends.

Silverstone: Your process can only be rational if there is some kind of an agreement on what the end is or what the beginning assumption is, and that is rare. The attempt to explain government decisions in rational terms misleads people. They are put in rational terms to give them legitimacy. But the effect of this process may be to remove any discussion of what the assumptions were or what the ends should be.

Langan: Where we have disagreement about ends, the question still is: "What's the reasonable thing to do in this situation?" For this I think we usually rely on process, a process which is not deductive or something that can be neatly formalized but that is our way of dealing as reasonable people with each other. The end product of this process may not resemble any one individual's account of what a rational solution of the problem would be.

Margulies: I think in government decision-making it's more likely that the process enables us to avoid making the choice and so the choice is forever put off. For example: We aggregate in order to look at the whole issue, then we say "Ah, but this is a pluralistic society", so then we disaggregate and send the decisions on back to somewhere else, at which point we call it a disorganized society. When we don't like it, it's disorganized; when we do like it then it's diversified and pluralistic. So we send it all back out there to make the decision; then we chide the people who make the wrong decision and then we aggregate and look at it all over again. Like so many Scarlet O'Hara's, we'll think about it tomorrow and tomorrow we'll find processes to postpone facing our dilemmas.

Breslin: We also "trade off". We pass this kind of bill and then we counteract it with that kind of bill. So we develop the kind of government which is trying to do a little bit for everybody.

Hollenbach: Concerning the previous paper, Ralph Dungan brought up that question about making decisions on principle and not on the basis of loyalties. Do you think it's possible to make decisions on principle? What does principle mean if you take this comprehensive notion of rationality?

Breslin: One issue comes to my mind immediately—the question of illegal immigration of aliens. What's the principled thing to do, what's the right thing to do, not even what's the politic thing to do? This is one of many issues that we are confronted with in government that we throw into the "too hard" file for later. I don't know who knows what the right answer is to that issue.

Haughey: Are your expectations that reason, if used well, will deliver that which it hasn't delivered so far? When faced with something which is as complex as some of the issues you mention, what are your expectations about reason in relationship to these questions?

Breslin: We seem to go back and forth between extremes. I think, in some respects, we are coming to the conclusion on some of these issues that we can't do anything about them, they are insoluble.

Haughey: Is this conclusion reached because reason has been exercised on them and found wanting or has reason been underemployed in attempts to solve the questions?

Breslin: I think it's been used. In the case of undocumented aliens there has been much research on it. All kinds of thinkers are throwing up their hands.

Haughey: Is that because there's a quandry at the level of principle? We don't have the principles to resolve the question?

Breslin: A little, yeh, I think—I don't know! The alternatives are so distasteful. In other words, we could erect a wall around the U.S. and say "You just can't come in any more."

Margulies: But do we include in our consideration all the alternatives? Why should we have borders between countries? Why should there be a difference between being a Mexican and an American? Maybe it is an issue which is too big for us to take on.

Breslin: I think we are almost there right now, frankly.

Margulies: So we're just simply trying to stay within a set of processes around a sovereignty principle which is inadequate.

Breslin: No, it's more than that—the problem of unemployment is a worldwide problem right now. As long as we have open borders we are solving some of the problems of other countries and we are making our problem worse. We could also respond in a violent way and use force. Force might be the rational thing. Having decided what our interests or concerns are, you can decide where you want to come out. If the way you want to come out is by not having so many people come into the U.S., we could then mobilize the kind of force that would be needed to accomplish the end.

Langan: Also, there are frequent situations where we may be clear about the end, even clear about the means, and of two minds about whether we want to pay the price. We might say, "Well, we know we can do this but do we want to take the means?" When you are in a situation where you say "I want the end, I see what the means are, and the means are so unpalatable that I doubt whether I really want the end," then reflective rationality is necessary.

Silverstone: Well, isn't it that the issue we're discussing is too big? There comes a time when you may have to recognize that there is only a certain amount of knowledge, technology, money. Bureaucrats cannot solve that big problem, but we can deal with some of the component parts of it. With regard to undocumented aliens, we have to ask what is our community going to do with regard for the people already here. "Are we going to make schools available to their children?" "Are we going to keep others out?" There are all kinds of ongoing problems that need to be dealt with even while recognizing that maybe we are stymied by the big problem. The undocumented alien is only a small part of the overall problem of the relationship of the U.S. with the Third World. We do not have a clear answer for that, and I doubt that we can formulate a good and fully acceptable answer in the near future. I avoid the big question which I cannot deal with anyway. HEW can come in and offer something in education for the kids of migrants and Civil Service can come in and offer a government job program.

McCormick: To what extent is not knowing what to do actually a way of restating or saying that we are committed to certain goods or values that we are very reluctant to let go of? For example, energy.

Margulies: I think we're also burdened with the American notion that problems can be solved but there are some which can't be.

Crahan: The question is, however, precisely why they cannot be. Such issues are being posed with limits to the responses that could be offered or the solutions that are possible for reasonable people to reach. In order to deal with the question of undocumented aliens you have to take into account economic conditions both within Mexico and the U.S. It means dealing with certain very basic structural elements within the international economic order. There is not the disposition within this country to deal with that particular problem at that level. So your response, your predicament in terms of response is determined by the parameters which you are accepting, the predetermined limits to the extent and nature of your response. The predicament is very much a function of the fact that conditions in Mexico that encourage migration are not created solely by Mexico.

Silverstone: I don't know that it's that clear that a new international economic order or transformation of world systems, or any plan that anyone has in mind, would reduce the migration problem. It might very well exacerbate the migration problem.

5
Responsibilities Regarding Morally Questionable Policies
Brian H. Smith

In the initial essay of this volume I examined the variety of contributions into the policymaking process that persons with different functions in government exercise, many of which involve a considerable degree of discretion and value conflicts.

The focus of this second essay of mine is to draw together several of the elements laid out in the first four essays and employ them to assist us in judging what to do when a specific policy has morally objectionable aspects and several options present themselves. I shall begin with a case analysis of a public event not related to government work but which graphically highlights all the dimensions involved in establishing a moral obligation for action to improve a social situation. I shall then discuss these dimensions in relation to the environment of government and explore what strategies are available to a public official who has decided that a policy or situation in which he or she is involved has negative moral implications. In the final part of this essay I will discuss what types of resources are needed both in an individual's personal life and in the institutional climate in government to nurture moral sensitivity and effectiveness among public servants.

THE KITTY GENOVESE CASE: THE DIMENSIONS OF MORAL DECISION-MAKING

One fall evening several years ago a young woman, Kitty Genovese, was attacked, robbed and stabbed on a street in Kew Gardens, N.Y. When her assailant came upon her she began to scream and resist. The man struggled with her, and finally stabbed her leaving her bleeding on the sidewalk. She dragged herself several yards into the doorway of a nearby building, all the while moaning and calling loudly for help. The whole process took several minutes. Later the police determined that a total of 38 people heard the screams or actually viewed the event from the windows of their apartments. No one did anything to help, not even call the police, and the woman subsequently died.[1]

The bystanders were not guilty of breaking any law, since New York State (like almost all states) has nothing in its penal code requiring citizens to come to the aid of others in grave public distress. It does seem evident, however, that there was some moral obligation facing those 38 people to try to minimize harm in this situation.

In fact, John Simon, Charles Powers and Jon Gunnemann in their book *The Ethical Investor* have used this case as an illustration of when and why persons have a moral obligation to take action for the elimination of harm or the promotion of some good in a public situation. They argue that four salient conditions established responsibility for action on the part of the 38 spectators in this case, and that these are transferable to other contexts:[2]

1) Someone or some group is experiencing a critical need.
2) Other persons are aware of this need or could be expected to have such knowledge.
3) These other persons have the capacity to act helpfully in the situation.
4) There is no other reasonable source of help available.

In the case of the attack on Kitty Genovese, there was a visible or at least audible manifestation of need of a person suffering serious harm. There were at least 38 persons who knew that something horrible was happening to her. They all had some ability to help without seriously endangering their own personal safety. It was also evident that there was no one on the street able to help the woman, and that there was a good chance she might die if one of the 38 did not at least call the police. Apparently there was no consultation among the 38 to see if anyone had done so. No one wanted to get involved. As a result, a life was lost that possibly could have been saved.

Aside from highlighting the conditions which establish the moral obligation to intervene in a situation harmful to other persons, the case also dramatizes that good moral decision-making requires much more than following a set of rules. While these can be helpful as general action guides, in approaching a particular situation they are meaningless unless there is something already present in persons enabling them to respect and *promote* the well-being of other people.

Moral principles even when based on some objective reality or culled from past human experience are useless if people have not developed a set of values which give life to principles and which sensitize them to the basic legitimate interests of other persons and groups. As the second essay pointed out, such values are more than subjective feelings; they result from a whole series of lived experiences shaped by family, community, education as well as personal commitment. In short, these constitute virtue and character and are formed gradually over a long period of time. These are the fundamental ground of all morality.

In the neighborhood of Kew Gardens where Kitty Genovese was murdered, public virtue and character were lacking not only in the individual spectators but in the community itself. A sense of solidarity and mutual concern for one another was sadly missing, and this was a crucial factor in the environment which dulled a sense of personal responsibility and moral awareness.

In addition to basic apathy, the Kew Gardens case also points to the lack of moral imagination on the part of those involved. All were so frozen in their own isolated positions that they did not seem to see that possibilities existed for ameliorating the situation in some way. This moral atomization or blindness illustrates the problem highlighted in Chapter 3 which illustrates how people can become so fixed in their narrow role responsibilities that they often lack the flexibility to see their capacity to improve wider social situations of which they are a part.

Finally, these 38 people were unwilling or unable to foresee, or be concerned about, the probable consequences of their choices—namely, that inaction would lead to the death of Kitty Genovese. Presumably no one made a conscious link between what they could or would do and the impact of their choice on the life of the endangered person. This also pertains to the issue raised in the previous two essays, namely the necessity for vision beyond the present, immediate situation and the need to assess the foreseeable consequences of one's action or inaction for oneself and for others. Not only did Kitty Genovese die, but the inaction on the part of the 38 people was a further erosion of the moral fiber of the neighborhood itself.

Hence, I would argue that a morally responsible decision in face of public issues involves at least four different elements of sensitivity: (1) a human sensitivity to people and their legitimate needs which is concerned with promoting these as far as possible, (2) a set of guiding principles that encourage persons not only to refrain from unethical conduct but also to enhance the good of others when they are in need, (3) a practical ability to assess what is possible in a situation regarding strategies to minimize harm or promote good, (4) some foresight and assessment as to what the consequences of these options will be for one's own integrity and well-being as well as for that of others affected by one's choices.[3]

Moral decision-making would involve all four of these elements; no one of them alone is sufficient for determining one's social responsibility. Very often people understand morality as simply following a set of rules or a code of professional ethics with clearly articulated "do's" and "don't's." When morality is conceived of only in these terms it becomes too rigid to be applied in a complex world, or useful only in identifying cases of egregious wrongdoing.

Some persons, on the other hand, focus exclusively on the level of personal values and emphasize that each individual must remain true to what he or she feels is right. While commitment to a personally chosen set of values is an essential ingredient of morality, by themselves these values can become too privatized or subjective if they do not sufficiently take into account the needs and interests of other persons or the consequences of one's actions on the overall well-being of others.

Focusing only on the context itself or on the foreseeable consequences of action is also insufficient to make a good moral decision. Weighing consequences is necessary to make a realistic and practical moral judgment, but these assessments can become purely pragmatic or subservient to the self-interest of the person making the judgment. Action possibilities and consequences need to be measured by some general standards to avoid the danger of proteanization (constantly shifting loyalties) discussed in the third chapter on loyalties.

Hence, all four elements must be kept in healthy tension simultaneously: commitment to a set of values that include the legitimate interests of other people; awareness of some general principles that serve as action guides; an assessment of the specific situation and of practical courses of action available in the context, and an assessment of the consequences of various options for one's own integrity and the well-being of others. While there will usually be conflicts among these four elements, or certain ambiguities due to a lack of complete information, all of them play a crucial role in the crystallization of mature moral decisions. No one of them can be ignored without detriment to ourselves or to other persons affected by our choices.

APPLICABILITY OF THE ELEMENTS OF MORAL DECISION-MAKING IN THE ENVIRONMENT OF GOVERNMENT

Needless to say, the choices that persons with various kinds of responsibility in government make every day involve problems that are far less clear than the Kitty Genovese case. The conflicting political pressures facing elected and appointed officials, the discretionary judgments of administrators regarding applicability of regulations and program evaluation, the weighing of alternatives for policy recommendations by persons with different perspectives in a collegial context, the assessment of pertinent information by specialists, and the contribution to the overall operation of an office by secretarial personnel, all deal with issues in which moral obligation is harder to identify and fulfill.

Nevertheless, moral values and obligations are certainly involved since a vast number of these judgments have a significant bearing on how policies will affect the well-being of large numbers of citizens. Furthermore, the mere observance of rules or codes of professional ethics, while important for preventing egregious errors, will not guarantee that positive and possible moral good will be achieved.[4] Legal requirements and regulations can be helpful in minimizing errors of commission in government, but are not very useful for identifying faults of omission or for providing for better performance and positive initiative on the part of government employees.

Some policies or decisions can at times involve questionable moral implications and the behavior of public servants in face of these is often too acquiescent or uncritical. Examples would have to include failure to disclose "cover-ups" of misuse of resources or suppression of important information within the ranks of management, failure to insist on adequate precautions for employee or public health and safety, lack of conservation of scarce resources, saying nothing about favoritism in awarding of contracts, going along with ill-conceived or badly managed programs that reduce the quality of public services. All of these examples are illustrative of serious omissions of effort to minimize harm by officials who do not have a deeper sense of purpose and commitment to their work that goes beyond following orders, or minding their own business. Although technically not violating laws by looking the other way in face of such questionable actions, persons who observe such policies (or who are unavoidably involved in carrying them out) fail in their moral responsibility.

None of these examples are as dramatic as the Kitty Genovese case discussed earlier in this essay, but similar issues of moral import are at stake. In all of these situations there is serious harm being done not only to the integrity of government itself but to the wider public affected by such policies. Some people undoubtedly are aware of such practices when they occur, or should be, given their proximity to what is going on. There are a whole range of strategies that can be taken by such persons to improve a situation. If those with awareness of the problem (even if they are not directly responsible) do not take constructive action to minimize harm or at least inform those who can, morally questionable policies or decisions are likely to go unchallenged or poorly conceived programs continue at substandard levels of performance.

Hence, the principles of serious need, proximity, capacity, and last resort as outlined in the Genovese case all apply to situations where public servants observe questionable policies or patterns of behavior that are causing some harm to the government process or to the well-being of the public. Their oath of office requires that they put loyalty to the "highest moral principles" and country above "loyalty to persons, parties or government departments." This clearly implies more than merely refusing to violate professional codes of ethics or policy regulations but includes a positive orientation to promote good performance and eliminate harmful effects of decisions where they are seen or experienced.

POSSIBILITIES FOR INFLUENCING QUESTIONABLE POLICIES

In addition to the possession of some sense of positive commitment to the overall purpose of good government and some awareness of the foregoing principles, a sound moral decision to improve a policy or minimize a harm requires a careful analysis of the situation and a choice of strategies that will produce positive consequences. As we saw earlier, virtue and principles alone are insufficient to guarantee a mature and effective moral decision; practical wisdom in knowing the context and weighing the possible results of alternative courses of action is also essential.

Too often when strategies to improve bad policies are discussed in the literature or in public debate the courses of action analyzed are extreme or dramatic. The focus most frequently is on the behavior of very high officials in government or on cases of notoriety requiring some drastic action. For example, when Edward Weisband and Thomas Franck in their book discuss the ethical choices between loyalty to team and loyalty to conscience in public life they deal only with cases of well-known high government officials who have resigned in disagreement over major policy decisions of their superiors.[5] Charles Peters and Taylor Branch concentrate on the type of dissent in government which involves "blowing the whistle," or going public with complaints against bad policies.[6] Much of the literature on Vietnam and Watergate focuses on persons at very high levels of policymaking, analyzing why they failed to exercise moral leadership in face of mounting destruction and misuse of power or go public with their criticisms upon resignation.[7]

Useful and enlightening as such studies and memoirs are, they are not very helpful for middle or low level career civil servants who deal with issues long before they become major public crises and for whom resignation or "blowing the whistle" are frequently not effective or realistic options. Resignation in protest can (and should) be used more frequently by political appointees since their withdrawal from government when carried out for moral reasons can focus public attention on a bad policy. Those lower down in the ranks, however, usually cannot afford to resign, nor will their resignation attract much public interest in the problem at hand. "Blowing the whistle" by going to the media can be effective in cases where egregious misuse of power is involved, but does not serve any effective purpose to rectify the far more numerous and less visible errors in government that occur every day.

The practical wisdom needed to operationalize moral commitments and principles in the daily routine of government work requires far less dramatic action but involves imagination, persistence, willingness to be flexible, a shrewd use of existing procedures, and a constant focus on the overall purpose of government—service to the public. There is much an average government employee can do to promote better performance and to minimize harm when it occurs far short of resignation or going public. In fact, as was clear in the topography laid out in the first chapter, numerous possibilities for influencing policy formation and execution exist all along the decision-making continuum. Many of these discretionary judgments when executed wisely sometimes can contribute far more to improving the moral climate of government and program performance than singular actions taken only by those with the highest responsibility or by persons resorting to strategies outside normal channels.

SOME GUIDELINES FOR EXERCISING PRACTICAL MORAL WISDOM[8]

One of the first things a person can and should do who believes he or she observes patterns of behavior that are causing some serious harm is to check to see if their perceptions are accurate. Finding out what others perceive is a good way to clarify one's own perspective and prevent purely subjective elements from coloring one's judgments. This is crucial for avoiding factual errors in assessing a problem as well as moralistic claims in approaching it. Such cross-checking can also provide information on the source of the problem, who are the responsible actors, past and present, what is the range of abuses to be corrected and what is a feasible way to begin to tackle the issue.

Once a person has gone through such a process and concludes that there is something wrong that needs improvement it is often important to seek allies who share their concerns. One can act alone, of course, and represent a case to an immediate superior individually. In many instances this can be effective and the issue can be taken care of quickly and expeditiously. In some situations, however, this may not always be the most effective approach, especially if the superior disagrees or is part of the problem. Building a consensus among interested parties, sharing insights as to how best to proceed, weaving the judgments of others into the overall critique of the problem, establishing a common definition of what is feasible to accomplish, are all strategies to form a wider base from which to exercise responsible criticism or more effective constructive action to rectify a situation.

When a problem cannot be taken care of horizontally through discussion or common action with peers, and it is necessary to approach higher authorities, or those lower in rank, it is wise to minimize ego conflicts, and when possible, open confrontation. More can be accomplished by articulating one's suggestions or criticisms in terms of loyalty to established goals or norms of procedure than by attacking persons. Arguing for fairer standards of operation or more clearly defined objectives or better evaluation methods can be effective strategies to improve performance, minimize personal mismanagement, or avoid such abuses as "sweetheart contracts." In making such suggestions or working to implement such procedures in one's organization it is also crucial to allow time for ideas to sink in gracefully to avoid unproductive impasses and to link offensive policies to views rejected by higher authorities.

Promoting an open written record of significant transactions and conversations can also enhance the possibility that pertinent information and decisions will be known to all who need to know them. One can also improve performance or forestall abuses or mismanagement by following procedures that call for periodic reports. In addition, a person can take the initiative to provide ad hoc critiques where relevant, encourage written exchanges and disseminate the record more widely to persons affected by policies. A thorough knowledge of regulations also enables one to point to objective guidelines as valid excuses to avoid becoming involved in illegal or morally questionable activities. All of these skillful uses and mastery of information can be additional strategies for preventing abuses, minimizing harmful consequences and improving smooth operations.

Resorting to extraordinary methods—such as going above the heads of one's immediate superiors or approaching influential outsiders, including the media—need not be ruled out as strategies of last resort. These are not the ordinary nor usually the most effective measures to exert influence, however, and should be employed only after exhausting other possible approaches mentioned earlier and in cases of rather extreme need.

A final practical aspect which one must keep in mind in assessing probable consequences of action strategies chosen to improve a situation is that compromise remedies are often better than none at all. One must aim his or her sights high to be true to the oath of office, but it is impossible to achieve everything one hopes to accomplish in a short period of time or in a situation involving a high degree of complexity or large numbers of interested parties. A partial or temporary solution may be the best one, at the moment, and sometimes one must be willing to accept this in pursuing more thorough or lasting remedies.

People with high ethical standards often feel that compromise is wrong, or means surrender, and that morality is all or nothing. Doubtless there are immoral actions that a person must always avoid in public service—stealing, cheating, exploitation of fellow workers, exchanging official favors for personal gain, sabotaging the good work of other people, empire building, deception of clients or supervisors. So long as these types of actions are avoided and one tries his or her practical best to promote positive improvement or eliminate clear harm, one can live with a clear conscience even if the outcome is not always optimum. It is possible to fight another day, and so long as a person does not accept mediocrity as the norm he or she should not be disheartened by partial victories.

Effective moral decision-making in public service, therefore, involves a combination of sensitivity, principled commitment, practical wisdom and a willingness to live with the best outcome possible without cynicism or discouragement. I would argue that public officials who do not try to maintain all these qualities in some sort of effective balance in the face of frustration, mistakes and failures will miss many opportunities to improve the moral climate in government as well as the quality of the services delivered to the public.

We surely have witnessed harmful policies in government that resulted from unprincipled, ambitious people bent on serving their own interests or those of greedy supporters. This is clearly harmful to both the integrity of government and the well-being of the wider public. Bad policies, however, can also result from the inaction of good public servants who give up too easily, who separate their personal morality from their work situation in government, or who, turning their backs on a dirty situation, say "I have no responsibility," or "I do not want to dirty my hands." These types of persons are also obstacles to good government and tragic figures of a different sort.

Ordinary government personnel might never come upon

situations comparable to the Kitty Genovese case. Yet everyday they are part of public decisions and transactions that directly or indirectly touch the lives of vast numbers of people in need. They can make a difference, however seemingly insignificant, for the quality of life of these people. When public officials view their work in too narrow a perspective, however, they are likely to overlook many daily opportunities to improve government performance and the well-being of society at large.

RESOURCES FOR PROMOTING MORAL SENSITIVITY IN GOVERNMENT

In order to nourish one's moral sensitivities and deepen commitments to a set of fairly comprehensive values contact with one or several communities beyond one's work situation is very important. People need some wider experiences beyond their daily occupational pressures if they are not to dry up or become totally absorbed in performing job roles. Relationships in family, among a circle of close friends, in professional associations, in neighborhoods, or in a worship community all put one's daily work in a wider framework of meaning and give a sense of proportion to what one is doing. Such contacts also provide a needed source of strength and constructive criticism that are a support in times of discouragement and a stimulus to keep one's ideals in perspective.

Connected with this is the need to expose oneself from time to time to the sufferings of people beyond one's normal relationships—poor people, the elderly, the terminally ill, etc. Such contacts nourish a consciousness that what one is doing in government is meaningful for a wider public beyond one's immediate experience.

All of these relationships and contacts outside the daily occupational environment help one to keep alive a consciousness that public service is more than merely a job or stepping-stone to security or power. These experiences nourish a sense that government work is a vocation to serve and a realization that the way one's job responsibilities are carried out is an integral part of realizing one's deepest identity. In such a way, character—the foundation of all moral choices—is strengthened, and one is in a better position to balance conflicting loyalties when they emerge.

Within the institutional environment itself there is much that can be done to keep alive a healthy sense of purpose and practical moral wisdom. Younger persons can find assistance by consulting with more experienced persons in public service whom they respect and who can give good principled advice. This helps to confirm or clarify one's instincts and judgments, and also reduces the anxiety that one must always appear in control. Conversely, older or more experienced persons have much to learn from new people in government work who can bring a freshness to the bureaucratic environment.

Aside from the personal resources that can enhance character, sharpen principles and provide practical wisdom, there are structural factors that also can enhance better performance. Instituting channels for dissent, for example, is a recommendation of the new Civil Service Code. Such processes can serve to reduce frustration, encourage initiatives and minimize the need to resort to extraordinary measures to fight bad policies. Within departments, agencies and offices the establishment of new methods to articulate more clearly defined long range objectives and evaluate piecemeal strategies in light of them help to sharpen a sense of purpose and improve performance among employees.

There is no substitute for imaginative and effective leadership at the highest levels of public service. Elected officials, political appointees and supergrade civil servants all can set the kind of example needed for the effective functioning of government. Personal commitment, however, from middle and lower-level career persons is absolutely indispensable to this, as are carefully orchestrated structural mechanisms which encourage initiative and constructive dissent.

NOTES

1. A. M. Rosenthal, *Thirty-Eight Witnesses* (New York: McGraw-Hill, 1964).

144 PERSONAL VALUES IN PUBLIC POLICY

2. John G. Simon, Charles W. Powers, Jon P. Gunnemann, *The Ethical Investor: Universities and Corporate Responsibility* (New Haven: Yale University Press, 1972), pp. 22-25.

3. In articulating these different but related dimensions that are involved in producing a morally responsible decision in a social context I am borrowing from and adapting the ideas of James Gustafson. See, for example, his seminal article on the various factors to be weighed in moral decision-making, "Context Versus Principles: A Misplaced Debate in Christian Ethics," *Harvard Theological Review* Vol. 58, No. 2 (April, 1965), pp. 171-202.

4. Harlan Cleveland, former Assistant Secretary of State in the Kennedy Administration, referred to the inadequacy of a written code of ethics for instilling a sense of moral responsibility in public officials:

When I was in government, I concluded that a written code of ethics could never be comprehensive enough or subtle enough to be a satisfactory guide to personal behavior as a public executive. Louis Hector, a lawyer who served on the Civil Aeronautics Board, put it succinctly: General prescriptions, whether in the forms of do's or don't's, are bound to be "so general as to be useless or so specific as to be unworkable." ("Systems, Purposes, and the Watergate," *Public Administration Review*, Vol. 34, No. 3 [May/June 1974], p. 267. See also his book *The Future Executive: A Guide for Tomorrow's Managers* [New York: Harper and Row, 1972], p. 103.)

5. Edward Weisband and Thomas M. Franck, *Resignation in Protest* (New York: Grossman, 1975).

6. Charles Peters and Taylor Branch, eds., *Blowing the Whistle: Dissent in the Public Interest* (New York: Praeger, 1972).

7. Daniel Ellsberg, *Papers on the War* (New York: Simon and Schuster, 1972). James C. Thompson, "How Could Vietnam Happen?: An Autopsy," *The Atlantic*, April 1968, pp. 47-53. James C. Thompson, Jr., "Getting Out and Speaking Out," *Foreign Policy*, No. 13 (Winter, 1973-74), pp. 49-69. Jeb Stuart Magruder, *An American Life* (New York: Atheneum, 1974). John W. Dean, *Blind Ambition* (New York: Simon and Schuster, 1976). H. R. Haldeman, *The Ends of Power* (New York: Times Books, 1978).

8. In this section of the essay I am drawing heavily upon the ideas of Dr. Carl J. Hemmer, Chief of the Population Policy Development Division of the Office of Population in AID. Carl has participated in several seminars and courses conducted by Woodstock for government personnel, and he has shared with us many of his own practical insights for making moral concerns effective in public service.

Morally Questionable Policies
Conversation

Haughey: I'd like to begin this discussion with asking you whether the Genovese case described in Brian Smith's essay is a good analogue for your own responsibilities and the needs you perceive which you might or might not respond to.

Silverstone: I wonder about the facts of the case. Is it possible to assume that the 38 on-lookers really didn't know what was going on? That they had reason to fear for their own lives and those of their families by becoming involved? That there was no reason to believe that calling the police or any action they could perform would really help Kitty Genovese? They would have to have faith that the police would come and would do something and that the system would not intimidate them later. I always had the feeling a lot of assumptions have been made about the moral deadness of the people in that case.

Margulies: I wish you hadn't picked this case because it always horrified me.

Silverstone: To judge these people, you have to assume that they believe there's an action they can take that will be effective. To make that assumption one has to assume, in turn, that they have a certain amount of faith in the system or faith in the police, in how the police act and what the police will do to those who report it.

*Christiansen: Brian gives you an abbreviated account of the events. Kitty Genovese was first attacked on the street; she got to

* Member of Woodstock staff, Woodstock Theological Center, Washington, D.C.

her apartment. The intruder then got to the hallway, beat her, went on to ransack the apartment. She began to call for help and then he killed her . . . in the window . . . in sight of the neighbors who were looking at the situation.

Margulies: All any of them had to do was pick up the telephone, make a call. They didn't have to identify themselves, all they had to do was say, "I hear someone screaming—I think she is in terrible trouble—The address is such and such." And this went on over some time. It was flagrant and clear and nobody wanted to take any step. It could have been done with no risk.

Dungan: Did people perceive that there was no risk? We're being very objective and rational to say they saw no risk to themselves. "The police will come though it will take them an hour to get here and then they will come around and start asking questions and I will have to take time off from work and my family will be attacked." Think of a black person witnessing a terrible crime and wondering whether to call the white cops or not. "Do I call the establishment?"

Langan: I think that reaction presupposes a degree of alienation from the institutions of society that is itself a profoundly important social development.

Crahan: In that period Kew Gardens was a middle to upper-class neighborhood. It's not an area solely of large apartment buildings, but primarily of garden apartments and private homes. It was a white neighborhood. These were not people one would assume would be intimidated by the possibility of getting involved with the police. There were studies done afterwards both by the police and outsiders trying to understand why this happened. The people who witnessed it were in their apartments or homes. The threat to them was not there. If you were in a neighborhood where crime was much more prevalent, that would be another thing but this was a low crime area.

Haughey: Let's stick with the question of the relevance of this case to executing responsibilities in government agencies.

Crahan: The applicability of the Genovese case to the moral responsibilities of government officials relates to the perception of need. The fact that members of the Kew Gardens community did not feel personal responsibility in Kitty's grave need may have flowed from the fact that this was a community in which the perception of need was of individual and nuclear family needs. This was not a community in which there was a tradition of social or economic problems being dealt with by pooling resources. They were, by and large, sufficiently advantaged to be able to meet their own needs. There is an analogy in U.S. political culture. Need is most often defined in terms of individual needs and the government bureaucracy usually attempts to be responsive to individual needs or to groups expressing individual needs. When the decision-maker attempts to think of responsibilities in making decisions in relationship to needs, one can appreciate how the needs of the constituency that are being dealt with can be defined in very personal terms. Generalized social and economic needs do not bulk large against these other things.

Silverstone: How is the Genovese example relevant to the government? There might be critics, as far removed from Washington as we are from Kew Gardens, who would ask: "How is it that all these high officials sat around while people were being napalmed in Vietnam for years? Genovese was one person in a neighborhood. The Vietnam war was not one Kitty Genovese being wiped out, but mobs of people who had done nothing to anyone." Well, the officials may have thought that the napalming served some higher purpose; that it takes fire to fight fire; and that no efficacious and honorable alternatives were available. Common folk in Kew Gardens, and the Best and the Brightest in Washington. Neither may have seen the issue as clearly as those who are far removed from their situation at the particular moment of decision, or nondecision. And both may reasonably have believed that there was nothing efficacious to be done at that moment to save the particular lives whose destruction they witnessed.

Smith: If we started with the Vietnam case or with a human rights case in El Salvador, we could immediately face the problem about not knowing all the facts and being at a distance, etc. Those are legitimate considerations. But when you take a very simple and dramatic case, what shows up clearly is that morality has to do with more than information or principles. It has to do with the ability of one human being to put oneself in another human being's position and feel his suffering. Unless that capacity exists, you can't even start value talk or moral judgment discourse. It's hard to discuss Vietnam unless you can presume the ability to go beyond self and consider the interests of other people. What I think the Genovese case shows is that there was something lacking there in terms of the moral character of a whole community. It's much more complex in government, of course, but unless you start with some sort of ability to feel, whether you're in a bureaucracy or in a neighborhood, you can't possibly be moral.

McCormick: Let me try to provide a bridge from that case to government decision-making. I don't want to deny what you said at all, Brian. Compassion (or passion, which is the beginning of com-passion) is presumed in moral discourse up to a point. But it seems to me that when you are dealing with decision-making in government we have three models with which we can deal in terms of the different relationships between people. 1) There is the Kitty case where you have people related to other people as human beings. They are looking on there and there are certain claims made upon them because of what they see. 2) At the other extreme there is the person who is hired as a guard to prevent robbery. He is hired by contract to do that and has to run certain risks in order to fulfill that contract that other people don't. You can't put a government official in either of those categories. Somebody working in government is not simply related to human concern or human charity, nor is he related by justice to a particular deed—in this instance, a particular prevention. Therefore, 3) it seems to me he's related by contract to a general thing somewhere in between those two cases. There's a justice angle in there in his omissions. But it's not the same type of justice where I am hired for a particular job. A government employee with power who would consciously do something, or look away from something he could possibly do something about, or prevent some abuse—I think would be involved in the area of justice.

Margulies: The weakness of the case for people like ourselves is in its dramatic quality. When you can identify an individual so in danger, the action to be taken is quite clear and very secure. You pick up the telephone, you dial 911 and say someone's being murdered at such and such address. When we move from Kitty Genovese to several thousand Vietnamese, something happens. It gets diluted by the sheer masses. It's no longer dramatic, it's a general concept. Then people talk about it as a concept instead of as a life or death of individuals. It's easy for people in government to interpose certain kinds of observations such as: it belongs to the policeman or it doesn't belong to me, or the issue is too complicated or if I act, what difference will it make? The nicest trick in the world to keep yourself secure is to assume impotence on your part. That keeps one somehow immune.

Dungan: That may be the ethical consideration that we are really discussing here . . . that we have so desensitized ourselves in terms of risk-taking that we are really neuters as a society . . . not only as individuals but as a society!

Gessert: I have a lot of uneasiness with what Jonathan said about risk-taking. I also had some uneasiness about the aptness of this analogue to government decision-making because the Kitty Genovese case seems to me to be very clear-cut, and even napalm bombing does not seem to me to be all that clear-cut. In the context of government it would be exceedingly rare except in cases where there is a relatively crystal-clear violation of a clearly accepted law or principle such as a wire-tapping of the democratic opposition or the cover-up. I think Watergate is a closer analogy to the Genovese case than policy in Vietnam. But laying that aside and turning to the four pre-conditions of moral action, I wonder if there is not a considerable difference between the first two and the latter two. The first two seemed to me to be absolutely essential for a moral response. With respect to the third, I am not sure that one needs to make the moral calculation that something I can do will be effective before responding to some situation. The same with principle #4. To sit back and make the judgment that there's no other reasonable course of help available

. . . (i.e. using the last two of your four principles) seems to me to be much more grounds for or an excuse for inaction, to provide that opportunity for sitting back and calculating whether what I'm going to do will be effective will produce paralysis.

Smith: I want to react to that. *The Ethical Investor*, which articulates these four principles, notes that if you want to apply them in more complex situations, like government or business, the 4th principle isn't always very helpful because in a bureaucracy or a complex situation where you don't know how much other people know, it really doesn't help to weigh "Are you the last resort or not?" The argument of the authors of this book is that in a bureaucracy or organization you should *not* wait until you feel you're the last resort but you should act on the basis of your competence.

Christiansen: The point of the Kitty Genovese case in the *Ethical Investor* is to establish lines of responsibility and particularly to establish what moral responsibility the university has as a corporate investor and what actions it might take in stockholders' meetings on moral issues that were raised about the practices of the corporation and its investments, in South Africa, for instance. The most specific point was to establish the responsibility of the remote actor, that is, one who does not have primary responsibility, maybe not even secondary responsibility, but someone who has knowledge and some capacity. The gist of Brian Smith's study is: "Just when does a person in a bureaucratic position at some middle level have a moral responsibility to act as a last resort to remedy some grave harm being done?"

Dungan: I would maintain that a government person at any level has multiple opportunities to intervene in decisions or policies or issues that involve ethical or moral judgment. I would likewise maintain that the infrequency with which this is done is not due to moral insensitivity, but to a general unwillingness to take even small risks well short of heroic virtue. I mean, to have somebody frown at you—whether I get my promotion or look good or bad, or be included on the guest list of the next session, become much higher priority issues than the issues with which we deal. To tell you the truth, I'm shocked. I feel a little like Rip Van Winkle because I have been out of Federal government a while and I'm coming back. Unless I am wrong, there's less willingness to take risks than there was 10 or 15 years ago . . . much, much less.

Margulies: Some years ago when Elliott Richardson became secretary of HEW, we had a briefing for him and were urging him in that first briefing to take some action on the perennial issues of health care and service in hospitals. He stopped the discussion early to inquire: "I have got to know one thing. What's my share of the final decision?" "If I have as much as one-sixth of the final decision then I will want to pay close attention to it and I'll take some action on it." I sat there thinking that I was well down the list from Elliott Richardson, and I realized that his 1/6 became diluted to 1/64 to 1/128 when it came to me. Though it reminded me that my decisions were not critical, it never convinced me, and I don't think it ought to ever convince me, that my decision is of no consequence. It still matters. If I may go back to long before I was in government, it was my habit regularly to antagonize the Medical Society in the positions they took, which was easy, because they were always wrong! And they haven't changed! People would come up to me afterwards and say, "Gee, I wish I could do that". It's more than just a threat to status or security. It's what was hinted at . . . the need for approval, the need for acceptance, it's easier if you go along, then you'll be looked at as one of the boys, part of the group. I have regularly violated this pattern of behavior, not because I'm heroic, but because I discovered at an early age that you can and become quite immune to the after effects.

Breslin: But how do you evaluate those beneath you in the bureaucracy when they behave the way you're advocating?

Margulies: It's a very good point. Let me say, I have always told people under me that if they make a decision I will back them. I think if the boss takes a stand from time to time, other people begin to function differently; it's not a revolution, but I think it's meaningful.

Breslin: It makes a difference whether you are encouraged to speak up or asked constantly, "Why are you disturbing this office?"

Silverstone: I remember in the early sixties what we were all told in effect: "If you can't stand the heat in the kitchen, get out". Whatever the intent was, the effect was to suggest to people that they better shut up and carry out orders. What I'm saying is that encouraging or discouraging speaking up also runs in cycles depending on the climate of the country or the style of the administration.

Margulies: In general the discussion has exaggerated the importance of the decisions and the risks that we are talking about. What one can contribute isn't that great, whether you say "yeh" or "nay". While we tend to exaggerate both the risks we might take and the contributions we might make, I don't think we exaggerate the importance to you as a person to make the decision based on what you believe in. One's character is at stake.

Part II
Theology and Government Decision

6
Does Religious Faith Add to Ethical Perception?
Richard A. McCormick

Thus far this volume has studied value perception and decision-making from several points of view. The task of the remaining essays is to focus explicitly on religious faith (and its source, revelation) and its relation to decision-making—and again, from several perspectives. The particular question I want to raise can be posed in any number of ways. Let me try just a few. How does religious faith affect decision-making in government—or in any other area for that matter (e.g., the practice of medicine, the profession of law)? Does one's faith add to one's ethical perceptions, and if it does, what does it add? Is not a morally wrong judgment morally wrong independent of religious belief? Is not a right decision right whether one is a believer or not?

Theologians have been deeply concerned with this question in recent years. They formulate the question variously. For example is there a specifically Christian ethics? Does Christian faith add material content to what is in principle knowable by reason? Is Christian morality autonomous? Is Christ the norm for the morally good and right, and in what sense? These questions may appear academic, at the margin of real life. Actually, the proper answer to them is of great importance.

For instance, if Christian faith, rooted in God's revelation, tells us things about right and wrong in human affairs that we would not otherwise know, then it is clear that decision-making in government risks integrity unless it is Christianly informed and inspired. Furthermore, the answer to the question raised affects public policy. Public policy, while not identical with sound mor-

155

ality, draws upon and builds upon moral conviction. If Christian faith adds new material (concrete, behavioral) content to morality, then public policy is even more complex than it seems. For example, if Christians precisely as Christians know something about abortion that others cannot know unless they believe it as Christians, then in a pluralistic society there will be problems with discussion and decision in the public forum.

Moreover, the answer to these questions affects the churches' competence to teach morality authoritatively, and how this is to be conceived and implemented. Thus, if Christian faith and revelation add material content to what is knowable in principle by reason, then the churches conceivably could teach moral positions and conclusions independently of the reasons and analyses that recommend these conclusions. This could lend great support to a highly juridical and obediential notion of Christian morality. The very processes we use, or do not use, to judge the moral rightness or wrongness of many concrete projects (e.g., donor insemination, in vitro fertilization, warfare, poverty programs, apartheid) would be profoundly affected. The question, then, is of enormous importance.

FAITH AND ETHICS

Before entering the discussion of this question, some precision must be given to the terms "faith" and "ethics". By faith, I refer to *explicit*, Christian faith, not a faith that remains implicit or nonthematic. I say this because there is a sense in which even explicit nonbelievers can be said to encounter the grace of Christ, be touched by it and therefore be living the life of faith even though it remains unrecognized as such.

Next a word on the term "ethics" (as it is used in the question: does faith add to one's ethical perceptions?). There are four levels at which the term can be understood where rightness or wrongness of conduct is concerned. Only one level is of special concern, at least in terms of the discussion as we find it in recent theological literature.

(1) First, there is what we might call an *essential* ethic.[1] By

this term we mean those norms that are regarded as applicable to all persons, where one's behavior is but an instance of a general, essential moral norm. Here we could use as examples the rightness or wrongness of killing actions, of contracts, of promises and all those actions whose demands are rooted in the dignity of the person.

(2) Second, there is an *existential* ethic. This refers to the choice of a good that the individual as individual should realize, the experience of an absolute ethical demand addressed to the individual. Obviously, at this level not all persons of good will can and do arrive at the same ethical decisions in concrete matters. For instance, an individual might conclude that his/her own moral-spiritual life cannot grow and thrive in government work, hence that this work ought to be abandoned. Or, because of background, inclination, talent (etc.) an individual might choose to concentrate time and energy on a particular issue rather than on others.

(3) Third, there is *essential Christian* ethics. By this we refer to those· ethical decisions a Christian must make precisely because he/she belongs to a community to which the non-Christian does not belong. These are moral demands made upon the Christian *as Christian*. For instance, to regard fellow workers as brothers and sisters in Christ (not just as autonomous, to-be-respected persons), to provide a Christian education for one's children, to belong to a particular worshipping community. These are important ethical decisions that emerge only within the context of a Christian community's understanding of itself in relation to other people. Thus, to the extent that Christianity is a Church in the above sense and has preordained structures and symbols, to this extent there can be and must be a distinctively Christian ethic, an essential ethics of Christianity which adds to the ordinary essential ethics of persons as members of the universal human community the ethics of persons as members of the Church-community.

(4) Fourth, there is *existential Christian* ethics—those ethical decisions that the Christian *as individual* must make, e.g., the choice to concentrate on certain political issues not only because these seem best suited to one's talent, but above all because they seem more in accord with the gospel perspectives.

CHRISTIAN FAITH AND ESSENTIAL ETHICS

The problem that has above all concerned theologians involves ethics in the first sense only, i.e. *essential* ethics. In light of the foregoing precisions, the question could be worded as follows: does explicit Christian faith add to one's ethical (*essential* ethics) perceptions of obligation new content at the material or concrete level? This is the more precise form of the question now agitating theologians under a different formulation: sc., is there a specifically Christian ethics? But this latter formulation I judge to be too vague and sprawling, and one that allows discussants to seem to disagree with each other, when in reality they are not addressing the same question. More concretely, it should be readily granted that revelation and our personal faith do influence ethical decisions at the latter three levels (existential, essential Christian, existential Christian). One's choice of issues, and the dispositions and motivations he/she brings to these issues can be profoundly affected by one's personal appropriation of revealed truth, by one's prayer life, and by the community in which these develop. It is this level and these modalities that are highlighted in most literature when it refers (cf. below) to a "style of life" and "intentionality," a "new dynamism and power," a "special context."

A few statements of opinion on this question will help give the flavor of the discussion. John Macquarrie, the well known Anglican theologian, states that the Christian ethic is not distinctive in its ultimate goals or its fundamental principles. These are shared with all serious minded people of all traditions. Therefore the distinctiveness is not to be found in the concrete moral obligations derived from an authentic humanity but in the degree of explicitness surrounding the notion of authentic humanity. "The distinctive element is the special context within which the moral life is perceived. This special context includes the normative place assigned to Jesus Christ and his teaching—not, indeed, as a paradigm for external imitation, but rather as the criterion and inspiration for a style of life."[2]

J.M. Aubert prepares the way for his own answer by studying the question in St. Thomas.[3] Thomas' point of view is gathered from his treatment of the relation of human virtues to

Christian virtues, and from his discussion of the relation between the law of Christ and human morality. With regard to the virtues, Aubert maintains that Thomas clarified a long patristic heritage by explaining the autonomy and value of human virtue. An earlier Augustinian concern to avoid Pelagianism tended to smother the human with the overwhelming gratuity and supremacy of the theological virtues. Thomas recovered this human aspect with no compromise on the supremacy of the theological order. For him charity was the form of the virtues, suffusing and dynamizing them, but leaving them intact as the genuinely human expressions or ways of charity.

With regard to law, Thomas taught that the law of Christ should animate and transfigure all of human life. This implies that human life already has a moral content to which charity will give a new sense. But Thomas insisted that the law of Christ adds of itself no new particular moral prescriptions. It introduces a new dynamism and power. The resultant new life is essentially a more total and divinized way of leading a human life, a human life having its own proper demands which man perceives by reason and conscience.

On the basis of his study Aubert concludes that it is faith which is the truly distinguishing (or formal) cause of the specificity of Christian morality. But this must be properly understood. Since there is only one destiny possible to all men, there is existentially only one morality common to Christians and non-Christians. That means that there is a material identity between Christian moral demands and those perceivable by reason. However, faith operates a distinctiveness in the manner and intentionality of living these common moral demands. That is, it renders explicit the presence of charity. The Christian builds a life style on this explicitness. Therefore the specificity of Christian morality is found essentially in the very style of life, the manner of comporting oneself and of accomplishing the moral tasks which the Christian has in common with other men—a manner more dynamic, more assured, more joyous, more capable of following the example of Christ dying for other men. For it is ultimately the law of the cross which remains the essentially Christian model of the manner of practicing the moral law. . . .

In several valuable studies Joseph Fuchs, S.J., pursues in

depth the notion of "Christian intentionality" mentioned by Aubert.[4] It is Fuch's thesis that prescinding from this intentionality Christian morality is, in its materiality and concreteness, human morality. Therefore both Christians and non-Christians must seek the answers to moral questions by determining what is genuinely human. It is the intentionality brought to the authentically human which specifies Christian morality.

How are we to understand this intentionality? To explain it, Fuchs recalls that in the moral act there are two aspects: the specific act itself and through it one's self-realization with reference to an Absolute. This self-realization in relation to an Absolute is the decisive element in morality, even though we are not reflexly conscious of it. Thus there is "a certain intentionality which transcends and fulfils the individual moral act." Now the Christian does not relate himself to God only as the Absolute, but to God as Father, to God who gave us His love in the person of Christ, and who is in His Christ our salvation. It is this deep-seated stamp on our consciousness which is distinctive of Christian morality. Or, as Fuchs puts it: "This Christian intentionality is what makes the moral behavior of the Christian truly and specifically Christian, at every moment and in every aspect, even when it appears at first to be simply conduct conforming to human morality."[5] Everything the Christian does is an expression of this personal, conscious, and freely willed relation to the Father of Jesus Christ. This intentionality is present to us without explicit and systematic reflection on our part.

FAITH AND ITS INFLUENCE ON MORALITY

While Christian intentionality is the decisive element in Christian morality, there is another important aspect which Fuchs underlines. The Christian knows in faith and acknowledges certain realities which he alone can acknowledge: the person of Christ, the Holy Spirit at work in us, the message of salvation, the Church, the Christian community, the sacraments, teaching authority. Our relationship to these realities belongs to our being and must be realized in our conduct. It will do so at the level of a deeper and richer motivation.

Franz Böckle (University of Bonn) pursues the line taken by Fuchs and lists three ways in which faith exercises an influence on morality.[6] First, faith in God's redemptive act in Jesus Christ gives to the radical act of self-determination (fundamental option) its basic ground and sense. This basic decision *(metanoia)* is the basis of the moral life and stamps all our activity, as Fuchs notes. Secondly, faith deepens and renders secure the insights important for individual acts. Here Böckle distinguishes "morally relevant insights" from "moral judgments." Faith has a direct influence only on the insights, not on the moral judgments themselves. Finally, Böckle argues that faith forbids the absolutizing of any created good.

The English Jesuit philosopher Gerard J. Hughes approaches the question by exploring the Christian justification for moral beliefs.[7] Does the Christian, he asks, base his moral beliefs upon grounds not available to the non-Christian? Hughes rejects the opinion that derives the substantive content of our moral knowledge from specifically Christian sources. The teaching and example of Christ provide, rather, a stimulus, a context and a motivation. For instance, we cannot read the New Testament seriously without being forced to re-examine our current moral values and beliefs. Here Hughes is close to Böckle's distinction between morally relevant insights and moral judgments. The Christian revelation continues to inject a divine discontent into our secular moral thinking and to throw light on the status of the moral life as a whole, though the implications of this discontent must be sought by the ordinary methods of ethical reflection.

Karl Rahner is one of the great theologians of this century. Rahner's thought on this problem can be summarized as follows. Since Christian ethics is the objectification in Jesus Christ of what every man experiences of himself in his subjectivity, "it does not and cannot add to human ethical self-understanding as such any material content that is, in principle, 'strange' or 'foreign' to man as he exists and experiences himself in this world."[8] However, a person within the Christian community has access to a privileged articulation, in objective form, of this experience of subjectivity. Precisely because the resources of Scripture, dogma, and Christian life are the fullest available "objectifications" of the common human experience, "the articulation of man's image of his moral good that is possible within historical Christian communities remains privileged in its access to enlarged perspectives on man."

These are but a few statements by contemporary thinkers of a position that is traditional within the Catholic community, at least since the time of Aquinas.[9] The Roman theologians F. Hurth and P. M. Abellan summarized it as follows: "All moral commands of the 'New Law' are also commands of the natural moral law. Christ did not add any single moral prescription of a positive kind to the natural moral law . . . That holds also for the command of love . . . The ethical demand to love God and one's neighbor for God's sake is a demand of the natural moral law."[10]

This tradition must be carefully understood. It refers above all to the intelligibility of moral norms and asserts that while there can be mysteries of faith, there can be no mysterious ethical norms which are simply closed off to human insight. Thus "human insight and reasoning" must be understood in its broadest sense. That broad sense would include two clarifications. First, it does not exclude the fact that the individual values that generate a norm can experience a special grounding and ratification in revelation. Quite the contrary. Thus our faith that God loves each individual and calls each to salvation deepens our insight into the worth of the individual.

Secondly this broad sense of "human insight and reasoning" suggests that there are factors at work in moral convictions that are reasonable but not always reducible to the clear and distinct ideas that the term "human reason" can mistakenly suggest. When all these factors are combined (cf. Langan), they suggest that the term "moral reasoning" is defined most aptly by negation: "reasonable" means not ultimately mysterious.

This position is found in Suarez, Vermeersch, H. Küng, A. Auer, B. Schüller and a host of other Catholic theologians. It is also broadly shared by Protestant authors like Bultmann, Cullmann, E. Troeltsch.[11] Recently, however, there has been a small reaction against this analysis. It is found particularly in the writings of B. Stoeckle, J. Ratzinger and Hans Urs von Balthasar.[12] They put great emphasis on the idea that for the Christian, Christ "makes himself present as the only norm in every situation" (von Balthasar), that his word is "the ultimate decisive moral norm" (Schurmann). These statements are not false, of course, but they do not raise the issue as to *how* one originally knows God's will, whether through faith alone as a distinct manner of knowing or through human insight and reasoning. Jesus' word is the "ultimate decisive norm" even when one accepts the fact that Christ simply recalled and renewed with his authority natural moral demands—sc., those available in principle to human reasoning processes.

Thus far some current statements. I should now like to develop a possible understanding of the matter in the hope that it may provide a structure within which the relation of religious belief to decision-making in government can be enlightened. I shall proceed in two steps: the origin of moral judgments and the relation of Christian perspectives to these judgments.

Origins of Moral Judgments

The first thing to be said is that moral convictions do not originate from rational analyses and arguments. Let me take slavery as an example. We do not hold that slavery is humanly demeaning and immoral chiefly because we have argued to this rationally. Rather, first our sensitivities are sharpened to the meaning and value of human persons and certainly religious faith can play an important part in the sharpening. As Böckle notes, it can influence our insights. We then *experience* the out-of-jointness, inequality and injustice of slavery. We then *judge* it to be wrong. At this point we develop "arguments" to criticize, modify, and above all communicate this judgment. Reflective analysis is an attempt to reinforce rationally, communicably, and from other sources what we grasp at a different level. Discursive reflection does not *discover* the right and good, but only *analyzes* it. The good that reason seems to discover is the good that was already hidden in the original intuition.

This needs more explanation. How do we arrive at definite moral obligations, prescriptions, and proscriptions? How does the general thrust of our persons toward good and away from evil become concrete, even as concrete as a code of do's and don't's, and caveats? It happens somewhat as follows—and in this I am following closely the school of J. de Finance, G. de Broglie, G. Grisez, John Finnis, and others who are heavily reliant on the Thomistic notion of "natural inclinations" in explaining the origin of basic moral obligation. We proceed by asking what are the goods or values man can seek, the values that define his human opportunity, his flourishing? We can answer this by examining man's basic tendencies. For it is impossible to act without having an interest in the object, and it is impossible to be attracted by, to have interest in something without some inclination already present. What then are the basic inclinations?

With no pretense at being exhaustive, we could list some of the following as basic inclinations present prior to acculturation: the tendency to preserve life; the tendency to mate and raise children; the tendency to explore and question; the tendency to seek out other men and obtain their approval—friendship; the tendency to establish good relations with unknown higher powers; the tendency to use intelligence in guiding action; the tendency to develop skills and exercise them in play and the fine arts. In these inclinations our intelligence spontaneously and without reflection grasps the possibilities to which they point, and prescribes them. Thus we form naturally and without reflection the basic principles of practical or moral reasoning. Or as philosopher John Finnis renders it:

> What is spontaneously understood when one turns from contemplation to action is not a set of Kantian or neo-scholastic "moral principles" identifying this as right and that as wrong, but a set of values which can be expressed in the form of principles as "life is a good-to-be-pursued and realized and what threatens it is to be avoided."[13]

We have not yet arrived at a determination of what concrete actions are morally right or wrong; but we have laid the basis. Since these basic values are equally basic and irreducibly attractive, the morality of our conduct is determined by the adequacy of our openness to these values. For each of these values has its self-evident appeal as a participation in the unconditioned Good we call God. The realization of these values in intersubjective life is the only adequate way to love and attain God.

Further reflection by practical reason tells us what it means to remain open and to pursue these basic human values. First we must take them into account in our conduct. Simple disregard of one or other shows we have set our mind against this good. Second, when we can do so as easily as not, we should avoid acting in ways that inhibit these values, and prefer ways that realize them. Third, we must make an effort on their behalf when their realization in another is in extreme peril. If we fail to do so, we show that the value in question is not the object of our efficacious love and concern. Finally, we must never choose against a basic good in the sense of spurning it. What is to count as "turning against a basic good" is, of course, the crucial moral question. Certainly it does not mean that there are never situations of conflicted values where it is necessary to cause harm as we go about doing good. Thus there are times when it is necessary to take life in the very defense of life, in our very adhering to this basic value. That means that taking life need not always involve one in "turning against a basic good." Somewhat similarly, one does not necessarily turn against the basic good of procreation (what Pius XII called a "sin against the very meaning of conjugal life") by avoiding child-bearing. Such avoidance is only reproachable when *unjustified*. And the many conflicts (medical, economic, social, eugenic) that justify such avoidance were acknowledged by Pius XII. Suppressing a value, or preferring one to another in one's choice cannot be simply identified with turning against a basic good. My only point here is that particular moral judgments are incarnations of these more basic normative positions, which have their roots in spontaneous, prereflective inclinations.

Even though these inclinations can be identified as prior to acculturation, still they exist as culturally conditioned. We tend toward values as perceived. And the culture in which we live shades our perception of values. Philip Rieff in *The Triumph of the Therapeutic* notes that a culture survives by the power of institutions to influence conduct with "reasons" that have sunk so deeply into the self that they are implicitly understood.[14] In other words, decisions are made, policies set not chiefly by articulated norms, codes, regulations, and philosophies, but by "reasons" that lie below the surface. This is the dynamic aspect of a culture, and in this sense many of our major moral problems are cultural. Our way of perceiving the basic human values and relating to them is shaped by our whole way of looking at the world. (Cf. Clarke.)

Let me take an example from another area of concern, that of bioethics. In relating to the basic human values several images of man are possible, as Callahan has observed.[15] First there is a power-plasticity model. In this model, nature is alien, independent of man, possessing no inherent value. It is capable of being used, dominated, and shaped by man. Man sees himself as possessing an unrestricted right to manipulate in the service of his goals. Death is something to be overcome, outwitted. Second, there is the sacral-symbiotic model. In its religious forms, nature is seen as God's creation, to be respected and heeded. Man is not the master; he is the steward and nature is a trust. In secular forms, man is seen as a part of nature. If man is to be respected, so is nature. We should live in harmony and balance with nature. Nature is a teacher, showing us how to live with it. Death is one of the rhythms of nature, to be gracefully accepted.

The model which seems to have "sunk deep" and shaped our moral imagination and feelings—shaped our perception of basic values—is the power-plasticity model. We are, corporately, *homo technologicus*. The best solution to the dilemmas created by technology is more technology. We tend to eliminate the maladapted condition (defectives, retardates, and so on) rather than adjust the environment to it. Even our language is sanitized and shades from view our relationship to basic human values. We speak of "surgical air strikes" and "terminating a pregnancy", ways of blunting the moral imagination from the shape of our conduct. My only point here is that certain cultural "reasons" qualify or shape our perception of and our grasp on the basic human values. Thus these reasons are the cultural soil of our moral convictions and have a good deal to say about where we come out on particular moral judgments.

Once the basic values are identified along with their cultural tints and trappings, theologians and philosophers attempt to develop "middle axioms" or mediating principles. These relate the basic values to concrete choice. The major problem any professional ethic faces is to reinterpret the concrete demands of the basic values in new circumstances without forfeiting its grasp on these values.

THE CHRISTIAN PERSPECTIVE AND MORAL JUDGMENTS

There may be many ways to explain the influences of Christian faith on the moral norms that guide decision-making. For instance, the very notion one entertains of the Supreme Being can influence normative statements. If one thinks of God above all as the creator and conserver of order, then this yields a certain attitude toward human interventions into the givenness of the world. If, however, one also believes God is the enabler of our potentialities, then a quite different normative stance becomes feasible, as James Gustafson has pointed out.[16] (Cf. Haughey.)

My own view on the relation of Christian belief to *essential* ethics would be developed as follows. Since there is only one destiny possible to all men, there is existentially only one *essential* morality common to all men, Christians and non-Christians alike. Whatever is distinctive about Christian morality is found essentially in the style of life, the manner of accomplishing the moral tasks common to all persons, not in the tasks themselves. Christian morality is, in its concreteness and materiality, *human* morality. The theological study of morality accepts the human in all its fullness as its starting point. It is the *human* which is then illumined by the person, teaching and achievement of Jesus Christ. The experience of Jesus is regarded as normative because he is believed to have experienced what is to be human in the fullest way and at the deepest level.

The Second Vatican Council stated something similar to this when it asserted that "faith throws a new light on everything, manifests God's design for man's total vocation, and thus directs the mind to solutions which are *fully human*."[17] It further stated: "But only God, who created man to His own image and ransomed him from sin, provides a fully adequate answer to these questions. This he does through what he has revealed in Christ His Son, who became man. Whoever follows after Christ, the perfect man, *becomes himself more of a man*."[18]

Traditionally, theologians referred to moral knowledge as originating in "reason *informed* by faith." The word "inform" is important. It does not mean *replaced* by faith. It is in explaining the term "inform" that we may hope to see more precisely how faith influences moral judgments at the *essential* level.

I have noted that our concrete moral judgments are applications originating in insights into our inclinations toward basic human values or goods. I have also suggested that our reasoning processes about these basic values can be distorted by cultural biases.

Let us take an example. It can be persuasively argued that the peculiar temptation of a technologically advanced culture such as ours is to view and treat persons functionally. Our treatment of the aged is perhaps the sorriest symptom of this. The elderly are probably the most alienated members of our society. More and more of them spend their declining years in homes for senior citizens, in chronic hospitals, in nursing homes. We have shunted them aside. Their protest is eloquent because it is helplessly muted and silent. But it is a protest against a basically functional assessment of their persons. "Maladaptation" is the term used to describe *them* rather than the environment. This represents a terribly distorted judgment of the human person.

Love of and loyalty to Jesus Christ, the perfect man, sensitizes us to the meaning of persons. The Christian tradition is anchored in faith in the meaning and decisive significance of God's covenant with men, especially as manifested in the saving incarnation of Jesus Christ, his eschatological kingdom which is here aborning but will finally only be given. Faith in these events, love of and loyalty to this central figure, yields a decisive way of viewing and intending the world, of interpreting its meaning, of hierarchizing its values. In this sense the Christian tradition only illumines human values, supports them, provides a context for their reading at given points in history. It aids us in staying human by underlining the truly human against all cultural attempts to distort the human. It is by steadying our gaze on the basic human values that are the parents of more concrete norms and rules that faith influences moral judgment and decision-making. That is how I understand "reason informed by faith."

In summary, then, Christian emphases do not immediately yield moral norms and rules for decision-making. But they affect them. The stories and symbols that relate the origin of Christianity and nourish the faith of the individual, affect one's perspectives. They sharpen and intensify our focus on the human goods definitive of our flourishing. It is persons so informed, persons with such "reasons" sunk deep in their being, who face new situations, new dilemmas, and reason together as to what is the best policy, the best protocol for the service of all the values. They do not find concrete answers in their tradition, but they bring a world-view that informs their reasoning—especially by allowing the basic human goods to retain their attractiveness and not be tainted by cultural distortions. This world-view is a continuing check on and challenge to our tendency to make choices in light of cultural enthusiasms which sink into and take possession of our unwitting, preethical selves. Such enthusiasms can reduce the good life to mere adjustment in a triumph of the therapeutic; collapse an individual into his functionability; exalt his uniqueness into a lonely individualism or crush it into a suffocating collectivism. In this sense I believe it is true to say that the Christian tradition is much more a value-raiser than an answer-giver. And it affects our values at the spontaneous, prethematic level. One of the values inherent in its incarnational ethos is an affirmation of the goodness of man and all about him—including his reasoning and thought processes. The Christian tradition refuses to bypass or supplant human deliberation and hard work in developing ethical protocols within a profession. For that would be blasphemous of the Word of God become human. On the contrary, it asserts their need, but constantly reminds men that what God did and intends for man is an affirmation of the human and therefore must

remain the measure of what man may reasonably decide to do to
and for himself.

THE INFLUENCE OF FAITH

If this is a satisfactory account of the relation of Christian
faith to decision-making (at the *essential* level), it means that faith
informs reason because the reasoner has been transformed. This
transformation means practically: (1) a *view* of persons and their
meaning; (2) a *motivation* in the following of Christ; (3) a *style* of
performing the moral tasks common to persons (communitarian,
sacramental, cross of Christ, Holy Spirit). I think it quite possible
that persons with such a view, motivation, style, might come to
some different practical conclusions on moral matters, as indeed
the historical Christian churches have. But these conclusions will
not be in principle unavailable to human insight and reasoning in
the broadest sense. That is what is meant, I believe, by the two
assertions we find in Catholic Christian tradition. The first admits
that our reasoning processes are "obscured by the sin of our first
parent" and that revelation is necessary so we can know "expeditiously, with firm security and without error those things that
are not in principle impervious to human reason." (DB 1286) Second, notwithstanding this realism about our sinful (even if re-
deemed) condition, this tradition refuses to bypass or supplant
human deliberation and hard work in normative ethics.

What does all this have to do with decision-making in government work? In private seminar-discussions, our collaborators
from the government sector repeatedly have indicated that their
faith does have an influence on their decision-making and conduct; yet, secondly, all found it hard to isolate this.

Here we see in combination the strong conviction that religious faith does influence decision-making, yet the inability on
the part of very articulate and experienced people to show very
specifically what this influence is. This is, I believe, to be expected and for several reasons. First, religious faith does not
originate new moral claims at the essential level. At this level, the
relation of faith and concrete ethics is one of informing reason, or

what is the same, transforming the reasoner, not eliminating or replacing him. It does this at a very profound level, what I have called the prethematic level, or the level of insight associated with our spontaneous inclinations. Thus, faith and reason are closely intermingled and it is difficult to sort out their independent influence.

Secondly, the levels at which religious faith does have a profound and original impact (essential Christian, existential Christian) are different from different individuals, and are experienced differently. That is because the claims originated by faith at these levels relate to individual talent, capacity, training, spiritual growth, etc. This means that it is difficult to generalize on the relation of faith to decision-making.

Finally, many deliberations and decisions in government work are concerned not directly with basic human goods, but with alternative strategies and perceived differences of means to achieve these goods. Such strategies—and differences in strategy—are probably best illumined and explained by disciplines and studies not directly related to faith.

On a December 1977 visit to London, Governor Edmund Brown, Jr., was asked how his belief in Catholicism affected his politics. He replied: "I do think one's values determine decision-making. And very simply, theological assumptions affect the shape and direction of government decisions." The first statement is correct and obvious. As for the second, Governor Brown did not specify how theological assumptions affect one's values. Had he tried he might have had a great deal of trouble. Or better, where our common moral tasks are concerned (and is not that preeminently the work of government—the common good?), he might have found himself speaking of a view of man and the world, a motivation, and a style of approach and performance. Indeed, he did precisely that. When asked about his own frugality, he remarked: "The closer leaders can be to the life-style and the ways of the population they serve, the better the democracy." Jesus said some remarkably similar things. Brown's statement is profoundly biblical—and utterly reasonable. We should expect such a conjunction after the Incarnation.

In sum, one need not be a Christian to be concerned with the poor, with health, with the food problem, with justice and rights. But if one is a Christian and is not so concerned, something is wrong with that Christianity. It has ceased to be Christian because it has ceased to be what its founder was—human.

NOTES

1. I borrow this usage from Norbert Rigali, S.J., "On Christian Ethics" *Chicago Studies* 10 (1971) 227-247.
2. John Macquarrie, *Three Issues in Ethics* (New York: Harper and Row, 1970) 89.
3. J.-M. Aubert, "La Spécificité de la morale Chrétienne selon Saint Thomas," *Supplément* 92 (1970) 55-73.
4. Joseph Fuchs, S.J., "Gibt es eine specifisch Christliche Moral?" *Stimmen der Zeit* 185 (1970) 99-112; "Human, Humanist and Christian Morality" in *Human Values and Christian Morality* (Dublin: Gill and Macmillan, 1970) 112-147.
5. "Human, Humanist and Christian Morality," p. 124.
6. Franz Böckle, "Glaube and Handeln" *Concilium*, 120 (1976) 641-647. Very similar to Böckle's distinction between insights and judgments is Helmut Weber's notion of a biblically inspired understanding of man and the world. Cf. "Um das Proprium Christlicher Ethik" *Trier theologische Zeitschrift* 81 (1972) 257-275.
7. Gerard J. Hughes, S.J., "A Christian Basis for Ethics," *Heythrop Journal* 13 (1972) 27-43.
8. James F. Bresnahan, S.J., "Rahner's Christian Ethics" *America* 123 (1970) 351-354.
9. For further literature cf. Richard A. McCormick, S.J., *Theological Studies* 32 (1971) 71-78; 34 (1973) 58-60; 38 (1977) 58-70.
10. F. Hurth, P.M. Abellan, *De Principiis, de virtutibus et praeceptis*, 1 (Rome: Gregorian University, 1948) 43.
11. Cf. Bruno Schüller, S.J., "Zur Diskussion über das Proprium einer Christlichen Ethik" *Theologie und Philosophie* 51 (1976) 331.
12. Cf. *Theological Studies* 38 (1977) 65.
13. John M. Finnis "Natural Law and Unnatural Acts" *Heythrop Journal* 11 (1970) 365-387.
14. Philip Rieff, *The Triumph of the Therapeutic* (New York: Harper & Row, 1966).
15. Daniel Callahan "Living with the New Biology" *Center Magazine*, 5 (July-Aug. 1972) 4-12.

16. James Gustafson, *The Contributions of Theology to Medical Ethics*, (Milwaukee: Marquette University, 1975).

17. *The Documents of Vatican II* (New York: America Press, 1966) p. 209.

18. *Ibid.*, p. 240.

Faith/Ethical Perception Conversation

Haughey: I have two questions. Has your own experience of the Christian faith as you've grown up in it led you to believe something different than this thesis? More specifically, has your church, Catholic, Episcopal, Lutheran, whatever, taught you that materially distinct ethical perceptions or concrete moral insight will or should flow from your faith? Secondly, does the McCormick thesis coincide with your professional experience?

Simon: Let me begin concretely. I think of a colleague like Sidney Yates who is a Jewish member of the House from Chicago. I don't see my voting record that much different from his, and yet I do feel that somehow my faith is affecting what I do. Somehow my background is affecting me though I can't pinpoint how it is.

Haughey: If your experience is that both of you end up with the same perception of what ought to be voted up or down, then it would seem to confirm the thesis of this paper. If this is so, then what role is your Christian faith playing in the conduct of your affairs in Congress?

Simon: I can't give a specific answer to that. Probably my interests in the food and population problems are motivated by it. But I have a hard time separating faith and family background here; for example, the attitude of my father has had a great influence on me.

Haughey: So faith is a fleshy thing, in the sense that it has come to you through concrete people.

Simon: Agreed. But that can also lend to another possibility on how faith affects decisions. I think of Thomas Jefferson who was a Deist, in the traditional sense, but he was so influenced by the Christian culture that his outlook also was informed by the faith of others in material and specific ways.

Trickett: I have usually seen the role of faith in my life operating in a different way than is treated in this paper. How many of my actions in the world does my faith inform? Do I do the right thing under great pressure or when I'm in a threatening environment irrespective of the group's approval or disapproval? I would say that my track record is very poor in this regard but faith then is very important because it says I'm not that track record—I'm the hope in what I can be and I will be what I can be and I'm moving towards what I can be because that's what I really am and this isn't what I really am. That's the role faith plays rather than as seen in the paper.

Haughey: You're using faith, it seems to me, more in the sense of what would ordinarily be called hope.

Trickett: Probably. While reading the paper I jotted down Hebrews 11, 1—"Faith is the assurance of things hoped for and the conviction of things not seen."

Haughey: Also you are seeing faith as a way of perceiving yourself rather than of perceiving an issue to be resolved or to throw light on an ethical question.

Trickett: What I'm saying is that due to my faith I have an assurance that I am not what I appear to be so I don't get terribly anxious and all wrought up because somebody can't tell the difference between me as a Christian and anybody else. I suppose I get some of this from Luther and his insistence that our good works don't justify us but our faith does.

Hennigan: I'm glad you mentioned Luther because I think he was the origin of the strong anti-Reformation tendency in the Catholic

Church of my youth which distrusted personal judgment or existential faith as used in this paper or self-generated ethical judgment. Growing up Catholic, as I experienced it, had a strong emphasis on the values of religious cult, separation from all the world, almost a denial of the values of human experience, and finally a reliance on religious precept as opposed to an inner sense of guidance or conscience. In the Cardinal Spellman years of my youth, there was a clear Catholic position on many public issues both in the metropolitan New York area, where I then lived, and nationally, not to mention on every personal question about which little seemed left to personal discretion.

Lowell: Basically, I would agree. The thesis of the paper goes against the line of spiritual formation at least of Catholic lay persons in our generation.

Mitchell: I think the part about the origin of moral judgment is important. You sense something is out of joint and your faith has a lot to do with your sensing it is out of joint. The out-of-jointedness is felt from within the faith. But when you try to say why it's out of joint you have no more to draw on, really, than anybody else.

Hennigan: Yes! Because by the time you get to specific issues, these can be dealt with in human terms of discourse.

Trickett: One of the books I read a few years ago was *Gideon's Gang*. Gideon's Gang was a whole bunch of people in a crisis situation, who didn't discover until about two-thirds of the way through the fellowship they developed what faiths they all had because they were too busy marching, trying to correct the rights and wrongs; then someone positively thought that in order to be a real fellowship they would have to develop a creed—and then the whole thing began to fall apart trying to write down what they believed in.

Mitchell: I'm thinking about the slave trade as I remember it historically. The Methodists in England were influential in bringing about a change in the laws. Their opposition to slavery came out of their life of faith. As they tried to convince the nation and change the laws, they moved to ethical argument about what was human. It wasn't presented as the conclusion of some particular religious system although obviously the question arose from within that religious system because they sensed the out-of-jointedness of slavery with being human. When the judgments are actually made, people are making them out of a faith context, but when you start to explain and argue, you move into the public arena and therefore you move into the essentialist area of ethics and you don't use the content of the faith there.

Simon: Your example pulls us away from the micro view to the macro view. But when you look at the macro view, you see faith as a very positive thing sometimes and sometimes being a negative thing. Some of the religious wars were things we're not very proud of.

Brian Smith: I have an uneasiness about this paper. It relates to the contention that Christian faith modeling itself after Christ's example helps you to be more firm in your choice or more secure in following it through to conclusion. Well, what about the good Jew, what about the good Buddhist, what about the good humanist? They're sometimes far more tenacious in their motivation, style of service, concern for humanity, or self-sacrifice, than a Christian is in a given case. The paper sounds like Christian faith gives one an added motivation other people don't have.

Langan: There is not much sense of tragedy in the paper—not much sense of the painfulness of choices as they are actually worked out in the concrete. How correlate its basic optimism with, say, massive moral failure on the part of Christians in response to anti-Semitism in Europe in the 1930's and 40's? That's only one instance of massive Christian moral failure. Any theory that's going to be satisfactory has to take these kinds of facts very seriously.

Mitchell: But then you get into the problem of the difference between making moral judgments and not following them. You can know what is the better thing and not do it. You can choose not to do it.

Simon: It's not just the 30's and 40's. My recollection is that five or ten years ago, Glock and Stark's study on Christian Anti-Semitism found Lutherans, Catholics and Southern Baptists showing appreciably more anti-Semitism than Unitarians or those who belonged to no church. And I'm not at all sure if you took a poll on capital punishment you might find a very similar pattern reaching a conclusion that is not a Christian conclusion.

Haughey: What conclusion would you cull from that?

Simon: That we have to be very cautious about how informed our faith is; it's too easy to assume that because we think we have been informed by faith that ergo the conclusion is consonant with our faith.

Langan: The paper, I think, underestimates the difficulties of the pressure of culture on the way faith works. The Germans thought that there was something wrong, something out of joint, to use Bob's phrase. But ingrained social passivity in the culture plus authoritarianism had accustomed them to live with the sense that something was wrong and not do anything about it. I would like to think that the German culture and the American culture are significantly different. If that is so that might be more to the point than the difference between Christian and non-Christian.

Hennigan: Yes. My recollection of history makes me believe that the values of the church in Germany had become coterminous with certain national values. This came about because the German State as it existed before 1914 or before 1918 attempted to set up a kind of prescriptive social ethic, that led to the appeal of Naziism which in turn really was a new eschatology for the German people. The paper leaves out a great deal of what the content of that faith is, even what the content of the regular human decisions is: I find this study articulates for me a great deal of what I think my faith brings to my work life. It doesn't operate as a *deus ex machina* delivering new data into my decisions. It does operate though, on the comparative choices one makes while there's room to make a choice on the areas you're going to work on. It's more operable there than it is in decisions taken in particular cases because by then the die is usually cast on the terms of choice.

Trickett: I tried to answer several questions for myself. What are the marks of a Christian? Is it an institutionally defined identity? Does a Christian have to know he's a Christian? Was the good Samaritan a Christian? I saw a greater diversity in the works of God than could be contained in an institutionally defined way of seeing what a Christian is. So I wonder if there's not a trap in this paper in the narrowness of concept of what a Christian is. We've developed creeds that say what we're not. Maybe we can define what we are as something inside of what we're not. I find it much easier to define what I'm not than what I am in my daily life. I can say what I'm against much better than I can say what I'm for. The other thing that I had to deal with is, if I could define one, could I detect one?

Haughey: If one were to buy or subscribe to this paper there really wouldn't be any way of detecting at the public policy level if one were a Christian or not since humans and Christians arrive at the concrete level with the same conclusions. Or can. Or should. I take it that's what you mean.

Trickett: Yes.

Clarke: I wonder if the study doesn't leave itself open to the charge of a certain triumphalism by what it doesn't say. It omits the fact that everyone, not only Christians, brings some world-view, some motivation, and some style and personal integrity to what they do.

Haughey: Isn't it an abstraction to talk about any people as if they could operate without some faith? There's always the danger that one has to imagine a population that doesn't exist in order to make a point. The content which "the human" has is never very clear to me because who's ever just human, *sans* faith of some kind?

Lowell: I thought of this paper when I read an article last week in the Archdiocesan paper, *The Catholic Standard*, by Monsignor Higgins who was critical of a Catholic columnist who, in turn, had been criticizing certain Catholic bureaucrats and legislators. The latter, according to the unnamed columnist, were making decisions about government policy on abortions without reference to their Catholic faith. Monsignor Higgins found this writer totally out of order for making such criticisms. Without using the same words, Msgr. Higgins took essentially the same position as this study. Msgr. Higgins in his turn was criticized editorially in the same issue. The *Standard* asserted that it was wrong for a person who claimed to be a practicing Catholic to fail to incorporate the content of his faith into his public decision-making. I found myself theoretically in agreement with Monsignor Higgins, although I had always assumed that my being a Catholic must have made some difference in the content of the decisions I participate in, without really being able to say what that difference was. I got some comfort out of this study for that reason.

Haughey: So it did speak to your experience; maybe not to your image of yourself but to your experience.

Lowell: Yes. I guess so. Except that there is a third possibility and that is my faith is not influencing either the substance or the context and I am just not recognizing it.

Ford: It did not speak to my particular starting place or where I think I am, on several scores. For one, there is a marvelous logic in the mind of the author which is not mine and I wonder if it is that he is Thomistic. He has an emphasis on reason, human reason. In my more historical sense of things I'm more struck by uncertainty about "reason" and more struck by how reason differs from person to person, from time to time, and situation to situation, and self-interest to self-interest than I am by its potential to arrive at what is good and true for all the peoples concerned with a given issue. I wish I were with him rather than where I am because he's coming out with more optimism about the nature of man and mind than I've been able to generate. I did not feel where he comes out catches my experience for what it's worth. In the Judeo-Christian tradition there are emphases and these can deliver content that would not be there if one were Islamic or Buddhist.

Haughey: He doesn't deny that there are unique emphases— what he would deny is that those unique emphases influence the concrete moral decisions in such wise that they can be traced to those emphases.

Ford: I would say that if one were the type of Christian that he should be they would make a difference.

Lowell: It is interesting that some people who do not perceive themselves as permitting their religious beliefs to affect their decisions are very suspicious that others who adhere to other religions bring their religious content to their decisions. I was warned a few years ago by several black employers to watch out for another employee who was a Black Muslim because "he's going to bring his religious beliefs to bear on the decisions that he makes here." People were just waiting to catch him bringing the content of his religious beliefs to bear on his decisions. These same people would not perceive themselves as doing that. It's much easier to suspect someone else than to acknowledge the possibility that you do it yourself.

Ford: Also, we are both late 20th century Americans which would probably influence the situation.

Langan: This problem would have to be thought through in different terms if we dealt with non-Western cultures and traditions where the relations between faith, reason, and culture are very different.

Betty Smith: An awful lot of Christian people would like to think that they acted differently but operationally they don't see how they do when the occasions arise. Both to themselves as well as to other people observing them they really don't look distinctive in many ways.

Trickett: I'd like to conclude that faith is a mystery and that writing about it is very difficult, and maybe even more mysterious.

Haughey: This paper contends that the *distinctive* Christian contribution to government decision-making has less to do with the ethical perception one might have and more with life style, the style of one's life. Could you talk about this, or concretize this from your own experience or observation?

Trickett: The opportunity for a Christian's contribution lies more in the interpersonal interaction, than in any application of Christian ethics to the policy decisions themselves. It is much more difficult, for example, to know what constitutes good stewardship of God's gift in extracting the energy in plutonium, than to know what relationship one ought to have as a Christian with those we work with. The general absence of good moral casuistry on energy related problems which are immensely complex is a weakness in the Church's mission.

In lieu of this, distinctiveness of the Christian appears to me to be less in the application of Christian ethics to complex issues than in the uniqueness of the source of that ethic. From that source the commandment is to love. Love can become a motive, a power, an attitude, an enabling and redeeming reality. It is our failure to fully appropriate this gift of love that makes the detection of Christians amongst those active in government decision-making in our society difficult.

Betty Smith: I find the distinction of life style as separate from ethical perceptions unreal. For me, one's life style is the current evidence of a personal integration of all the meaningful experiences one has had. A major orientation of one's life style originates in one's ethical perceptions and necessarily colors many aspects of behavior. In my own work, I am particularly concerned with issues of equity and I presume that everyone in any level of government must be similarly concerned. Government being the instrument of advancing the common good, it seems essential that all those toward whom a particular government program is directed have equal access to its benefits. This implies endless considerations in the day-to-day operations of a government program. For example, in announcing programs, in providing technical assistance, in review of grant applications, in appointments of consultants, in modifying budgets, determining responses to special requests, etc. the role is one of stewardship in the equitable service to all.

Ford: I personally don't think of ethical perception and "life style" as separable. The perception is the total way we have been programmed by our families, childhood, education, culture, experience, religion, etc.; it is that which we bring to our decision-making jobs, and constitutes the lenses through which we "see" (or distort) and react to new stimuli, problems, etc. Culture is probably the heaviest influence here, with variations on that stemming from the different mix of the other ingredients such as our biological givens. Our life style is substantively dependent upon the underlying ethical perceptions one has accumulated.

7
Government Career
and Commitment to Progress
Robert A. Mitchell

There are many reasons why people take government jobs. For some, it is simply a way to make a living. For others, the work itself is important because it is a service to the nation and its people. For still others, government work is attractive because it is close to the levers of power; it is where the action is. Some people just like to live in Washington.

Clearly there can be a mix of many motives in any one person. Moreover, an entirely different kind of motivation can influence a person's decision to follow a career in government. There are, for example, Christians in government service who look on their work as a "vocation"—a religious enterprise. For people of this mentality, their work in government has a religious significance; it is somehow or other involved with God's saving purposes. In this view, the religious value of work is not confined to the good intentions of the worker nor to the virtues he or she may practice on the job. The task itself is important and not merely the way in which it is undertaken. *What* one does, in other words, has some part in God's plan of salvation.

Christians of this mentality frequently have a love for this world and a commitment to its development which is part and parcel of their love for Jesus Christ. To put it another way, it is precisely *because* of their love for Christ that they are committed to social and political progress. For them a passion for human development is not the prerogative of agnostics and atheists. It is also part of being Christian.

This attitude toward government work, however, raises a

184

further question. Is such a mentality really Christian? How can a commitment to something as secular and this-worldly as social and political development be viewed as a religious enterprise? What kind of an overall outlook, what kind of a vision can bring together in faith such seemingly disparate elements as salvation in Christ and the progress of this world?

This question is an old one. In some ways it is as old as Christianity itself, since it involves the relationship of Christianity and culture, the Church and the world, the religious and the secular.[1] Moreover, there is no one response that completely satisfies all who ask the question. The churches have struggled for an answer at various times in their history. A good part of the Second Vatican Council, for example, touched in one way or another on this topic and many theologians today are forced to grapple with the problem as they seek a deeper understanding of commitment to Christ in faith.

Can a commitment to social and political development be viewed as a religious enterprise? Can work in government be considered a "vocation"? As we shall see throughout this essay, the answers given to these questions can have an important influence on decision-making, not in the sense that they provide new ethical norms and ethical rules, still less in the sense that they yield definite programs for agencies to adopt. The influence of the theological perspectives involved operates more indirectly, affecting motivation, vision and style of life, to use Richard McCormick's categories in the immediately preceding essay. The influence on decision-making, in other words, is indirect. Yet it is no less real and important. For reflective Christians, it can shape the attitude they take toward their job, the meaning they give to progress and development, the value they see in their work, the significance they attach to social problems—in brief, how they live their faith in the modern world.

In this essay, I will not attempt to develop any one answer to the question I have posed. Instead I will present the ideas of three Christian thinkers: Teilhard de Chardin, Johannes B. Metz and Gustavo Gutierrez. I will also try to show how their analyses could influence the attitude government workers take to their jobs.

TEILHARD DE CHARDIN

Teilhard's life was consumed by the desire to bring together in a single unified vision two things which are frequently seen as contradictory: commitment to human progress and belief in Jesus Christ.

He wanted his fellow believers to "see"—to share his vision about the place and importance of this world in God's plan of creation and redemption. He wanted nonbelievers to understand that the "builders of the earth" would be caught in a dead end unless they saw the relevance of a personal God drawing all persons to himself in Jesus Christ. He was afraid that men and women would "go on strike"—turn away from the problems of the world—unless they saw how commitment to human progress and belief in God necessarily go together.

The key to Teilhard's vision was his understanding of evolution. While it is impossible in this brief essay to give an adequate treatment of his thought, I would like to indicate how Teilhard saw the connection between commitment to the human enterprise and belief in Jesus Christ.

As a paleontologist, Teilhard accepted evolution. Human beings are clearly its product. But more than that, the human person is the key to understanding evolution. To explain the movement of life in which forms of living and nonliving things have succeeded each other in a certain order, Teilhard postulated his famous law of complexity/consciousness. There is, he insisted, a "within" as well as a "without" of things. The "within" is consciousness: reflective thought in man and various levels of spontaneity or centreity in lower forms of life and even in pre-life. The "without" is the material organization or structure of things. The law of complexity/consciousness simply states that "consciousness is that much more perfected according as it lines a richer and better organized material edifice."[2]

In the course of evolution, as the "without" became more complex and the "within" grew in intensity, certain critical thresholds were passed. One obvious example of this was the beginning of the human race. At a certain point in the complex development of the human organism (the "without"), reflective thought came into being (the "within"). Something completely new and startling began to exist on the face of the earth: men and women capable of thinking, choosing and loving. A critical threshold was passed.

For Teilhard, evolution did not stop with the arrival of human beings. It continues in the social organization, interaction and development of people. Over the course of many years, men and women spread out over the whole surface of the globe, developing cultures, societies, nations and states. More recently, forced by the confines of the globe on which they live, human beings have been impelled to ever increasing interaction with one another. The development of science, technology, communication and transportation, for example, has begun to tighten this network of human interaction. The "noosphere," to use one of Teilhard's neologisms to describe this phenomenon, has come into existence and is evolving steadily and dramatically.

This indicates an extraordinary development which is now occurring in the human race. There is a growing complexity in the "without" which at this point is primarily social rather than biological. This complexity is, nevertheless, part of the total phenomenon of man. In the logic of evolution, it points to another "critical threshold" somewhere in the future, where there will be another beginning—a change in "the within" as dramatic and as qualitatively different as that which took place when human beings first appeared. From all present indications, it will be an explosion into a new kind of unity, involving a collectivity of consciousness, a higher level of knowing and loving. It is the "Omega Point."

All this, Teilhard maintains, can be "seen" by looking at the evidence of science and the phenomenon of man. Using a more philosophic type of analysis, Teilhard insists that the growing unification of men and women must follow the lines of the development of the person. It must respect freedom: integrate differences and not destroy them; result in a unity of persons and not in their obliteration or in loss of their identity. He further claims that an analysis of the human person indicates that Omega already exists, is personal and is drawing men and women forward through the power of love. Omega point, therefore, is that moment in the future when mankind as a whole will be united in knowledge and love with a "super-personal" being who has been drawing the movement of evolution forward, ever since it first began.

But it is as a believer, who tries to integrate this vision with his Christian faith, that Teilhard is of greatest interest to us. Using the sources of revelation, he identifies Omega with Christ, Jesus of Nazareth, the God-man, who was born in a manger, who suffered, died and rose from the dead to redeem man. Through this same Christ God created the world—an evolving world as we now know. Through this same Christ, who at a certain point entered the process of evolution and who now reigns gloriously, God is drawing human beings forward to a new personal union with the divine: the Omega point, the end of the world, the Last Day, the Final Kingdom. This is the knowledge that Christians have, that is preached by the Church but which in no way goes counter to the vision Teilhard has already proposed. On the contrary, his vision complements it, completes it, and infuses it with new meaning and added hope.

There are, of course, difficulties in integrating Teilhard's vision with all the data of the faith, but that need not detain us now. What is of interest is how the main lines of his vision can shed light on the question that was posed. How can a commitment to social and political development be viewed as a religious enterprise?

The answer is fairly clear. The continued development of mankind is at least a necessary condition for the final coming of Jesus Christ. Only when the social development and interaction of men and women have reached a certain stage will the "critical point" necessary for this new level of existence be reached. This ongoing evolution depends on the conscious and free activity of human beings. Any contribution to this development, no matter how humble—anything that promotes the knowledge, growth, unity, interaction and progress of men and women—is directly related to the coming of the Kingdom. If it is performed with the understanding that it contributes to the final unification of men and women in Jesus Christ, it is a religious enterprise.

Not every action so contributes, of course. The human person is free and sin is a pervasive reality. Men and women can opt for selfishness and against the direction of greater unity and interaction. Moreover, some tasks would seem to make a greater contribution to human progress than others. Teilhard himself, for example, put great emphasis on the need to develop knowledge and research on an international level. But in the long view any work that contributes in some way to truly human progress has a great value from a religious point of view because it helps bring about the necessary conditions for the final coming of the Lord.

If Teilhard's vision were accepted (in its general thrust, at least, if not in all its details), government work would be measured in terms of it. In its thrust toward service, the common good, the development of the republic and its affairs both at home and abroad, government work should be oriented toward human progress and consequently have an important role to play in the ongoing process of evolution which must take place before Christ can come in glory. In the Teilhardian vision, government work can be a "vocation" for a Christian.

Moreover, a Teilhardian outlook could have some influence on individual decisions a government worker makes. While it would give no prepackaged answers and while it would in no way dispense one from the difficult task of gathering and analyzing necessary data, it would develop an orientation—a bias, if you will—a predisposition to choose what is seen as most conducive to increase the unity and deepen the interaction of the human family.

But how can a vision such as Teilhard's be really Christian? Isn't it simply a "sell-out" of the faith? Doesn't it attribute far too much importance to the world? Hasn't Christianity always urged us to renounce the world, in order to seek the things that are "above"? Believers "do not belong to the world"; "they are not of the world"; and they are consequently hated by the world.[3]

This theme of renunciation is essential in the Christian heritage and must somehow be integrated in any belief that pretends to be faithful to the tradition. A view of one's work as a religious enterprise must somehow incorporate this dimension of renunciation, else it could rapidly degenerate into the "wisdom of this age," with very little religious about it.

Teilhard himself was very much aware of this. In his little book *The Divine Milieu*[4] he analyzes at some length the place of renunciation and detachment in the life of a believer. He notes, first of all, that even in our most active moments renunciation and detachment play a part. He is referring to the common experience that worthwhile tasks require effort, concentration and discipline. This is true for the artist, the scientist, the thinker, the manager and the worker. In addition, progress demands of us a willingness to go beyond what we have achieved, to try new forms, new ideas, new approaches. The artist is never satisfied with his painting, the scientist and the thinker are always reaching for new theories, the manager and the worker look for improved products and better ways of achieving them. Effort and struggle are a part of every worthwhile human activity. Dedication to work demands a spirit of detachment.

But there is more to human experience than activity. At least half our life, Teilhard points out, is made up of what he calls "passivities." By this he means that we not only act, we are acted upon. We undergo diminishments, we suffer all kinds of misfortunes: opposition, accidents, sickness, physical defects, intellectual and moral weaknesses, death. These "passivities," however, are not completely negative. Provided they are accepted in faith and love—as Christ accepted the cross—they can serve the positive function of uniting us more closely with Christ-Omega. The "passivities" of life—frustration, failure, suffering, death—can purify the person of egoism and self-centeredness and thus bring about a closer union with God. These negative aspects of life, therefore, have a great value for the believer when they are accepted in a spirit of detachment and renunciation.

But before they are accepted, the "passivities" of life must be resisted. The first reaction must be to fight against diminishment, to affirm life, to struggle against difficulty, to resist suffering. Only when this becomes impossible should the passive attitude of loving acceptance become operative. Detachment and renunciation in face of the "passivities" of life is of crucial importance for Christian growth, but only after every effort has been made to overcome what threatens to diminish us. Commitment to progress and human development, therefore keeps the place of honor in Teilhard's vision of life.

JOHANNES B. METZ

Another thinker who develops the link between renunciation and commitment to development is Johannes Baptist Metz. I would like, therefore, to examine briefly some of Metz's ideas to see if they can shed any further light on our question: how can a lifelong commitment to social and political development in a civil service career be viewed as a religious enterprise?

Metz affirms that the modern understanding of the world is fundamentally oriented toward the future—a claim that would have delighted Teilhard. A striving after the "new" is the predominant spirit of the social, political and technical revolutions of our time. For modern men and women, the golden age does not lie behind but ahead. This can be seen in every important humanistic system of thought today. Marxism is a notable example.

Part of this modern mentality is that the world of today is by no means fixed or sacrosanct. The world is not a "given"—a set frame within which people live out their lives. It is rather the raw material out of which human beings fashion the future with the help of science and technology.

Despite this modern understanding of the world, a great deal of Christian thought has focused on the present—on the personal response of the individual to God's initiative as perceived in the present moment of his or her life. It has also focused on religious concerns: liturgical and sacramental life, individual prayer, marriage and the family. It has had little to say about the social and political movements which are shaping the future. This situation has been accentuated by the process of secularization, in which more and more of reality is seen to be autonomous and subject to its own laws. It is harder and harder for men and women today to see the divine hand in this world. They see only a human one.

The personal and the private, of course, are important for religious life. Religion cannot exist without it. But religious belief must find within itself an orientation toward the future and toward the great public issues of our day. Otherwise it will become fossilized and less and less meaningful to anyone who shares this modern mentality.

Christian belief according to Metz should of its very nature be oriented toward the future. The words of Revelation of the Old Testament are not primarily statements of information, nor mainly accounts of personal self-communication by God. They are words of *promise*. They are announcements or proclamations of what is to come. "This . . . proclamation and word of promise initiates the future: it establishes the covenant as the solidarity of the Israelites who hope, and who thereby experience the world for the first time as a history which is oriented toward the future."[5]

The New Testament does not change this orientation toward the future; it rather intensifies it. Christ's proclamation and promise of the Kingdom look to a future event, even though early Christians thought it to be very near. Moreover, the proclamation of the resurrection is more than information or statement of fact. It is a proclamation of promise for all believers. The message of the New Testament is necessarily oriented toward the future; it is a message of hope, of "creative expectancy."[6]

This future, furthermore, for which Christians hope is not something completely separate from the world or "above" the world, Metz, following on St. Thomas, would maintain. Human persons do not have two last ends—one natural and the other supernatural; they have only one last end—the future promised by God. Christian hope in its orientation toward the future cannot bypass the world. The one promised future which Christians yearn for includes this world.

But what about the Christian theme of renunciation mentioned above? Does not the New Testament require the renunciation of this world? Indeed it does, Metz insists. But the renunciation called for by Christ is not a "flight out of the world, but a flight with the world 'forward.' "[7] What Christian renunciation requires is the rejection of the world that lives solely in its present and that refuses to orient itself to the promised future. It is the world enraptured with itself and its own self-glorification which can only conceive the future as a function of the present world situation. Christian renunciation is not a refusal to be engaged in the world; much less does it mean that a Christian despises the world. It is a rejection of the world's complacency, sinfulness, selfishness and vanity for the sake of the future promised by God. Far from demanding flight from the world, Christian renunciation calls for the initiative to change and renew the world toward the Kingdom of God.

How do Christians do this? Do they have a program for the world which has somehow been given to them by revelation? Can the Bible or the Church give men a plan for changing and renewing the world toward the promised future?

By no means, answers Metz. Christians have no more information about particular political and social programs than anyone else. The process of secularization has taught us about the autonomy of many processes in the world. Moreover, we live in pluralistic societies. Not only Christians but all people are involved in the problems facing men and women today.

But Christians do have something which comes from their knowledge of the future announced by God. These are the promises of the biblical tradition: liberty, peace, justice, reconciliation. These should function in the activities of Christian believers in two ways. First these promises should impel Christians to take an active part in the public and political arena as they strive, in any way they can, to change and renew the world toward this kind of future. Secondly, these promises should enable the Christian to maintain a critical attitude toward the present conditions of society. The promised future can come, in the final analysis, only from God's power. Before this future is finally given, the promises can only be partially realized. This critical function, therefore, is not a negative one. It is not a total rejection of the present. But this critical function does make Christians restless. They see the present as provisional; they refuse to rest content with any experienced lack of liberty, peace, justice and reconciliation in the present world situation. They necessarily adopt a "critical liberating function" in society.[8]

As examples of this critical liberating function, Metz cites three. First, he cites the need for believers to be continually concerned about the individual and his fate in the face of every abstract idea of progress and humanity. The individual can never be seen as only a function of society's progress technically directed. Believers must always be concerned to help and protect the poor and the oppressed in every move towards progress. Secondly, believers should refuse to canonize any party, any group, any nation, any class, any system as necessary carriers of the promised future. All must be constantly subjected to critical scrutiny in light of the Kingdom promises. Finally, believers should continually mobilize the critical potency that lies in their central tradition of Christian love. This tradition cannot be restricted to the interpersonal sphere of I-Thou relations. It must become the unconditional determination to bring justice, liberty and peace to others—even enemies, who are included in the reach of Christian hope. This structural dimension of love does not seek to avoid all conflict. It is not a "wishy-washy," "milk-toast" attitude toward injustice in society. It could, at times, even call for revolution in favor of freedom and justice for the sake "of the least of our brothers" whenever "the status quo of a society contains as much injustice as would probably be caused by a revolutionary upheaval."[9]

But to return to the question at hand. How can a commitment to social and political development be viewed as a religious enterprise? In the type of theological thinking exemplified by Metz, the answer is fairly clear. Believers would become involved in the social and political arena not only because of the natural attraction such tasks might have. They would become involved precisely because they view such activity as an imperative of their faith. They see that the future, promised by God in revelation, is proclaimed not only for themselves as individuals. It is proclaimed for the world. There is only one promised future for all. Their faith, therefore, impels them to move the world forward by becoming involved in the social and political developments of the day. The renunciation of the world, demanded by Christ, prevents Christians from ever "buying" the world situation as it is, from "selling out" to the vanity and complacency of the world. In the light of the promises of the Kingdom, believers are always restless, always critical. So believing and so acting, the commitment of Christians to social and political development is a religious enterprise. It is a "vocation."

If these ideas of Metz are accepted (once again, in their general thrust, if not in all their details), government work has a privileged position. Because of its necessary involvement in the political and social arena, it is clearly a unique way in which believers can live out a commitment, made in faith, to labor for the fulfillment of the revealed promises of the Kingdom. Government work—and at many levels—can have a high religious value.

And once again, this kind of religious understanding can have an influence on individual decisions government workers make. It gives no detailed information, no plan, no program for social and political progress. It does, however, operate "around the edges" in questions of public policy. In fulfilling the "critical liberating function" which is theirs, believers will always have a concern for the fate of individuals, especially the poor and oppressed. Believers will refuse total commitment and total loyalty to any party, nation or system. These too must always be subject to the critical scrutiny of the promises. Finally, believers will stretch their imagination to bring to bear on social problems their central tradition of Christian love. And they will never despair, because of their belief in the future promised by God. All this will, in some way, affect the individual decisions they make.

GUSTAVO GUTIERREZ

Thus far, in examining explanations of how a commitment to social and political development can be a religious enterprise, our attention has been focused on two representatives of the first world. But thinking about this problem has not been confined to Europe and North America. Theologians of the third world have also developed ideas which have a bearing on our question. This is particularly true of some recent theological thinking in South America.

I would, therefore, as a final example, like to examine some of the ideas of Gustavo Gutierrez as they relate to this question.

Once again no effort will be made to give a complete exposition of his thought. Only a select sample of his ideas will be considered in an effort to see how one other thinker has tried to explain the religious value of political and social involvement.

Gutierrez writes out of the Latin American experience. He is less concerned with the growth of science and technology (than was Teilhard, for example); he is likewise less concerned with the secularization process that has occurred in western culture and the excessively private and personal nature of much recent religious thought (than was Metz). Indeed, Gutierrez claims, excessive preoccupation with these realities is a result of looking at the current scene with the eyes of the first world.

The dominant concern of many third world Christians is the pervasive poverty, underdevelopment and oppression of their peoples. It is not surprising, therefore, that Gutierrez begins with an analysis of what he sees to be the Latin American reality. He notes the disfavor with which the idea of development (desarrollo) and developmentalism (desarrollismo) are viewed by so many in that part of the world.

This is a change from the 50's—the decade of developmentalism—where there was great optimism regarding the possibility of achieving self-sustained economic development. According to the accepted thinking of that decade, this would be accomplished by ending the stage of foreign-oriented growth and beginning a process of inward development. A modern independent society would follow on the expansion of the internal market and full industrialization. This thinking presupposed that the "underdeveloped" countries were simply behind the "developed" ones and were obligated to repeat more or less faithfully the historical experience of the "developed" countries in their journey towards modern society.

The decade of developmentalism, however, was a failure. It did not bring about any improvement in the situation. The gap between rich nations and poor ones widened. While developed countries continued to increase their wealth, two thirds of the world population continued to struggle in poverty and frustration.

For this reason, another idea began to gain ground in Latin America: the theory of dependence. In this view, underdevelop-

ment is the end result of a process; it is perceived "as the historical by-product of the development of other countries. The
dynamics of the capitalist economy lead to the establishment of a
center and a periphery, simultaneously generating progress and
gaining wealth for the few and social imbalances, political tensions and poverty for the many."[10]

Their awareness of "dependence," maintains Gutierrez, has
led many Latin American thinkers to see that they must take into
account not only economic factors but political ones. Only by
breaking free of dependence will third world countries be able to
bring about any meaningful change in their situation of poverty.
For these thinkers, real progress in Latin America is not possible
within the framework of the international capitalist system. And
conflict will be implicit in the process—a conflict of class struggle
between the oppressors and the oppressed.

In other words, as a result of the analysis they have made of
Latin American reality, many have become radicalized. Timid
reformist efforts, characteristic of the decade of developmentalism, are no longer seen as sufficient. "Only a radical
break from the status quo, that is, a profound transformation of
the private property system, access to power of the exploited
class and a social revolution that would break this dependence
would allow for the change to a new society, a socialist
society—or at least allow that such a society might be possible."[11]

According to Gutierrez, therefore, the need in Latin America
is not for development. It is for liberation. *Liberation*, at this level
of meaning, expresses the "aspirations of oppressed peoples and
social classes, emphasizing the conflictual aspect of the economic, social and political process which puts them at odds with
wealthy nations and oppressive classes."[12]

The influence of Marxist thinking on this analysis is clear and
explicitly noted by Gutierrez. It by no means, however, demands
a commitment to atheistic communism nor the acceptance of any
existing socialist state as a model. Latin Americans, committed to
liberation, are seeking to find their own unique way to build a new
and more just society.

A growing number of Christians have become committed to

this process of liberation and are actively involved in the shared efforts to abolish the current unjust situation and to build a different society, freer and more human. They have, therefore, attempted to think through their faith in an effort to see the relationship between their commitment to liberation and their belief as Christians. In a very different context, therefore, Gutierrez raises the question: how can a commitment to social and political progress be a religious enterprise?

Liberation, he notes, is a biblical theme and one closely connected to salvation. Christ came to save us—to free us—from sin and from all sin's consequences. Sin, however, is more than an individual, private or merely interior reality. Sin is also a social historical fact, the absence of brotherhood and love in relationships among men. It has a collective dimension. It is evident in oppressive structures, in the exploitation of man by man, in the domination of peoples, races and social classes. It can be found not only in the acts of individuals but also in situations and structures. There is a sphere of sin, the " 'harmartiosphere': a kind of parameter or structure which objectively conditions the progress of human history itself."[13] Sin, therefore, involves more than particular instances of unfaithfulness. It also appears as a fundamental alienation which is at the root of all injustice and oppression.

As a result, the salvation promised in Christ encompasses not only the forgiveness of personal sins but liberation from this fundamental alienation. Seen in this way, liberation has many levels of meaning. It can mean political liberation in the sense described above. It also means the liberation of man throughout history as he assumes conscious responsibility for his own destiny. Finally, it means liberation from sin and admission to communion with God. These three levels of meaning are distinct, yet they mutually affect each other; they are all part of a single all-encompassing salvific process.

Salvation, therefore, becomes a much richer concept than when it is applied to individuals. It includes temporal progress without being reduced to it. There is only one promised Kingdom. (In this, Gutierrez agrees with Metz.) But the main obstacle to the coming of the Kingdom is sin, just as the root cause of oppression

and injustice is sin. Total liberation from the fundamental alienation of sin can be achieved only in the final coming of the Kingdom in the complete union of men with God and of men among
themselves. The *growth* of the Kingdom, however, involves
every liberation from oppression and injustice throughout history. And, conversely, every liberation from oppressive and unjust structures brings about a growth of the Kingdom. It follows,
therefore, that the commitment to build a more just society is a
salvific work, although it is not the sole component of salvation.

In other words, the growth of the Kingdom is a process
which occurs in liberating historical and political events, although
the fullness of the Kingdom can be found in none of them, since
none of them will have conquered the root alienation of sin. Only
the final coming of the Kingdom can bring about this radical
liberation. This realization enables the believer to understand that
political liberation is part of the process of salvation, but not its
total embodiment. A new and more just society is not the complete fulfillment of the promise. The growth of the Kingdom is not
its final coming.

But it is time to return once again to our question: how can a
commitment to social and political development be a religious
enterprise? From a perspective such as that of Gutierrez, the
answer is fairly obvious. The commitment to build a more true
and just society—a commitment to political liberation, as he ex-
plains it—is an effort to overcome oppressive and sinful structures. As such, it is part of the process of salvation in Christ from
sin and its effects. By becoming actively involved in the struggle
to abolish situations of injustice and build a new society, men and
women contribute directly to the growth of the Kingdom. When
this is seen and chosen in faith, such activity is, of its very nature,
a religious enterprise.

Because of the more radical meaning he gives to political
liberation in the Latin American context, some of Gutierrez's
thinking may be less immediately applicable to the situation of a
U.S. government worker. The totality of his thought is more
meaningful for revolutionaries, for those who want to overturn
the present system and establish a new one. Such convictions
usually are not found in the Washington bureaucracy. Yet a good

deal of his thinking—especially as it regards the connection between the growth of the Kingdom and the changing of unjust structures—can be enlightening for those of a reformist mentality. The perception that sin can have a structural dimension need not demand that the structure be overthrown, if one is honestly convinced that a large part of the injustice can be overcome by progressive structural reform. In this view, the commitment to improve society, to work for more just and human systems in the social, political and economic order would likewise be a participation in the process of salvation and the growth of the Kingdom.

If this perspective were adopted, it would also influence individual decisions a government worker makes. Once again, it provides no answers. But it does cause a greater sensitivity to the plight of the poor and the oppressed not only in the United States but in much of the third world. And it heightens the realization that the lot of the poor cannot, for the most part, be improved without some structural changes in the economic and political systems that determine so much in the world today. All this would necessarily have some effect on the choice and implementation of many government programs.

CONCLUSION

I would like to conclude this essay with these observations.

1) In discussing some of the ideas of these three men, I have touched on only one aspect of belief, namely our specific question: how can a commitment to social and political development be viewed as a religious enterprise? For this reason, I have not mentioned at any length some central realities involved in Christian belief—e.g., prayer, the community of believers (the Church), worship and sacramental life, etc. All of these are essential in the life of believers and must be integrated with whatever view they have of the religious importance of the work they do. Because this paper has been selective, it may give the impression that these other realities are unimportant, that the only concern for believers should be the effort to bring about human progress

with the consequent neglect of the more traditional activities associated with their faith. Nothing could be farther from the truth. For these three men, the two aspects are important. It is not a question of either-or. It is a question of both-and.

2) Each of the three men has a particular angle from which he views the relation of the believer to this world. For Teilhard, it is evolution; for Metz, it is the future; for Gutierrez it is liberation. But despite these differences there are clearly common convictions. All three believe in some form of human progress and have hope for the successful outcome of the human enterprise. All three, in the last analysis, anchor their hope in God's revealed promises and in his saving power, rather than on mere human effort. All three likewise give great importance to the final coming of the Kingdom—to the end of the world—as part of the content of Christian revelation. All three believe that Christ's effective love operates outside as well as within the Church—that all men and women are offered, in some way, the gift of salvation. And all three see a commitment to real human progress—correctly understood—as a direct contribution to the building of the Kingdom. These are the common elements in the answer each one gives to the question: "how can a commitment to social and political development be viewed as a religious enterprise?"

3) The ideas of these three men result from their reflection on their faith and what they perceive to be the experience of modern men and women. The validity of their ideas must be judged by their inner consistency, their faithfulness to revelation, and the accuracy of their reading of the human situation. The teaching Church has not officially endorsed their ideas—nor should it. The work of all three men—as would be expected—has been criticized by other thinkers and theologians. No one need accept all that they say. The purpose of this paper has been modest: to examine some answers that have been given recently by religious thinkers in the hope that their ideas may widen perspectives and indicate different ways in which the question may be approached. Believers may answer the question differently. Indeed some may never ask it at all. But reflective men and women of faith, actively committed to social and political prog-

ress, can scarcely avoid thinking of the problem. The search for integration between their life and work necessarily demands some answer to the question.

NOTES

1. Cf. H. Richard Niebuhr, *Christ and Culture* (New York: Harper and Row, 1951).

2. Pierre Teilhard de Chardin, *The Phenomenon of Man*, tr. Bernard Wall (New York: Harper and Row, 1965) p. 60.

3. John 17, 14-16.

4. Pierre Teilhard de Chardin, *The Divine Milieu*, tr. Bernard Wall (New York: Harper and Row, 1968).

5. Johannes B. Metz, *Theology of the World*, tr. William Glen-Doepel (New York: Herder and Herder, 1969) p. 87.

6. Ibid. p. 89.

7. Ibid. p. 92.

8. Ibid. p. 117.

9. Ibid. p. 120.

10. Gustavo Gutierrez, *A Theology of Liberation*, tr. Caridad Inda and John Eagleson (Maryknoll, New York: Orbis Books, 1973) p. 84.

11. Ibid. pp. 26-27.

12. Ibid. p. 36.

13. Ibid. p. 175.

Government Career and Progress Conversation

Haughey: All the way back at the beginning of our Christian lives we received and accepted a perspective about how God views and is interacting with this world. Even now my personal relationship with God is somehow compenetrated with my understanding of God's relationship to the world. Presumably in some implicit way this has an impact on how I do my work and see the work of government, its purpose and my purposes in it. Do you reflect on this at all? Do your friends in government talk about these things, do you think? Your work is a work of hope. Does that hope have any shape to it? If it does, would that shape be similar to that of the three theologians analyzed in this paper?

Ahearne: Yes, the general advancement of mankind towards the Kingdom would be a congenial attitude of most of us who are Christian, but if you were to get much more specific than that, the vision would begin to fade away.

Hennigan: The reason why it's hard for people to go beyond some sort of subjective expression of the religious or theological meaning of government is the complexity of the institutions we deal with and work in. There are so many possible combinations or consequences of actions and very few of us can see how these work in one single area of decision much less all of them going on at one time. This doesn't reflect a lack of religious interest but simply a certain humility before the complexity of all this. One hopes that what he does moves things towards a good but it's very hard to test five, ten or fifteen years ahead because of all the uncertainties of what that may be.

203

Simon: I don't think there are very many who would feel comfortable answering your question as you pose it, but even among those not claiming to be religious there is a sense of the purposefulness of life. I think the majority of people believe that there's some purpose—some overall purpose—to their lives. People in Congress, secretaries, people who work in factories, people in housework have that sense as far as I can tell. The phrase we all hear, "Everything works out for the best"—if you were to ask people, "What is the theological implication to what you just said?" they'd be startled. There is a feeling but it is not precise.

Trickett: I think also there's a profound limitation in the sense that you have a sense of being part of a body in your neighborhood and church but in the professional world you have a sense of being an individual in a world of ordered missions, of defined objectives and confined scope. There's an aloneness to it. Just a quick example. If there's a family in the neighborhood—someone stricken with cancer or with great problems, you get together whatever the race or religion to figure out what they need, what you can do. The wives organize things and you share something of what you have. In the professional world you don't seem to have this sharing. It doesn't seem that the system prohibits it, but in some ways people do not think it appropriate, it does not fit in the job description. I have worked with some people for twelve or fifteen years in my work in government but the family I'm talking about has been in our neighborhood a year and a half and there was a demonstrated need. This simple example should give some indication of how much we might fail to bring our world-view to our work.

Ahearne: I spent many good years with a large group of people, the military, who would definitely say there's a lot beyond simply having a job to do. I'm sure there are hundreds of thousands in that group who are very definitely motivated beyond the specific tasks they are trained to perform, who tend to view a ten- twenty- thirty-year time frame as having an objective purpose. They tend to have that very close cohesiveness that you're talking about. I think they view themselves not as individuals but as members of a large group who have an overriding purpose that transcends their individual purposes.

Simon: Office coherence, a sense of common mission, aren't all that rare in government. The other day, as is my custom, I dropped in unannounced and visited the Department of Labor—this time the Black Lung office, the Office of Coal Workers Compensation, they call it. As I found myself all of a sudden talking to these people I sensed their enthusiasm. Though they're handling forms and everything else they weren't just handling papers. The woman who was in charge of that section had really instilled a sense of purpose in them. There was real leadership there! She had given them a sense of what they were about and it was a thrill to come in and see that. People in Senate offices and House offices, too—very few of them put in eight-hour days. I just left the office at 20 minutes to eight, where I have never asked anybody to come in early or stay late, and there were two people still in the office when I left. That dedication is there for many.

Betty Smith: I see a lot of people who would be very hard put if you asked them to consider what they're doing in terms of very large massive social change. But I think they would talk very readily in more middle-range terms about creating opportunities for improving people's circumstances, so that it's not exactly moving society towards some generically better future but it's in the terms of some very specific population that one deals with, and hopefully improves the circumstances of the individuals in that group.

Hennigan: I think it's quite appropriate in the kind of political process that we have where there is no single power, where you have a system of checks and balances, that personal commitment is basically to the process by which a myriad of good acts are worked out. Our process doesn't lend itself to a sweeping vision such as Gutierrez'. Our people concentrate on the pieces they can influence. There is a faith in and commitment to the process. We Americans find a sense of vision and of fulfillment in smaller areas but we trust the larger process we are working in even though we can't see exactly the shape it's leading to. I think we usually operate in trying to see the personal meaning in what we do rather than the shape of the institutions, or the future.

Haughey: What do theologized world views such as you read in this paper do for you? Is there any value for you in these kinds of attempts to name the relationship between the human enterprise and God's purposes?

Trickett: I think there is. When I arrived at the Atomic Energy Commission twelve years ago I was not met by Father Abbot at the door. There was not a discussion dealing with God's purposes for the world. But in the absense of Father Abbot it is at best a groping exercise where you take the Sunday into the Monday-Tuesday-Wednesday unassisted. These theologies, therefore, are extremely good.

Ahearne: I found this study very useful. It puts a theological expression on groping feelings.

Mitchell: Does it come through with any reality in the kind of life you have and the work you do?

Ford: I need these kinds of views to address the "so what" of our human condition. I found the views of the four theologians very revealing (the fourth one being Mitchell).

Hennigan: Yes, as we mature professionally we begin to feel the need for larger visions. Theology can help one to see a much broader religious dimension because it includes what we find ourselves dealing with professionally and humanly. The larger visions bridge the gap between religion and life.

Simon: I do a lot of reading and I discovered, all of a sudden, in taking a closer look at what I was reading that I was reading a lot of junk! So I started a habit of reading something every day at least ten years old. It's amazing how that habit has enriched my perspective. That sense of perspective is something you can get not just from theologians. I have just been reading a little bit of Sigmund Freud who talks about what moves nations. He says nations tend to move on the basis of passion rather than interest. It has started me thinking and has generated much reflection in me. So what I'm saying is, these over-views are quite helpful.

Haughey: You all seem to agree that a believer who works in government has an implicitly theological world-view. That world-view is continually being reinforced, I would presume, within your own community of faith, that includes spouse, friendships and worshiping community. Are you satisfied that these provide a sufficient source of refurbishment of your theological world or does theologizing from the outside of your circle, as it were, seem like it would have any value for you?

Betty Smith: Where you get your rejuvenation, is your question. That's kind of an interesting one because I really hadn't thought about it.

Ahearne: I find that in government you tend to get concerned that the process is just, because on any given issue that you are working on it may seem to be getting nowhere and it can get very discouraging. You can struggle for years in your job trying to get something accomplished and are met so much of the time with frustrations or blind alleys, if not defeats, that you need rejuvenation to try to continue that effort. Maybe rejuvenation isn't the right word for it, it's a maintenance of the spirit, a maintenance of belief, that although it may be a consistently frustrating effort nonetheless it's worthwhile. Even if it doesn't succeed.

Haughey: Maybe there's a distinction needed between the need for new myth and rejuvenation. In the case of rejuvenation you stay with the same horizon, the belief system you had known, and try to be more motivated in it. But a new myth would furnish perhaps a brand new way of looking at myself and the relationship of the political enterprise with God's purposes.

Betty Smith: I think this distinction between rejuvenation and a new myth is rather useful. Rejuvenation can come more readily from within the context of one's everyday world. But if you're looking for a new myth, that's more likely to come from a new experience—not one that's been commonly shared over a long period of time—or from a new author. That's a very exciting idea.

Ford: Rejuvenation of what, for what? For what do I wish to be rejuvenated? Personally I would hazard a guess that most of us find stimulus and great meaning in liturgy or catechism or music or sacraments. But at the same time I would imagine that for many of us individual study, prayer, conversation with people of different communities and different faiths is also necessary and enriching because you've got to be pushed to know what you've gone to the well to get rejuvenated *for*!

Lowell: I deal with individuals part of the day and with systems part of the day. To the extent that I deal with persons I need rejuvenation but to the extent that I deal with systems whose reality I'm not able to confront immediately or understand in any way close to their entirety, I need a new myth. For example, after a course I had a couple of years ago I began taking my lunch to the office to read John Rawl's book on justice. I did that for months (because it took me months). I found it immensely enriching. Gutierrez had the same effect on me. I am certain that both now affect my approach although if you ask me what actions I take because I've now been exposed to Gutierrez and Rawls I wouldn't know, frankly. I think this kind of paper has the same effect. It enhances your perspective. It makes you think in ways that make you go beyond where you are even when you think you've arrived. I realize that there's more to this justice business than I had imagined. And Gutierrez is helping me to bring my faith to bear on the problems that I deal with, but again I have to admit I can't put my finger on exactly how. Sometimes I think maybe it's better that way. I mean I'd hate to think I'm . . .

Haughey: Deductive—

Lowell: Well, subversive. After all, I deal with people who have other faiths and I don't want to get into a kind of competitive situation where my religious beliefs are competing with some-body else's in a government setting.

Trickett: My experience is that the Church posits certain basics and if I had a great mind I could get from those things to my daily world, but I don't have that kind of mind—and I need someone with that kind of mind to come into my world, share it, help to structure it, and help to redeem me out of my limitations. In its present state the Church's basics alone are not adequate for the rejuvenation I need. In other words, I'd say that the Church does not have an adequate doctrine of vocation.

McCormick: I've known any number of basically reflective people who've undergone certain spiritual experiences, and de-veloped a certain amount of enthusiasm, after which they've tried to analyze or relate it, but have just gotten so far with it. Then they read someone like Teilhard and they say "Oh yeh". He's taken them where they're spontaneously ready to go and pro-vide the larger world-view which provides them with an articula-tion by which they can put things together. The spiritual experi-ence has started personally and then gone reflective and then they'll find somebody who will take them beyond that.

Ford: Something jumps out at you, from a printed page or a sermon or something that crystallizes or captures an amorphous yearning, or you're heading in that direction and you find some-one who's been there and who can elucidate this. It's a combina-tion of inner and outer stimulus.

Hennigan: But what I think must complete what you're saying, Dick, is that what are needed are prophetic people who try both to dream and apply visions of this kind.

Ford: Who can apply it not in the distant future but in terms of the present situation.

Ahearne: The vast number of people, I think, are at such a stage that in approaching this kind of a paper they would be helped by it. It would be a substantial step for most people.

Hennigan: My point was that this of itself doesn't evoke an action response. It helps to give meaning, significance and value to what one is doing, but it leaves one with a sense of passivity that a model in the form of a person would not.

Simon: But different people have totally different needs—and means for rejuvenation. There is a kind of charge in this study and in these theologians I find a tone of optimism that I think is awfully important.

Betty Smith: But what Hennigan says is a very real problem. One can come through these kinds of ideas, but you need roles and you need some very practical notions of "Well, what does that really mean?" "This is really fine but I'm still just sitting here plodding my way along." That's probably one of the biggest problems for most people, this thing of finding embodiments of the application of great visions.

Hennigan: Yes, the person who moves me from general optimism to concrete hope is the person who can ground his vision, bringing it down to earth by specific actions that matter and are imitable.

Langan: There are two functions that a paper like this can serve. First, it can provide a means of integration, that is, some sort of integrating vision. This can be done once and for all. When it does, something like a conversion takes place; and that's very important and valuable. Second, it can assist the search for hope, which has to do with the movement towards a good that is difficult to attain, a good that we get to through suffering. We want the integrating vision to be both comprehensive and realistic enough to include all these moments of reversal and also to serve as an energizing or motivating factor. Theology has certain unique advantages in the task of providing an integrating vision. In the task of sustaining hope there are a lot of other things that have to go on besides theology, such as a vital community life and on-going individual prayer.

Mitchell: Which of the three theologians appealed to you most or spoke relevantly to your understanding of the meaning of your work?

Trickett: de Chardin's concept of an 'Omega' point fascinates me because it ties together my material and spiritual worlds. The parallel with the 'critical mass' of nuclear physics is obvious as a critical spatial geometric and material relationship which is uniquely 'just right' for a massive transformation of form and release of 'locked in' energy. This can be seen too in people, who go through the white heat of critical suffering from which they frequently emerge more completely whole as persons, though not always physically. The excitement of de Chardin for me is his willingness to see that the unity of mankind can be positively contributed to by our daily work *in this world*. How much more exciting and meaningful than 'renunciation' as rejecting participation in the world, or redemption by good works.

Betty Smith: I kept agreeing/disagreeing with the three thinkers depending on the extent to which they approximate my notion that God has a very special plan and tasks in mind for each of us. Whether we know how it is advancing the social and individual development of others or of society in the larger sense is not particularly at issue. The implication of the conceptual framework of the paper is that anyone's work, to the extent that it is intended to fulfill God's plan, has religious significance and is the necessary means through which one's salvation is achieved. The notion that God "intends" something specific which enables an individual to participate creatively in his plan for society as well as in one's own salvation is a source of considerable optimism and freedom for me.

8
Public Policy and Christian Discernment

Thomas E. Clarke

The title of this essay is likely to induce nervousness even in some who fully accept the relevance of religious commitment to engagement in political processes. The term "discernment" (traditionally termed "discernment of spirits") might seem to suggest a ouija board or seance or divine computer approach to public decision-making. "It has seemed good to the Holy Spirit and to us" (Acts 15:28) may have been appropriate language for the first notable decisional process of the Christian Church, but for a complex, technological, secular and pluralistic American society confirmed in the wisdom of keeping religious ideology at a safe distance from the halls of government, this kind of language seems clearly intrusive.

There is a point to the demurrer, and it helps me to indicate from the beginning the limited character of this essay. I will be focusing primarily on political decision-making as engaged in by persons in government, more particularly by persons whose values are Christian. Like other essays in this volume, it seeks to enlighten Christians about the decisional aspects of their lives in government. Shall I vote for this or that particular piece of legislation? What recommendation should I make to my supervisor on the basis of the analysis I have made?

But there are others besides Christians who serve in government. There are also limits to the acceptable influence of religion in American politics. And besides the personal aspects of political decision-making there are technical and institutional aspects, highly complex and difficult to integrate with moral values and religious commitments. A full treatment of Christian discernment and political decision-making would have to attend, therefore, to this broader problematic, namely, whether and how, in a secular, pluralistic and increasingly complex technological society, the tradition of Christian discernment may throw light on decision-making in its institutional aspects. My essay will touch only briefly, at the end, on this more difficult question. My chief concern will be to help Christians in government toward a practical integration of their faith and values with the political decisions which they make.

The first part of the essay is more theoretical in character, and reflects theologically on discernment as a distinctly Christian approach to decision-making. The second part is briefer and somewhat more practical, speaking of the role in personal discernment of prayer and other supports. The conclusion will, as I have indicated, point the way to what might be said in a fuller treatment that would attend to the institutional features of public decision-making.

For committed Christians in government this essay holds out some aspects of their specific religious heritage—story, values, techniques—which may assist, illumine and enliven their participation in political processes. Others, hopefully, will be helped, if they are led to the sources, religious or humanistic, from which their own aspirations to integrity derive.

The need for what is here termed "discernment" stems from a few facts of universal human experience that are shared by government people no less than by others. Saul of Tarsus put the first fact rather starkly: I find myself all mixed up, not doing what I want to do, doing what I don't want to do; how the hell can I get out of this mess? (Rom 7:15, 24) The second fact is not unrelated to the first: we lie to ourselves and to one another. If there are any readers who have not experienced, in themselves and in others, this lack of freedom and lack of truth in decision-making, they have no need for the present essay. But one does not have to be a gloomy critic of public life to say that it verifies, like other sectors of human life, both light and darkness. We may choose not to curse the darkness, but we refrain from acknowledging it only at the price of conniving in its growth, especially when we possess resources capable of curtailing it.

It is not objective complexity, then, but our proneness to

subjective complicity in moral evil, which is the target of what is here understood as spiritual discernment. Illusion and addictiveness are the names of the enemy. Ultimately this essay has a very practical goal: to help people to deal with the various moral obstacles to good decision-making, and, more positively, to provide them with some suggested helps to grow in their ability to make good decisions.[1]

THE CONTEXT OF DECISION

A theoretical reflection on Christian discernment needs simultaneously to draw upon the resources of Christian doctrine and the insights of secular disciplines. Only a summary presentation of such a synthesis is possible here. The reader may be helped by keeping in mind the following three frameworks of discourse:

1) The triadic framework of creation, fall and redemption, or: native human endowment, deprived human condition, restored human potential.

So much of public life is built around conflict that it seems appropriate to accept in the Christian view of things the centrality of conflict between good and evil. Good derives from creation by an infinitely good and wise and provident God. Evil comes about in the Fall, through the abuse of the gifts of freedom by creatures made in God's image. Redemption through Jesus Christ and the Holy Spirit counteracts evil, without removing the necessity of struggle with it as long as human history runs its course. Creation, fall and redemption are not so much temporal phases of human history as dimensions of daily human experience. Viewed from the standpoint of "ultimate concern," what happens in any government office each day is simultaneously an act of continuing creation, a struggle with evil and a campaign for the prospering of good.

2) The utility of certain models of human life represented in the Christian sources.

By model I mean an image or concept drawn from some elementary human experience and utilized metaphorically or analogously for the expression of an ultimate interpretation of life. Corresponding to the triadic framework just given, the following arrangement of models is proposed:

Creation	*Fall*	*Redemption*
Light	Darkness	Enlightenment
Freedom	Bondage	Liberation
Integrity	Brokenness	Reintegration
Health	Sickness	Healing
Peace	Estrangement	Reconciliation

3) The triad of intrapersonal, interpersonal, societal as descriptive of what constitutes the human in its totality.

What is here in question is the expression of a Christian understanding of the human, employing some tools provided by sociology and anthropology. The findings of these modern disciplines have helped us to see that human life is constituted by (a) individual personhood (interiority, subjectivity); (b) relationship (intersubjectivity, interpersonal communion); (c) climates of life (society, symbols, structures and institutions, etc.).

A few things need accenting with respect to this important triad. First, climates are not totally extrinsic to personhood and relationship. Just as our physical bodies are/are not our selves, so the climates which we generate by personal action and interaction are/are not our individual and shared selves. We are responsible for the several worlds which we create or acquiesce in, and they profoundly influence our inner selves and the ways in which we relate to others. The point is of major importance for decision-making. Not only the formal and deliberate structuring (juridical or organizational) of a decisional process, but a wide variety of informal climates, ranging from accepted habits of speech and address, physical settings, the influence of tradition and custom, stereotypes and mind-sets, etc., exert a profound influence on how individuals think and feel and behave, how they relate to other individuals and to groups, and how groups of various sizes and composition will think and feel and behave. The opposite is also true. Personal attitudes and freely-chosen or accepted relationships will be capable of affecting the various climates which influence the outcome of decisions.

If these three frameworks are brought together and taken as

a basic religious perspective on what happens each day in the complex world of government decision-making, the following might be said, from the viewpoint of faith, without extravagance. Robert Mitchell's exposition of three theologies of involvement supports the view that, each hour of the day, in the complex and usually prosaic processes of public life, the history of human salvation is being enacted. Conflict and cooperation on many levels are characteristic, but at the deepest level what matters is the conflict of powerful forces of evil and good. Depending on what metaphor seems appropriate, the process and the struggle may be described in terms of enlightenment, liberation, reintegration, healing or reconciliation. The agents of the struggle are human persons, all of whom carry within them both darkness and light, bondage and freedom, sickness and health, etc. As the struggle rages, their interpersonal relationships embody varying proportions of evil and good, darkness and light, etc. And from their interaction emerges over a period of time a whole gamut of climates—customs, laws, regulations, social habits, shared assumptions and stereotypes, etc.—which both give expression to the evil or good already present, and also tend to confirm that evil or good.

Of the several metaphors or models mentioned, the most significant, from the viewpoint of spiritual discernment, are enlightenment and liberation. For the evil which afflicts human life consists primarily in (1) illusion and ignorance, and (2) addictiveness or enslavement. To extend the statement of Paul quoted earlier, human misery consists in our not really knowing what we are doing and in not really wanting what we are doing. What modern psychology and psychiatry have revealed of the unconscious, of hidden motivations, meets a major theme of Christian spirituality, the lack of self-knowledge as hindrance to spiritual growth.

The themes of enlightenment and of liberation are interwoven, of course, for at the deepest human level consciousness and commitment, enlightenment and freedom, all but coincide.

Now it is precisely in decision that the heart of the struggle we are describing is had. However complex, however difficult to locate, it is decision by persons in relationship within structures that shapes the life of the world. And, to pick up a theme already mentioned, what is most significant in decision is the quality of goodness, not the degree of correctness. Now we may say that the quality of goodness is constituted by the degree of enlightenment and freedom present in the decision. Here the focus is less on what is chosen than on the process of choosing. What goes wrong with government or with business or with any other area of human life is not so much that people choose the wrong things as the fact that they fall short of choosing humanly, primarily because of illusion and addiction. Where sin reigns not only in human hearts but in relationships between persons and in the resulting climates of life, illusion and addiction become the polluted moral air which people breathe. Similarly, when grace abounds in any area of human life, what results is not precisely that people begin to choose the right object but rather that they begin really to choose. As illusion yields to freedom, the quality of life, verified centrally in the shaping of the future through decision, makes its way out from human hearts into human relationships and then into the variety of climates which begin to participate in light and freedom, and in turn, in the completion of the circle, invite individuals and groups to real choices.

DISCERNMENT AND DECISION-MAKING

We are finally in a position to comment directly and pointedly on the title of this essay. What does Christian discernment have to do with political decision-making? Christian discernment is a distinctive approach to decision-making, rooted in the Christian interpretation of the meaning of life and providing the decision-maker(s) with vehicles, supports and challenges drawn from the integral life of the Christian Church. One special characteristic of discernment in decision-making (hereafter DM) is its holistic accent, which hopefully will appear in what follows.

The goal, then, of Christian discernment as a way of political decision, may be described as the enlightenment and liberation of persons in communion within society for shaping the future through good decision-making. The principal obstacles to good decision are illusion and addiction. Because our affective and cognitive faculties are so closely linked, liberation from bondage involves also enlightenment from ignorance and error. Our addictions—inner, shared, societally embodied—hinder our seeing the truth as it offers itself here and now; and our blindness—inner, shared, societally embodied—deepens our helplessness to escape bondage. In all three dimensions (to advert to the other models), alienation, fragmentation, sickness are experienced. As a result, we find ourselves doing what we don't want, not doing what we really want. Confirmation of this dismal portrait is easily come by: watch the evening news, or reflect on one of our poorer days on the home and work scene.

Thus far the bad news. But "where sin has abounded, grace has abounded yet more" (Rom 5:20). The paradoxical simultaneity of sin and grace—recall Luther's *simul justus et peccator* (simultaneously just and sinful)—is a capital affirmation of the Christian interpretation of life. That grace is present and that it eventually triumphs is an affirmation of faith, not of reason or experience, though both of these may add supportive "evidence." Implicit in our being Christians at all is the conviction that good DM is possible—not in the style of the first Adam, in paradise, but in the style of the second Adam, who pilgrimaged from womb to cave to exile to home to road to synagogue to mountaintop to prison to cross to tomb—and beyond to garden and to glory.

It is possible, drawing upon the models already suggested, to describe what good DM looks like. The following is not a complete and systematic portrait, but a description of some of the important features.

1) There is a vast spectrum of human decisions, ranging from a deep once-in-a-lifetime conversion experience or the shared decision to secede from the Union to the decision to move one's desk closer to the window or change the brand of paper clips used in the office. Theologians in recent decades have written much of "basic options," i.e., fundamental reorientations of a person's life in relationship to God, other humans, the creation. Such basic options, while not everyday occurrences, are nevertheless somehow present in the lesser choices we make, which will be more

congruous or less congruous with them, depending on the quality and consistence of our fidelity.

2) A second consideration concerns the reality of virtue, habit and character. These terms point to the fact that facility, spontaneity, and stability in choosing the good can be developed. Together with an understanding of "basic option," this consideration can help us to be at ease with not being too explicitly conscious in everyday life of having to make choices that are in line with the Gospel. It will also help preserve us from "decisionitis," so that we let ourselves be, without undue anxiety, in the flow of a life which has been chosen in the light of the Gospel. This does not exclude the need we all have to reflect on the quality of decision in our lives. But the need for deliberate reflection is a variable, contingent on temperament, stage of personal growth, type of work, etc.

3) What constitutes the core goodness of decision can be named with several terms, e.g., faith, love, righteousness. Here we choose the term freedom, understanding freedom (to be distinguished from free will) within the Pauline, Augustinian and Lutheran traditions as a quality of unimpeded moral goodness and self-realization in responding to life. In this sense we act freely when we do what we really want, and when we really want what we do. It is the freedom of self-realization. Its supreme exemplar is God himself, and its human sacrament is Jesus Christ.

4) Because of our fallen-redeemed condition, this freedom must come as liberating grace from God. The created forms and vehicles of this grace are multiple: the good example of others, our personal endowments, a happy childhood, solid education, the teaching of Christ and the Church, the positive influence of human and Christian community, etc. But the core-grace is the self-gift of God himself. The Holy Spirit is God himself (the one God) precisely as he gives us himself in the intimacy of indwelling. He is God as infinitely immanent in humans, in human and cosmic process. The key to good DM is the indwelling Spirit of God acting within us to liberate, enlighten, heal, integrate and reconcile in every aspect and dimension of human DM.

5) This action of the Spirit is not substitutional but evoca-

tive. It is the freedom of God expressing itself in and through the sacrament of our human freedom. We are not free in spite of but rather because of the gift of sharing God's freedom through the action of the Holy Spirit within us. Far from relieving us of the responsibility—and sometimes the burden—of empirical data gathering, rational analysis, the tedium of debate, etc., the action of the Spirit gives courage and stamina and humor for persevering engagement in a DM which remains totally human. If sometimes Christians speak as if their DM were on automatic pilot, it is because the Spirit often—not always—gives joy, facility, spontaneity, and because habits of sensitivity and responsiveness have reduced the elements of struggle and doubt, especially as these bear the mark of sinfulness.

6) If freedom through enlightenment by the Spirit is the heart of good DM, that action has a two-fold aspect: (a) positively, we are drawn by the attraction of good—we taste and see how good the Lord is or, as Augustine said, we are conquered by *delectatio victrix*, by victorious delight; (b) negatively, we are enabled to be disengaged from addictiveness, from our proclivity to absolutize what is relative, from idolatry in every form. As we have said, affective and cognitive dimensions of the human, and of the action of the Spirit in and through the human, are inseparable. What draws us to true freedom is the delightful vision of truth, God himself as infinite truth shining forth in every human value and freeing us from deceit and vanity in every form.

7) It is this interweaving of the models of enlightenment and liberation which makes the traditional term discernment of spirits an appropriate one even today. The pluralism of our society, the ever-growing complexity of the human processes within which DM is situated, the bewildering acceleration of change, the increasing domination of life by technology and system, the subtle and insidious invasion of the human person and human relationships by violent and manipulative techniques of "persuasion," all these point to the need for an approach to DM which can deal effectively with confusion, anxiety and threat. The tradition of the discernment of spirits offers an approach which, while it accents the role of the heart and of intuition (a term combining both aspects might be spiritual sensibility), refuses to let these substi-

tute for reason, empirical sense, authority, or any of the other contributors to DM. The tradition of the discernment of spirits also takes seriously the reality of conflict and doubt in DM, and prepares us to deal with frustration, opposition, interruption, fragmentation, provisionality and similar characteristics of our society today. It is able to deal with unprecedented objective complexity in DM precisely because it fosters a subjective simplicity, in the Gospel sense of purity of heart, singleness of purpose, poverty of spirit.

8) The degree of formalization and reflection in DM will vary with the nature of the decision to be made and with the subjective dispositions of the person or the group. It may be helpful to distinguish discernment (a) as a quality; (b) as a process; (c) as a formal method. As a quality, discernment (or discretion) should be found in every decision, even the most spontaneous and the least significant. As a process, informal or formal, discernment will become more conscious and systematic in proportion as the material for decision is objectively significant, but especially as we find ourselves having to deal with our own illusions and addictiveness. And there will be certain cases, relatively rare, when an individual or group ought to choose a formal method of discernment, one geared particularly to diminishing the force of addictiveness and heightening sensitivity to the attraction of the Holy Spirit.

9) An approach to DM by way of discernment will attend to all dimensions of the human, and it will seek to situate the particular decision within the flow of time in the story of the person or group making the decision. It is precisely this time-dimension which extends the scope of discernment beyond the present to past and future, and prompts it to have recourse not only to the empirical and the rational but to the resources of memory, imagination, and the heart-feelings which are stimulated by the exercise of these two faculties. Here the integral life of the Church, and particular liturgical and sacramental celebration, are paradigmatic. The Church lives, first of all, by remembering *(anamnesis)*, by proclaiming over and over again what God has done in Jesus Christ. She lives by story telling, by recalling her origins. In the Eucharistic celebration this remembrance is so

powerful that it makes the saving history of Jesus Christ present in the sacred signs as the power of the future. Similarly, the Church lives by imagining, by a dreaming hope which differs from optimism by its transrational character. Its power stems not from rational analysis of present favorable trends but from trust in the One who is Lord of the future. Power is generated for facing the challenge of the present moment of decision by a joyous, confident anticipation of a blessed future to be given by God. And, because the heart has reasons the mind knows not of, its engagement through remembering and dreaming brings elements of insight and courage which are irreplaceable.

10) Implicit in much that has been said is an acknowledgement of the important paradox that the total process of DM includes key elements, perhaps the most crucial elements, which are not directly pragmatic and decisional in character. Here is where leisure, contemplation, silence, a due regard for physical and psychic health, have their importance.

11) Finally, a word needs to be said on the communal and ecclesial aspect of all DM. Both sound psychology and the Christian faith insist that person is person only within community. Hence, whatever the forms of influence on individual DM by the various communities to which the decision-maker belongs, that influence is not extrinsic but constitutive. It is here that the various loyalties spoken of by David Hollenbach make their contribution. Conversely, the quality of communal decision will, by and large, be proportioned to the quality of individual decision in the members, as well as to the quality of their interaction and communication.

There will be occasions, even within the pluralistic context of American political life, when the discernment of Christians regarding the fulfillment of their political responsibilities will be communal in character. While prayer breakfasts or Christian study groups are not occasions for concrete political decisions, they are significant elements in a total process by which individual Christians are supported by communities of shared values and aspirations. Helping one another to remain attentive to the presence of deep human values within specific political issues is, at least in a broad sense, an exercise of communal discernment.

PRAYER AND DECISION-MAKING

If the preceding theoretical reflections have been at all suasive, they are likely to have generated in the reader the question, "Just how do I go about discerning the spirits in the context of my work in government?" Without entering the area of the very practical which John Haughey's concluding reflection will take up, here are some observations which touch the "how to" of Christian discernment.

First, let it be clearly stated once again that the goal of an asceticism of decision-making is, negatively, the progressive liberation of the decider from illusion and addiction, and positively, facility in choices that are truly human because more fully conscious and free. Such liberation is, obviously, the work of a lifetime. It aims not at facile choices in the midst of complexity but at the disposition or transformation of the one who makes the choices.

This ongoing transformation of the subject of decision-making is wrought in and through all the facets of that subject's life, not just through an isolated set of "spiritual practices." Still, prayer is an appropriate way of naming the congeries of specific strategies for growth in discernment. It is obviously not possible here to present even the rudiments of a description of prayer, its character, value, forms and criteria.[2] Some brief observations relating prayer to discernment will have to suffice.

Prayer in its most basic and pervasive character is nothing but faith itself as consciousness and commitment. It is the human person (or group) receptive and responsive to the absolute One whom we call God. It is verified wherever faith is verified, and so it can take place wherever we are responding to life in faith, not only in times and spaces apart from productive activity. But, given our fragility, some times and spaces apart—what is called formal prayer, as distinct from virtual or habitual prayer—are normally necessary. Alone, with a few intimates, or with the great throng of believers in liturgical celebration, one needs to exercise one's faith in a situation and posture of heightened awareness and dedication.[3] Between the exercise of faith in situations of formal prayer and its exercise in other situations the relationship is one of reciprocity and interdependence. Sometimes we need to leave our gift at the altar, and go first to be reconciled with our neighbor, before we are truly disposed to pray. At other times we need moments of solitude, of shared prayer, of spiritual counsel, where we may find the courage and humility to go to the neighbor in a reconciling spirit.

There are many, many ways in which prayer heightens our ability to discern. By enabling us to stand, simultaneously, in the presence of the shining truth that is God and the bag of untruths that is ourselves apart from God, prayer enables us to deal with illusion. By bringing us the warm experience of being loved by God, prayer frees us from the petty pseudo-loves which keep us from making genuine choices. Prayer is remembering, *anamnesis*, the way that the Christian individual in community returns to communal and personal roots and brings the power of story to bear on the conflicts and decisions of life. When we remember how God has loved us, how his amazing grace and unfathomable providence have brought us to the present moment endowed with a rich heritage, it is far more likely that we shall make noble, grateful, confident choices.

Prayer is also an experience of dreaming hope. The word of God in Scripture is powerful in our lives because it is a word of absolute promise: "I will be with you always." Without hope, no one would bother to get out of bed in the morning. It is hope—dreaming hope—that makes the world go round. It is the deficiency of hope that begets non-decisions, the compulsivities of routine or novelty that strive to substitute for our unwillingness to face life—and death.

The fruit of prayer may also be described with reference to John Langan's essay on rationality. Genuine prayer practiced over a period of time has a clarifying and liberating impact at the core of the person, and so tends to heal and order each of the elements involved in decision. Reason itself, in the narrow sense, finds itself enhanced and more free as a person becomes enamored of the rectitude, the shining truth, of God himself, especially as manifest in Jesus Christ. Experience, the heritage of the past, which can be a deadening hindrance to creative decision when it is mired in mere nostalgia, is set free by prayer to become what Johannes Metz terms "dangerous memories", the power of the future.[4] Similarly the riches of intuition, insight, imagination are unlocked by prayer in its aspect of dreaming hope, enabling reason to let go of paralyzing caution. So for the other companions of reason analyzed by John Langan. Their integration for purposes of good decision requires something more than a pragmatic ordering of their respective contributions. It is only within a conscious and freely sustained personal relationship to the Absolute One, whom we call God, that the human organism becomes a fully apt instrument of significant choices.

There is space only to mention the fact that prayer for the Christian takes place with the help of a remarkable panoply of traditional resources: Let me enumerate only some of the principal ones:

1) Prayerful reading of the Bible, in solitude, intimate groups and large Church society, together with other kinds of "spiritual reading."

2) Liturgical celebration, and particularly the celebration of the Eucharist.

3) The enriching practice of the examination of conscience (today frequently referred to as the "consciousness examen").

4) Spiritual direction from an experienced and wise counsellor.

5) The cultivation of silence and solitude, especially for extended periods in the form of a spiritual retreat.

6) Experience of life in Christian community, in family, parish or other kinds of groupings.

7) The practice of the "works of mercy," to which today may be added "the work of justice," that is, efforts to heal and transform those structures of life in Church and secular society which deprive people of their rights and render it difficult or impossible for them to live humanly and to participate in the decisions which shape their future.

For most of the decisions made in the various contexts of government, as these have been described by Brian Smith, nothing needs to be added to what has been said. Let the reader recall the distinction made above between discernment as quality, as process, and as method. A Christian in government who has been working at being transformed in truth and freedom along the lines we have described, will make most good decisions without needing any special method. Such decisions will have a discerning quality. There will be occasions, when decisions are more important, have major moral consequences, or find the decision-maker not fully detached, when some kind of a process of discernment is called for. The details of such a process can be quite varied, ranging all the way from a little time spent in prayer of petition to a more sustained effort to deepen one's inner attitude of detachment. And, on relatively rare occasions, it will be helpful to engage in a formal method of discernment of spirits.[5] In such a method, prayer in solitude, the prayerful reading of Scripture, immersion in the Gospel mysteries, and similar exercises, are combined with a testing of one's heart in the presence of the possible options, with peace, joy, freedom, hope, love as the basic indicators of the choice which ought to be made. Sharing what happens in the experience of prayerful discernment with a director is an immense help, by way of support in adversity and by way of challenge to illusion.

CONCLUSION

Theological reflection on decision-making is still in its infancy. The present essay, focusing on the help that needs to be given to Christians engaged in government, has not dealt with some of the larger aspects of political decision-making within secular, pluralistic American society. By way of conclusion, it may be useful to point to some important avenues of future investigation, where Christian discernment might make a distinctive contribution to secular processes:

1) Among the assumptions of such a prospective study would seem to be the following:

    i) Religious and ethical pluralism among the participants in political decision-making is a fact, which does not of itself exclude viable political life, and in fact has distinct advantages for enriching that life.

ii) Political life is secular in character, that is, it does not include in its formal constitution any particular religious ideology. This does not preclude among the participants in public life religious motivations which are influential in shaping personal decisions within government, and so at least indirectly influential in shaping public decision as such.

iii) Decision-making in government today is increasingly institutional and technological in character. While persons and groups of persons and their decisions are necessarily involved in public decision-making, personal and interpersonal choices become embodied in processes, methodologies, statutes, and the like, and so achieve a more impersonal and objective character.

iv) Nevertheless, public decision-making remains human and moral in its character. Hence all that has been said regarding Christian discernment needs to be applied to it, with all due respect for its pluralistic, secular and technological character. Thus, for example, the human myths and dreams which are embodied in public decisions need to be noted, as do the values and norms which are implicit. The categories of illusion and addiction, of truth and freedom, which have been accented in the account of Christian discernment, are important for assessing not only the attitudes of persons but the institutionalized forms of decision-making.

2) Proceeding from these assumptions, an approach to political decision-making could transpose into secular, pluralistic and technological idiom many of the basic features of Christian discernment which I have described. Here are some of the leading features of such an approach, in question form:

i) What are the concrete agencies within American government within which the power of myth and symbol are to be integrated with the more narrowly rational and pragmatic elements of decisional process? To what degree and in what way can the workings of memory (in the return to roots), of imagination (in making a place once again for Utopian dreaming) and of feeling (particularly as fed by memory and imagination) be integral to governmental options? And how does one deal with the manifest blocks to such an integration, e.g. a prevailing mood of cynical and despairing pragmatism, or the growing enslavement of memory, imagination and feelings by media of communications in the employ of a technology which progressively controls the lives of human beings?

ii) How can concrete institutional choices embody commonly shared human values, articulated with sufficient clarity and with such verve as to enlist the commitment of the American people and of those who serve them in government?

iii) Through what instrumentalities will public decision-making disclose and deal with the hidden illusions and addictions present not only in human hearts but in the powerful climates which shape people's attitudes and behavior, including the institutional processes of decision themselves?

iv) Correspondingly, how can the clarity of truth and the serenity of freedom become objectivized in institutions which in turn foster truth and freedom in persons and groups? How do enlightenment and liberation, so prominent in Christian discernment, become institutionalized in a secular, pluralistic and technological society?

v) How can conflict, which also moves from persons and groups to structures and institutions and back, be dealt with creatively, so that it serves the purposes of enlightenment and freedom, and eventually the purposes of harmony and peace among persons and groups which, however much they differ in religious ideology and articulation of moral values, share a common humanity, common story, common destiny? Here is one area where the tradition of Christian discernment and the best of secular approaches to group relationships, communications, etc. would seem to converge. On both sides there would seem to be a conviction that conflict is not necessarily destructive. The tradition of Christian discernment contributes various suggestions: the role of silence, the need for solitary reflection, the deliberative assumption of the viewpoint of the other party, the testing of the quality of one's own spontaneous convictions, etc. Investigations into public decision-making in the American context might ask just in what way some of the methods employed in Christian discernment might be adapted to a more secular, pluralistic and conflict-ridden scene.

It will be some time, undoubtedly, before theology sheds any major light on the extension to public decision-making of the fruits of the perennial tradition of Christian discernment. In the meantime, Christians involved in government are already in a position to profit by that tradition for the various kinds of personal choices within the framework of government which they are called on to make.

NOTES

1. It may be helpful at this point to distinguish between a correct decision and a good decision. A decision will be correct to the degree to which it corresponds to the pragmatic requirements of total non-moral reality as well to general moral principles. A decision will be good to the degree to which it is, as a concrete human choice, characterized by the freedom and truth already spoken of. Correctness in a choice has to do with conformity to standards which are rationally ascertainable. Goodness has to do with the quality of the choice itself and of the processes and relationships which constitute it. Not every correct decision is good, nor every good decision correct. For example, two couples having marital problems may decide to terminate their marriages, and in each case an objective and knowledgeable observer would approve, seeing, for example, that there is such a basic incompatibility that neither marriage should have happened in the first place. Both decisions, then, are correct. But in looking at the way in which each couple has come to its decision, there may be notable differences. In one case, for example, the climate of decision, the quality of the exchanges and of the consultations made may have been destructive of truth and freedom, leaving the partners not only separated but humanly diminished, likely to carry a residue of self-reproach and bitterness into whatever relationships life will now offer. In the other marriage, which objectively might be no less tense and difficult in the issues being faced, the decision-making process may have taken

place with a notably higher degree of truth and freedom, because the couple spoke and acted in light, not darkness, and because their choice to separate was a genuine exercise of freedom, not a shared neurotic enterprise.

One could also describe decisions which were good but incorrect. For example, ten years after voting for an important piece of legislation, a senator may see that his analysis was faulty or that he had not included all available data, and so he now views his vote as mistaken. But if these deficiencies originated from human fallibility and not from resistance to the truth, the decision was a good one.

It may be said further that (1) it is more important that our decisions be good than that they be correct (though this latter is not unimportant); (2) by and large concern for the goodness of decisions will be favorable, not unfavorable, to the likelihood of correct decisions. The presence of spiritual freedom and truth eventually improves not only the moral quality of persons and relationships but the pragmatic effectiveness of choices. (3) It is for the sake of goodness, not correctness, that recourse to the religious roots of decision-making is had. Not least in our own day do we need the reminder that life's absolute imperative is not to succeed or to avoid all mistakes but "to do justice, and to love kindness, and to walk humbly with your God" (Micah 6:8).

2. There is an abundance of classic and contemporary writings on prayer, and each one must find or be helped to find what is suitable. One simple approach which many have found helpful is L. Boase, *Prayer in Faith*, Huntington, Ind., Our Sunday Visitor, 1976.

The classic (and much criticized) comprehensive manuel in the Roman Catholic tradition is A. Tanquerey, *The Spiritual Life*, Westminster, Md., n.d.

Two other general introductions are: J. de Guibert, S.J., *The Theology of the Spiritual Life*, New York, 1953, and G. Thils, *Christian Holiness*, Tielt, Belgium, 1961.

3. In a recent essay I have tried to show how the triad of intrapersonal, interpersonal and society may be applied to prayer. Cf. "Toward Wholeness in Prayer," in *The Wind Is Rising: Prayer Ways for Active People* (eds. W. Callahan, S.J. and F. Cardman), Quixote Center, Hyattsville, Md.

Each of the fourteen essays in this collection represents a more or less biographical approach to an understanding of contemporary prayer; contributors are drawn from Roman Catholic laity, religious, and clergy.

4. Cf. J. Metz, "The Future in the Memory of Suffering," in J. Metz (ed.), *New Questions on God*, Concilium Volume 76 (1972), pp. 9-25.

5. For some recent contributions to the theory and practice of individual and communal discernment, see the following essays, all in *Studies in the Spirituality of Jesuits*: J. Futrell, "Ignatian Discernment," volume 2, number 2, April 1970; J. Toner, "Method for Communal Dis-

cernment of God's Will," volume 3, number 4, September, 1971; J. Futrell, "Communal Discernment; Reflections on Experience," volume 4, number 5, November, 1972; L. Orsy, "Toward a Theological Evaluation of Communal Discernment," volume 5, number 5, October, 1973.

Discernment Conversation

Haughey: Let's begin in your world and the relationship between the accomplishment of your professional tasks and praying. Is there any connection? Do you ever "discern" what decisions you ought to make by praying about the matter to be decided?

Betty Smith: Let me start. I have come to believe very strongly in Divine Providence. I have learned that I must keep my commitment to God steady, while professionally expending intellectual and physical energy in pursuing what seems right according to my own lights and take matters in the directions they ought to go in so far as I can see where this ought to be. Notwithstanding all this I've found a sort of hanging loose is necessary so that if God chooses to move me in a different way then I can be moved. I've had so many experiences in the course of a lifetime where my whole career has changed radically. I didn't have a planned career. I moved from one set of circumstances to the other and always in unexpected ways. Every job I have had I'd stay in until suddenly something else propelled me another way to another kind of activity. I don't know whether this is praying, or discerning, or what. I feel as though I get a tremendous amount of individual personal assistance in all kinds of what could seem to be ridiculous ways. I always find a parking spot in difficult places— tonight when I came down this street I was late and I said "Lord, you better find me one since Georgetown is an impossible place." So I turned around the corner and there was a lovely place. I don't consider this any privileged kind of gift or position to be in. I think this kind of relationship many people have with God, though maybe they define it differently than I do. I happen to feel that it's very personal; it's helped me to avoid a lot of pitfalls. For

232

me there's a real interface between my own personal religious convictions and the things that happen to me in my own professional level. I don't pray about the decisions as such. They work themselves out. Don't misunderstand. I do pray but I think there's a sort of a constant reliance based on an assumption that I am to make use of all the talents that I have and if I do this with a good intention the outcomes are going to be worked out in a very appropriate way.

Simon: I identify with Betty in having a rather tough time defining prayer. The connection between prayer and action intrigues me. If I may use an illustration from my first campaign, I remember running into a lady in Granite City, Illinois. I handed her one of my folders and asked her to vote for me. She said she had read what I stood for and she was certainly going to pray that I would be elected, but that she was not going to vote because she didn't believe in getting mixed up in politics! In the same vein, Sunday morning I'll hear in the Lutheran church where we pray a petition to help the hungry, but then we do nothing about it. And I wonder—Is that prayer?

Haughey: So for you prayer and life are not or should not be all that dissociable—that the activity of praying and actual living are much more intertwined one with the other than "Now I pray" and "Now I work"—

Simon: Yes! Jimmy Carter at one point defined how many times a day he prayed, and I would have an awfully difficult time doing anything like that.

Lowell: I can clearly say that I have never discussed with God the decisions I am expected to make in my government position. The thought of meditating in a prayerful way over a decision just doesn't occur to me. On the other hand, the request for light or grace or the ability to be helpful, the aspiration: "God, help me to say the right thing that will help this particular thing to move in a direction that is more conducive to what you have in mind for the world" . . . I can do that and do that. But it doesn't get beyond that, it doesn't become "OK, now let's talk a little about this—the substance of it, so that I know what message You have in mind for me to communicate."

Hennigan: Prayer in my life used to be centered around and was concerned with questions of commitment. But after a while, over a period of time I learned that it wasn't commitment that was so difficult, but detachment was the missing feature. In my professional work too much of my ego or self was involved in the rational process and prayer for me became less an affirmation in the commitment sense and more of a driving out of selfishness. In an attempt to arrive at accurate judgments or good decisions that I was involved in, I had to get in touch with the peculiar preferences or very human drawings I felt and simply stand back from the thing and to see myself in perspective. I find now in the stuff I deal with I can get to a point where I can weigh the possibilities more clearly, I think, and I have a feeling that my judgment is more disinterested than if I hadn't learned more detachment. Prayer is certainly less discursive. I don't find myself involved so much in verbal prayer nowadays. What I seek is a kind of intuitiveness that enables me to think with a kind of inner mind. As far as formal prayer is concerned, now it's either in groups or in liturgical settings where I need the sense of the community verbalizing and engaging in ritual to be really drawn out of myself and be replenished in my inner mind. The vocational sense I have about my work remains quite interior, it is not something you can share with many other people at work. I can share in the larger community which involves family, and people from a wide range of vocations, a body of relationships you might loosely call the "Church". It's this group of many people who are attempting to reach God in a variety of ways, it is with them that there's affirmation; from them one draws strength and prays in a different way than in a work situation. How to bridge these two worlds I'm not sure yet. I pray differently in each of them.

Ford: I'm concerned about the degree of certainty which a given individual thinks he can come to about God's will. That it is capable of being revealed in particular matters relating to public policy . . . I think that has been a rather dangerous thing in history. People felt too strongly that they knew God's will. I'm reminded of a story that was told about Churchill before he became Prime Minister while he was under the Chamberlain government. One of the chief members of the appeasement government was very active as a church layman and prided himself upon the fact that he never made a decision without first going into his closet praying for Divine guidance. Churchill complemented his colleague for his procedure, but he lamented the fact that he got such poor guidance in the closet.

Trickett: My own recent experience of prayer has made me much more quiet, wordless. I now have the impression that prayer for me is letting God see into my heart. I don't have anything I must do or say, but just be open to him being present to me better than I can be to myself.

Hennigan: Discernment for me is not passive but a very active process, linked in my mind with what I conceive of broadly as prayer.

Haughey: Now we have gotten to a point in our discussion where prayer and discernment come together. With respect to the essay itself, what aspects of it spoke to your experience?

Hennigan: I found the notions of addiction and enslavement highly pertinent. In other words narrowing, exclusivity, shutting out a whole range of concern, operating expediently, becoming comfortable with doing things easily and unreflectively—all of these are omnipresent possibilities in our lives here in Washington.

Lowell: Yes, to be specific about the enslavement part. I have worked for many different bosses and it is easy to observe the differences in the way I have behaved. The greater the freedom, the more likely the fullness of personal convictions will be brought to the work situation. As the paper indicates, the goodness of one's decisions hinge not only on enlightenment but on the atmosphere of freedom in which those decisions are made. I can think of decisions which weren't really good because what was lacking was the atmosphere in which you felt free to think things out, express yourself, argue and attempt to persuade others who participated in that decision-making process.

Ford: Let me give an example of illusion and addiction—from my own particular experience. For some years I was part of the business of making what are called National Intelligence Estimates. That function was established in the late 1950's following the Chinese invasion into Korea because of the surprise the Americans got when they found that there were all kinds of Chinese troops attacking Americans. The problem was that although American intelligence knew the intervention had secretly occurred, it didn't get its act sufficiently together to bring that to the attention of President Truman in time. In the course of reorganizing, among other things was created what I think was a splendid organization of senior scholars who were to look at the world with no policy or budget responsibility at all. They would not have the problem of defending any particular policy or plumping for any particular budget. They had no built-in bias emanating from addictions or illusions. The purpose of the National Intelligence Estimates was to present to the President of the U.S., whoever he happened to be, a picture of the actual world that confronted him, warts and all, apart from whatever U.S. policy was, or the party or the people wanted to think the situation was. In addition, the purpose was to help senior policy-makers to do away with the illusions they might be entertaining. I did this for years, but it was terribly frustrating because you couldn't see your estimates being included in policy at all. Policy seemed to develop without these inputs being factored in. For example, for years the Estimates said one thing about Vietnam, and American policy went another way, so no one was listening. But the paper at hand is good in reminding me, too, that illusion and addiction are universal things. I can see that as one got more senior in the National Intelligence Estimates operation one began to develop one's own illusions and addictions. Granted we weren't defending a particular budget or policy, nonetheless we did have certain lenses through which we saw reality. We all developed tendencies to which we became addicted or positions to which we were attached, especially if we had published or it was known that so-and-so had taken a position last month; you stuck to that and offered resistance to new stimuli or new information. What I'm saying is: we all fall short of the glory of God!

Betty Smith: I find that the more advanced you get in your career and the more focused you are in your particular area of decision-making, plus the more experience you've had, the more selective I've become, at least, in what I will accept by way of new ideas or orientations. If something fits with where you are, you react very positively and you accept it. If it doesn't reinforce or fit into your thinking (whether it's your world view or job view or whatever kind of view) I'm afraid you let in only what reinforces you and your illusions and addictions. But how do you know what's an illusion or an addiction? I'd like to hear something about the involvement of the Holy Spirit in all this. That seems like sort of the saving grace of the matter.

Trickett: I don't really understand discernment as it is used here. I think there are two kinds of discernment. One is where discernment is perceived as a special gift of grace as a result of which one becomes better able to see in a situation explicitly what is a good or what one should do. With that kind of discernment I get into all kinds of trouble. I get into a state of utter distress and feel I'm being totally forsaken. When moving in that direction I need God to redeem me out of that situation rather than to redeem that situation. So there is another kind. Discernment for me, in an experiential way, is a reading back into events and having the sense of being in the presence of God in them rather than of bringing God to them. What I discern is a presence. Does discernment mean making a conscious decision for a good course of action or can it mean simply a submitting or lifting up of any situation, "letting it be" and being open to God's redeeming of that situation—not necessarily through us at all; in fact getting our hands off it? In my daily work, this second way seems to be the main way of discernment.

Clarke: What you're bringing out is an element which is necessary in any kind of decision-making, namely the receptive or contemplative dimension which I would see as the first moment in the total process of choice. I have looked at Christian discernment from the viewpoint of human choice, but you are bringing out that it is really God who is making choices, making things happen, and our task is frequently not to make a choice but simply to be present to His Presence.

Henningan: I tend to view discernment as a kind of virtue or cultivated quality that the Christian has to work at to make himself open to the Spirit. I use the word "virtue" advisedly because it's something one has to work at and could get good at. Particularly this could grow through deepening one's relation to other persons, the counsel of others, even leisure, which can give you clarity about your life and its addictions.

Lowell: This study is very traditional. You can find in it all the words of one's youth that were used in a much more restrictive sense, like virtue, and habit and grace, but in a way that makes sense in today's market. I can take what I learned years and years ago and by just a little bit of shifting and a little bit of maneuvering I can move into a much more sophisticated understanding of my faith. This is so well grounded in what is traditional to me that I find it very meaningful. It enables me to build on that tradition without feeling like a revolutionary. It isn't a denial of my past.

Brian Smith: I wish you'd say something more about how you see the relative importance of the process of choosing and the actual end result of the choice—you seem to be saying it's the process which is the important thing. What goes wrong with government is not so much that people choose the wrong things as the fact that they fall short of choosing humanly, primarily because of illusion and addiction. A person could say "Well, the important thing is that I feel good about a decision". How do you relate the interior feelings of goodness with the question of the impact of the decision?

Clarke: I do try to indicate that the goodness of a decision, all other things being equal, tends to foster correct decisions. The more a person is free from illusion and from addiction, the more that person is really present to the data for decision, and is able to use the analytical tools and to see consequences. So goodness will promote correctness. I don't think that one should aim at "How am I going to grow through my actions?" Good action should not be preoccupied with how one is going to profit by it, even by goodness. But because of the goodness of action the actors become more human. So as they proceed to the next area of decision they are bringing a greater residue of goodness to bear on subsequent decisions.

Langan: There are perhaps two ways of extending what you are saying. First, the attitudes that a particular person has shown in good action will have all kinds of other beneficial results, even if the particular decision is somehow incorrect so that unforeseen undesirable consequences can be avoided or at least minimized. Second, part of what's involved in good action is a sense of responsibility for the correctness of one's actions so that the good agent conscientiously tries to do the correct or right thing.

Clarke: Just as the Holy Spirit will not substitute for the human elements in decision-making so also the goodness of the decision is not a substitute for a concern for correctness. Furthermore, as you indicate, John, it's deficient in goodness if there is not a concern for correctness.

Ford: I found it enlightening to have our government labors or what happens in any government office each day described as simultaneously an act of continuing creation, a struggle with evil and a campaign for the prospering of good. But most of the ambiguities and difficulties of our decision-making is not that they are choices between evil and good but you have to choose between competing goods. Of three or four courses of action all of which are moral and all of which conflict—which is the best or which is the least bum of these in the way this touches my work.

Trickett: In my world I'm given a number of policy options, they're givens. I'm asked to analyze these with respect to technical and sociological data and come out with what one might call the best fit with certain weightings. I would say if I look back over 31 years almost exclusively I could characterize those policy options as having the characteristics of pragmatic politics, rather than human values. Human values do not appear in the spectrum of policy givens. Let me be more specific. After I graduated from college I joined a group of people who were doing something in what we used to call atomic energy. We had started to build a nuclear reactor. After a while I inquired, what are we doing? And the answer I was given was: We're doing something that's very very important for National Security; as a result of this, this nation is going to be a lot more safe. We were actually making nuclear weapons or doing plutonium research for nuclear weapons. Now it turns out 31 years later we are debating whether having plutonium is in point of fact a good thing for the human condition. I would have to confess that long ago I did feel OK about the answer I was given to my question. But now, 31 years later, I have a much more profound sense of what we're about in a plutonium economy. So do we all. These persons who had started the thing were probably informed as best they could be by their sets of values and came to the decision they did just as Truman did in using atomic weapons in Japan.

Hennigan: I would conclude, Ken, that what we need is a process of discernment in public decision-making which takes a decision which was perceived as correct at one time and revokes or revises it when quite different contingencies and circumstances come about which makes a good decision no longer a correct one. Or where there were factors that were not perceived when it was first made but have grown either out of the consequences of that decision or the consequences of collateral decisions. How to build discernment or reflection into policy-making, which allows this kind of reevaluation or reassessment and process of orderly change to take place is a neat trick we haven't worked out very well yet.

Ford: I am very much helped by the attention to climate this paper gives and the reminder that this is not something that is simply there. It is something that's created. But it's not created in an unmotivated way. One has to really discern it, but doing something about it is another thing.

Hennigan: In a sense I think in our society, particularly one as affluent as ours is, the way we resolve the dilemma of an atmosphere gone bad is to create a parallel substitute institution that alledgedly will embody the values the first one was meant to pursue. Many new agencies in this city are instances of this. Another way was mentioned previously by Paul Simon the other night. He sensed a different climate and morale and motivation in the Black Lung section of the Labor Department. This, as he noted, was largely a function of leadership. Leadership is nothing more, basically, than trying to hold values out and motivate other people to work towards them, concretizing the possibilities, attracting people to "Let's choose this rather than that". This concretely is discernment for leader and led. For the former how to bring out what one hopes is the best course in a way that is not vanity. For the latter, to see the good presented and move towards it.

Clarke: Your example, Ken, makes me think of something I've been reading in the last few days, Jacques Ellul's *The Technological Society*. It's a pretty depressing view of how good and evil are not just in human beings and persons and their acts but are also in human relationships and then, beyond that, in various structures and institutions. There can be a societal embodiment of moral good or moral evil—certain customs, laws, ways of doing things can promote good or evil. Is part of what we're struggling with here the fact that persons who have within them good and evil—perhaps a lot more good than evil—may be a good deal better than the embodiments of the human which have taken place around them in the course of their lifetime? As you go from persons to relationships to institutions, you pick up these barnacles; a group of saints becomes a ship of fools. To the degree that this is the case the melancholy question emerges: Is public decision to choose the good a concrete possibility?

9
An Examination of
Job Consciousness

John C. Haughey

The first chapter of this volume attempted to draw up a to-pography of government decision-making. This last chapter will try to do the same except it will be an interior topography that is attempted. Instead of a sketch of the vast network of contributors to the decision-making process of government it will map out some of the influences inside the individual decision-maker which slant decisions in one direction or another. By so doing this chapter will seek to raise the consciousness of civil servants to some of the attitudes habitually entertained by them. These attitudes seldom become an object of reflection in themselves but are reflected in so many of the decisions they make.

I refer to these interior influences not as values but as attitudes although the difference between the two is slight. Attitudes, as I am using the word here, include values but are more complex. More complex, I say, because they congeal over a period of time and as a result of different experiences. The origins of our attitudes differ. Some are taught then tested and tempered over a period of time. Some are arrived at more experientially. Some are held together more by choice than by judgment. Whatever the origin or the reason for their continuance, attitudes as I use the word in this essay are the usual carriers of our values. Our attitudes, furthermore, are usually a cluster of inter-related values. They freeze into patterns of choice or judgment either of which in turn are major determinents of subsequent choices. For this reason attitudes are highly germane to decision-making.

The decision-maker's attitude toward his family and children would be an obvious example. This would be a complexus of values, affections, experience, concern. It would influence the way one sees oneself and one's responsibilities and how one executes those responsibilities not only at home but also in one's employment situation. The need to succeed and persevere at the job for the sake of the family will obviously have an effect on how one performs in it as well as the tensions one experiences and the risks one is willing to undertake in carrying out occupational responsibilities. The fact that this influence is constant does not mean that it is an object of one's consciousness in an on-going way. The attitudes which I mean to bring under inquiry in this essay are more subtle than this more obvious one.

The spirit behind this essay is not a didactic one—I do not assume to teach what the proper attitudes are. Nor is it a judgmental one—suggesting that the habitual attitude of a person is inadequate or unacceptable. It is meant only to be catalytic— an invitation to the reader to examine and locate himself or herself more clearly within the spectrum of attitudes described so as to understand the influences operating on them in the course of the performance of their tasks. The attitudes described in this essay come from real people, friends I have known who happen to be civil servants or from conversations I have had with their acquaintances or from notions I have picked up in interviews conducted in the course of composing this book. It should be obvious that the attitudes that are represented here are not exhaustive of the areas covered. They are merely samplings. These samplings have been chosen because they represent different points along a spectrum of attitudes held about common areas of interest or concern. I should stress here that these samplings do not correlate directly with attitudes held by those whose conversations are recorded in this book since many more people were involved in their manufacture than these.

Several things should be noted about these attitudinal samplings. First of all, although they have their origins from people I've counseled or known or interviewed, they have been composed by me with imagination and a good deal of selectivity. Secondly, my interest in each of the attitudes probed here has much to do with the religious values implicitly or explicitly contained in them. In part this is because most of the people I have known over the years tend by and large to be religious people or at least have definite attitudes about religion. I suppose also this is due to the fact that the religious values of government officials are a particular interest to me as a theologian. Finally I confess that I have a preference for one attitude in each of the categories analyzed below, but I've tried not to fit out the other attitudes with black hats.

The reader is invited to examine himself or herself in the course of trying to understand the vast differences in attitudes described in the following pages. Although a reader is likely to identify more fully with one viewpoint than the others, I presume the majority of readers will find a little of themselves in more than one of the attitudes described. After reading over widely different perspectives under each of the following five categories, readers should examine which most closely represents their own habitual attitude. They will also find it helpful to get in touch with opposite ways of viewing the same area.

This exercise can have two added effects besides raising one's consciousness to a new degree of awareness of the habitual attitudes one harbors. It could serve as a review of the entire volume since many of its topics are treated in more detail in the essays. It could also serve as an introduction to many of the issues raised in the volume for those who have not yet delved into it.

ATTITUDES TOWARDS THE SERVICE COMPONENT OF THE CIVIL SERVICE CAREER

a) (This person's attitude could be described as patriotic/secular.) 'I think that career civil service is the best way that I as a citizen can serve my fellow citizens. I love our nation and am happy to have a small part in serving its people. Within the area of my competence I do what I can to make our country a better place for people to live in. My responsibilities like those of all other civil servants are created in order that the civic units of society whether they be local, state or national can function and operate harmoniously. The importance of a civil service career derives from the fact that it is at the heart of society's well-being. It is right for citizens to expect from us who are civil servants a degree of altruism not only because they pay the salaries we make but also because of the nature of the employment which we have freely embraced.'

b) (This attitude derives from a biblical consciousness.) 'To confine the meaning of a civil servant to a merely secular understanding of that role is a disservice to those who are served as well as to me. It is not incumbent on me to take my cue about the nature of things solely from the definitions society puts upon them. As I see it, whatever elucidates the meaning of the service I do for my fellow citizens will add to my serving them better.

I have developed an understanding of myself and my role in society in terms of what I read in the Gospels. For example, one that I find pregnant with meaning is "The Son of Man came not to be served, but to serve, and to give his life as a ransom for many." (Mk 10, 45) I don't think Jesus intended to reserve the role of servant to himself but called any who took him to be their Master to the same style of life. It is endlessly consoling to me to know that the measure of greatness in the kingdom Jesus preached about was assigned to those who served the needs of others. And as far as I can see the needs he was talking about were not confined to a religious sphere but referred to ordinary needs. Furthermore, if Jesus could wax eloquent over a single act of service done by a Samaritan on his way from Jerusalem to Jericho, how much more eloquent would he be about those of us whose whole life is dedicated to serve the needs of our fellow citizens! If service done to one had such importance in his eyes imagine the dignity my work must have which serves hundreds, even thousands. Granted I don't see them face to face but is a person any less served by one whom he does not see than he is by one whom he sees?

My overall decision to embrace a life of civil service I take to be a vocation in the religious sense of the word because I am responding not only to those whom I am serving but I see Christ in some way in those whom I serve. The discreet decisions, therefore, that I make on behalf of the needs of those whom I serve in the course of the performance of my tasks can be deemed not only acts of meeting the needs of my fellow citizens but also acts of following Christ himself.'

c) (This attitude derives from what might be called a professional job consciousness.) 'As I see it, a job is a job is a job. Circumstances brought me into government work and the intrinsic value of my work plus the benefits which have accrued to me from my position make me content to stay an employee of the government for as far into the future as I can see. Career civil service has been an accident in my life. The only formal choice that I made to serve people came from the choice of my profession made early in my life which like all other professions is a service profession. The career civil servant aspect of my occupation is of no particular consequence to me. Whatever is good for me I really think is going to be good for the public I serve. I find the benefits of working for the government outweigh, at the present time at least, any benefits that I could have from working for the private sector.

A further elucidation of my attitude would have to add that I am nervous about people adding any religious or theological significance to the ways that society sees and intends the role of the public servant. It has taken centuries for church and state to separate themselves into two different spheres of interest. I am afraid that matters would be confused now if religiously motivated public servants attempted any rejoining of these dissimilar spheres of concern. Our society is pluralistic in its value perceptions and it would destabilize society if the private value perceptions of some civil servants imposed another meaning on the role they had in the public sphere. This mixes apples and oranges.'

d) (This consciousness derives from what might be characterized as a Christian realist's attitude.) 'My background is much too religious to identify with the patriotic secularist consciousness represented in the first position and at the same time too modern to identify with the kind of biblical consciousness represented by the second position. Let me give you a couple of reasons why neither of those makes me comfortable. I find much more complexity in myself and in the social realities our agency delves into to subscribe to either one of them. If those who were served by us civil servants were as simply in need as the man in the ravine in the Good Samaritan parable, then I could entertain the possibility of applying that parable to my life. But rather than being gripped with compassion I find I have to ward off cynicism about so many of those whom we attempt to serve in and through our agencies. What comes through more often than not is a tangled series of self-interested peoples and groups, each shrieking louder than the other for what they take to be their needs which seldom appear to me to be all that drastic, and are usually conceived of in ruthless despite of others whose needs are more pressing and whose voices are more frequently silent. In general what I'm saying is that the rhetoric of service on the one hand like the rhetoric of need on the other no longer describes the simple realities they might have described in the past. Consequently, I find it hard to retain the idealism I once knew when I am face to face with the power conflicts that greet those of us who would serve the public.

And as far as following Jesus is concerned or being like him, I'm afraid the modern understanding of Scripture robs one of those simplicities. I am not a student of the matter but I get enough of a whiff of their complexity from learned friends and priests to make me quite hesitant to use them directly to feed my own piety. They mediate a less accessible Jesus than heretofore thought . As some wag put it referring to the kind of critique the Scriptures have been subject to in recent years: "They have taken away my Lord and I do not know where they have laid him."

And as for my colleague with the professional consciousness who is afraid that we will revert to confusing Church and State I would like to relieve his anxiety. The religious people I know are so divided on so many elemental things that they will never constitute a single force in public life. I am one of those divided people. So fear not, I say to you, and to those of you who have such clear ideas about your role in society or your following of Jesus, I respect you and wish that I could reduce complexity to such simple terms.'

(The reader is invited to read or reread Chapters 1, 3 and 7, and the conversations subsequent to each since these are

germane to the subject of service dealt with in these attitudes.)

ATTITUDES TOWARDS ADVANCEMENT
IN THE CIVIL SERVICE CAREER

a) 'As I see it, service and position go together. If anyone wants
to develop a greater effectiveness in serving others, one must try
to advance. Power to serve is commensurate with the position
one attains to. The better the credentials I amass and the further
up the ladder I can get with my skills, the greater capacity I have
to serve people. In addition to these humanistic considerations, I
also think that advancement is good stewardship, in the Christian
sense of the word. As I see it, God has placed in each one of us a
series of potentialities which are meant to increase a hundredfold
if God is to be glorified by his creation of us. But striving for
advancement is a practical spelling out of this kind of stewardship, as far as I'm concerned. Anything less than this would
leave these potentialities unrealized and would not, therefore,
glorify God. I would be like the timid servant who hid his talent
without multiplying it and would be deserving of the castigation
he received in the Gospels.'

b) 'Linking service and position together seems reasonable
enough at first blush, but my own experience is that the service I
can perform today tends to become secondary to the position I
might attain to tomorrow. Present service possibilities are very
easily postponed or performed slovenly if it seems I can work my
way into a better position in which I will have greater leverage
and power. Leverage and power when used for the sake of those
who are served is, of course, a good thing but for me it's a more
than even chance that when I begin to pursue these things my
own self-interest overtakes my more altruistic motives and drives
me to attain to positions for my sake rather than others. One of
the telltale signs is that I find myself expending whatever creativity I have calculating my moves for the prospective position so
that my interest in or esteem for what I can or should be doing
now is proportionately diminished. Maybe more mature people

can keep these two things in balance, but I have found that once I begin to hanker after a position I have not yet attained to, the good that I can do in the one I'm in becomes quite remote by comparison to the need that I have to attain to the next. In effect, I sometimes wonder whether I'm using the served to serve my needs.'

c) 'The scope of my concern to serve does not extend as widely as those of my colleagues, apparently. If the public is better served by my advancement or by a greater development of my own skills, I am happy about that. But my own purview does not really find service of others an operative intention. At least, if by others one means people that one has no personal relationship with. The only people I am consciously serving are the members of my family. Perhaps my attitude remains focussed in this terrain because I have everything I can do to raise a family and provide them with the possibility of a decent life or at least a better life and a good education for my children. And I would think that I am not being irreligious about this since it seems to me the only commandment that we have been given by the Lord is to love one another. By striving to advance in my profession, it seems to me I am concretely loving those for whom I am responsible and who are closest to me. Greater stewardship or a development of talents or a greater degree of service of others and all of these other religious notions I do not find operative categories in the way I have come to look at myself or my advancement. My own advancement makes the family more secure so whatever upward mobility is possible for me I will pursue since its attainment would enhance the possibility of a better life for me and them.'

(The issue of advancement has been touched on in Chapter 5 and 8 and alluded to in the conversations following those chapters. The reader might review these sections of the book.)

PERCEPTIONS OF THE EFFECT OF THE NEED
FOR SECURITY ON THE HANDLING OF ONE'S RESPONSIBILITIES

a) 'I would have to admit that when push comes to shove my need for security in my job is a more operative dynamic than the good that might accrue to others from the proper execution of my tasks. My ordinary disposition would seem to be: Where will my action or decision or omission leave me in the agency? This concern certainly colors my choices and performance. I don't think this is particularly noble, but it's a fact. It's not one that's peculiar to me either, it's pervasive among those whom I know in government work. But who would say that it's peculiar to us bureaucrats?

You seldom find a bad person in the ranks. But most of us feel we have too much to lose and that no one will be there to back us up if we stand up for what is the right or better thing to do for the public.

The problem, then, is not so much that we do wrong but the amount of good we leave undone is incalculable insofar as we are affected by a fear of consequences that could result from actions we might take. I think one of the really significant things that is lost by our insecurity is pride and a sense of accomplishment. One finds a good deal of cynicism among bureaucrats. I wonder if it comes from a defensiveness we develop because we don't feel satisfied we're doing the job we're commissioned to do. It's easier to be cynical about the system than to find fault in ourselves who make up the system.'

b) 'I have always had a sense that the enormous government apparatus which I play a very small part in is terribly disconnected with real people's needs as I see them. So I don't feel guilty seeing that what I'm in is a game more or less. You learn the rules of the game and it carries its players relatively well if they learn to keep their expectations minimal and their capacity for tolerating inadequacy maximal. Since I don't walk around with any great sense of dedication to what I am about, I do not put myself out in my day to day performance. If I am going to be given credit for a particular input that is within range of my capabilities, then I am quite interested in expending effort in making it creditable. If not, I find myself very uninterested. I see many things that could be done better and I have many ideas about them but I have chosen to keep a low profile by comparison to what my contribution could be. When I did try to make a contribution in my first years in government I was either ignored or someone else was given credit for it. So I guess I would sum up my situation as being a combination of alienated and wanting to have attributed to me the contribution that I can make. In effect this means that only a small portion of what I could give is being used. It's an on-going decision for me to endure the present boredom for the future security I'm assured of simply by hanging around here.'

c) 'Around the time of Watergate I had what you might call a conversion. I saw the effect of a loyalty that was too narrow for the good of the people involved or the country. Through those revelations of otherwise astute and good men my eyes were opened about what was happening to me and many of us in my own agency. What I might call 'get ahead' habits in relationships had become second nature to me. By this I mean that the power persons had to advance me became the stimulus that had me relate to them. On the other hand I began to see that I developed a great lack of interest in those in my division who had no power to insure my continuance in the agency or ability to help me to move up in it. This came as quite a shock to me since I had always prided myself on treating people with respect and evenhandedly. In other words, quite unsuspectingly I had gradually learned to become inauthentic. I was caught in a web of sycophantish interaction and indebtedness that I wouldn't name and couldn't own.

What was eye-opening about the Watergate disclosures was the widespread manipulation of public power and exploitation of people to attain to greater security. And this from those who had less reason for being insecure than anyone else in the government. I began to see that security is a voracious need that is never satisfied and is prepared to make people mere means to satisfy its appetite. The more it is fed the more people are eaten up or cast aside or ignored. I have resolved never to subject myself to its tyranny again.'

d) 'Giving in to insecurity about the future is an omnipresent weakness in me and something that I must continually fight against. I do this by trying to be more of a believer that God is in charge of every detail, situation and circumstance not only in my life but in the whole of government and in fact the whole universe. So "God will provide" has become an adage that I try to subscribe to and which I have found reduces my propensity for anxiety. The most immediate source of insecurity I have is my place in the pecking order in my division and agency. This is a relatively subtle thing but it has enormous power to get me and others to take our sights off of the laudable objectives we have and get them focussed on how we're faring or whether we're being approved or noticed or getting ahead. I can lose both perspective and integrity though in an inch by inch kind of way by succumbing to the power of the pecking order. It affects how we relate to one another, it causes competition and back-biting and suspicion and a poor relational context within which to work. I have seen strong people, or so I thought, lose their self-confidence overnight when the approval they had sought from higher-ups was withdrawn and they were passed over.

There is nothing wrong, of course, with the desire to be secure, nor with actions taken to secure one's position, but what is quite difficult to sort out is whether I'm inadvertently shoring up my own future by the way I handle a matter for decision that affects others, especially the public. Having learned to make decisions on the basis of where they'd get me or where I'll be in the pecking order as a result of my input rather than dealing with cases or issues on their objective merits, I was departing from a morally neutral situation and entering into a situation in which I could be causing injustice or guilty of neglect of people's legitimate needs.'

(The reader will find it helpful to read or reread Chapters 1, 5 and 8 as well as the conversations which follow them in connection with the above issue of job security.

ATTITUDES TOWARDS THE SPECIFIC EFFECT ONE'S RELIGIOUS FAITH SHOULD HAVE ON THE DAY TO DAY JOB PERFORMANCE

a) 'My religious faith impacts most directly on the personal relationships I have with my co-workers. I feel I must help to create (insofar as that is possible for me to do) an atmosphere which for want of a better word could be called charity. This may sound pollyannish but I see it as critical for the well-functioning of the office and in turn the division and in turn the agency. I am not suggesting that I am the lone virtuous Christian trying to do this in a hostile atmosphere since I see the mode in which people relate to one another in our division is by and large one of respect. In addition to charity, patience is something I'm constantly called to exercise. The trick there is not to judge people who rankle me and others since negative judgments about people make it virtually impossible for me to deal fairly and easily with them. So, insofar as my faith has any specific effect on the secular reality of my work, it is in this area of the virtues I am called to practice, primarily the virtues of charity and patience.'

b) 'The way I see this thing about where my religious faith is meant to impact my government work is in the decisions I'm responsible for. God has a will about each of these. My understanding of how to discover this is that God reveals his will to us believers through the Church. The Church in turn teaches us norms which mediate and specify God's revelation to us. It's my responsibility to learn those norms well and to become more and more adroit in applying them to the matters I am faced with in government work. For me to be a faithful servant of God, therefore, means I must steep myself in learning his will as revealed to me through the Church so that a real contribution can be made by me in public affairs and in the policies and decisions taken by the government.'

c) 'The way in which my religion most directly affects my government performance is the belief I have in the efficacy of prayer. When I am faced with a dilemma that I cannot resolve, which is often the case, I withdraw from the office to a place of quiet where I can sort through the feelings I have about the matter to be decided. I frequently have to weigh things in an explicit faith atmosphere to get a sense of the fittingness of going in one direction rather than another with them. When I do this I don't believe that God is revealing to me a new content but I believe I can come to a better sense of the decision I must make. Admittedly this doesn't bring me to a sense of certainty but at least I have the satisfaction of having used explicitly religious means for arriving at a sense of what seems the better route to take.

The understanding I have of my religion does not confine the notion of God's will for me to matters that concern only me and my personal relationships. I have always been taught that God contours public life through those who make themselves his instruments. My way of responding to this belief is by being prayerful when faced with doubt about the right thing to do. If God has a particular will about the things I have charge over I must do my best to find out what it is by putting myself in his presence.'

d) 'It is both my experience and my belief that prayer is not an appropriate activity for the proper execution of my work or anyone else's work as a civil servant. I think what I owe my fellow citizens is to serve them as dispassionately and objectively and as rationally as possible. The matters that we are faced with are usually steeped in ambiguity and obscurity about their rightness or wrongness. The tools we have to pierce through this ambiguity are professional competence, systems analysis, computers, the experience of wiser co-workers and the checks and balances of an interlocking legislative, judicial and executive system. These are the processes that reasonable men have developed so that reasonable solutions can be arrived at. My understanding of God is that he is satisfied when we human beings can deal with the self-interest that we have in public matters and come to a freedom about what would be best for all concerned. God is pleased when human beings reason together and are reasonable about the social construction of their existence.'

e) 'I think what my faith supplies to my workday world is perspective. I think that perspective is continually freshened by my relationship to the believing congregation with whom I celebrate the mysteries of the life of the Lord. Through them and ultimately from him I find myself motivated to continue to do the best I can to make the little piece of world in which I am competent a better place for people to work in and citizens to be helped by. I do not see my religion feeding any information into my mind about the programs we ought to create to help the human enterprise nor anything by way of implementation. My faith does not supply me with a vision of the way God sees government or his will for it in any specifics. I guess it's more in the area of optimism and hopefulness as well as the long view that religion affects me. I can comport myself regularly in the office with a degree of peace and humor. Without that perspective the daily evidence would be dire enough to get me down as it tends to get everybody else down. When I feel inadequate to the immediate task facing me I do employ the prayer of petition asking God to help me and to help us in humanizing the enterprise we're in together.'

f) 'Anyone who thinks that they can connect their religion in any specific way with government employment either hasn't been in it very long or has a wild imagination. First of all, with regard to decisions, the amount of discretionary power any one of us has is really minimal. And the number of times even this slight degree of discretion involves religious values is virtually nonexistent. Government work is circumscribed by procedures and statutes and rules and if one is good at it one seeks to understand these well, work within them and apply them. Religious vistas I think are likely to have persons try to circumvent the constant need for nuts and bolts competence in the nitty-gritty of the job they're hired to do. Secondly, it is woolly-headed to view everyday politics and the work of government which undergirds as a process in which ideals are embodied or values as such are pursued. It is a process in which hard compromises are arrived at slowly, grudgingly and painstakingly. It is admirable for a person to think that what they're doing in government is trying to embody ideals or values or apply moral or religious norms to our society. They will be endlessly frustrated as long as they retain that image. A more accurate image would be fashioned if in it power plays abound and trade-offs are frequent and compromises that everyone can live with are the bottom line. Undoubtedly, the rhetoric of political principles and ideals serve some purpose since they raise the American political experience to the levels of axioms and principles. But what it really comes down to is that we have produced a number of procedures that reduce the possibility of self-interest or thwart personal greed and keep the majority moving in a direction which is relatively harmonious. These procedures will always be inadequate and will be under endless revision. That's the nature of our form of government—and it will always be so. I say all this as a religious person and am happy that my religion speaks to me of a world that transcends the niggling things with which bureaucracy is surrounded.'

(The conversations following Chapter 6, 7 and 8 will elaborate on the ways in which personal religious faith affects one's understanding and performance in public life. Chapters 2, 4, 6 and 8 also have direct relevance to some of the attitudes described here.)

ATTITUDES TOWARDS THE IMPORTANCE OR PLACE OF GOVERNMENT IN RELATION TO GOD'S PLAN OF REDEMPTION

a) 'I see secular government as definitely having direct religious meaning and import even though most modern governments would not describe themselves in such terms. Governments are no less in God's hands than the rest of created realities. He works out the salvation of people through the structures within which people's lives are organized whether they believe this or not. One of the best statements of this belief comes from Paul's letter to the Romans, Chapter 13. "There is no authority except from God and all authority that exists is established by God." "The ruler is God's servant." (Rom. 13, 1 and 4) To rebel against or oppose the authority of government is to "rebel against God". Even when this authority is gained unjustly or exercised abusively it still remains within God's hands and flexes to his purposes since there is no evil that human beings can generate that is stronger than God's goodness or beyond his power to draw good from it. I do not see our government as any less in God's hands than the churches are and I don't see those who conduct the affairs of government as any less likely subjects of God's empowerments than the ministers of the churches, even though the former would not in most cases see themselves as being led by God or see the government run in formally religious terms. God is not biding his time until theocracy as a form of government returns but even now "disposes all things mightily." If God is God and being Lord means anything, it must mean that governments, like flowers, are in his hands and yield to his purposes.'

b) 'Pursuit of this question belongs in the area of vain speculation. It has not seemed important to God to tell us what the destiny of any one nation is and therefore it is futile to speculate how governments are part of his purposes. I am reminded of the statement Jesus made to his disciples when they posed the same kind of political question to him. "It is not for you to know," he said, "the times or the seasons that the Father has picked by his own authority" for bringing about the fulfillment of Israel. (Acts 1, 7) It's as if Jesus were saying: "Some things are a little too macro to be part of your business." But at the same time and in the same context he promised his Spirit to them so they could do what was part of their business, namely to use the powers with which they were imbued to serve people. Sometimes Jesus saw this power in terms of justice (freeing the captives, liberating the oppressed and so forth, Luke 4, 18-19) and sometimes he saw it in terms of being witnesses to him in every political realm all the way to the ends of the earth. God will hold governments and those who work in them accountable for whatever use has been made of the powers and the resources with which he has endowed them and the opportunities he has accorded them for serving their people. Whether believer or unbeliever, it should be clear when this power is advancing and undergirding human dignity and when it is denigrating it. All we have to know is that, and that's all we do know.'

c) 'It seems to me an odious kind of zealotry to conceive of government in terms other than those by which the governed see themselves. The powers of our government are invested in the people. Government exists for the people, and through the people. Implicit in this understanding is the right of the governed to name the meaning of their government. But if a considerable portion of the governed see it in merely secular terms it behooves the rest to accept that and not attempt to add to it. The pluralism of our society requires this kind of etiquette. We should know enough history by now to know that religion and politics don't mix and that any attempt to mix them generates enormous suspicion, fear and resentment.

I would add to this political science judgment a theological reflection to undergird it. I think that government is basically secular in origin and if it had not been for the fall of human beings from grace it would have been unnecessary. It is necessary now in order to stave off further deterioration and fragmentation and to keep the minimal of social harmony that is possible for us. I think God looks upon government as such (if I might be so bold as to assume to know anything about God) as basically neutral. It is part of what is passing away and God gets interested in them only if they jeopardize the dignity of the individual citizens under them or that make their search for him difficult or impossible. Otherwise I think governments and their doings are not a direct object of his care or concern. After all, we were put in this world to save our souls and only if government jeopardizes the possibility of that would it become a concern to God, I should think.'

   d) 'I don't want to start off in the unknown and speculate. I want to start off in the religiously knowable and build my faith from there. I don't know what God thinks of government but from the scriptures which are his Word about what I'm supposed to understand, I believe that human activity has religious importance to the degree that it meets human needs or fails to meet them. If that is so, then it seems to me governmental activities and hence governments are at the center stage of God's concern. I find much food for thought, for example, in Matthew 25, 31 ff. In that scenario it becomes obvious that the norm according to which the divine Judge judges is whether the poor have been housed and clothed and visited, etc. Those who salvaged people in need, whether they knew it or not, were being saved through the very people whose needs they were serving. "Whatever you have done for the least of these, my brethren, you have done to me." And the more abject the served are, the passage suggests, the more religious the servers are, irrespective of any piety they brought to their actions. I presume the important thing about government, therefore, according to God's Word, is not governments as such but whether they're getting the job done. What's interesting too here is that it doesn't seem that individuals are being judged, it seems that nations are. Whole nations are blessed and named sheep or cursed and named goats.'

   e) 'I think people-building and Salvation are of a piece. I think that anything that helps people become more integral to their social realities and realize their social potential is a keystone to God's saving purposes. But that is what government exists for.

Isn't this what scripture says about God's purposes? He wants to save persons in their social realities which are inextricably part of their personhood. Israel is the prototype of this. And his choice of Israel was not only a choice to save people but to save all other peoples in their corporate reality through his chosen people. I don't hear the scriptures saying that God is interested in saving individuals from the social reality which is organic to them, unless of course it is hopelessly corrupt, but rather is interested in removing from individuals what keeps them from becoming a vital up-building part of the larger whole. If all of these things are true perceptions then governments must be very important in God's eyes since governments are critical to whether people-building happens or fails to happen, comes apart or comes together.'

(Readers of these opinions would profit from Chapter 7 especially and from the conversation which follows it.)

* * * * * * * * * * * * *

There are many other areas about which the decision-maker has attitudes that would have to be included in this essay if it posed as a complete inventory of interior influences. Since it does not, these few will have to suffice. This chapter extends to the readers an invitation to a degree of introspection that we modern people are not sufficiently versed in doing. The pluralism recorded under each of the attitudes was calculated to stimulate the reader's own self-examination. The ultimate purpose of this final chapter rests on the assumption that public servants' responsibilities will be performed with more objectivity if they are more aware of their subjectivities which are replete with "illusions and addictions", motivations and aversions, judgments and attachments, opinions and predispositions. A conversation does not follow this chapter because it is hoped the readers will be in dialogue with their deeper selves as a result of this exercise or possibly even motivated to converse with some of their colaborers about the inner life each has which affects our public life so profoundly.

Epilogue
John Rohr

Because of the unfamiliar territory charted in this volume, it seemed good to the authors to expand the customary concluding call for further reflection into a fuller and more specific statement of what particular avenues might be explored profitably. Having opened the topic of moral values in governmental decision-making in such a fresh and innovative way, the volume has elevated the conventional curtain call for further research from a modest disclaimer to an urgent imperative.

This volume has rendered signal service in showing how profitable an exchange between academicians and practitioners can be. It provides considerable insight into how practitioners see the relationship between personal values and their decisions in public life. It does this in no small part because the academics, so obviously at ease with disciplined moral discourse, guide the discussion with a sure but gentle hand toward solid ethical reflections. In so doing, they keep the discussions from the shoals of the slogans, invectives, and ritualistic incantations that impoverish so much of our contemporary debate on public morals and values.

There are two areas not dealt with in the volume that I would put at the head of the list of those to be examined the next time the Woodstock Center and its guests share their insightful discussions with a broader audience. The neglected issues are: (1) the moral significance of the oath of office and (2) the fundamental justice of the American regime.

OATH OF OFFICE

The significance of the oath to uphold the Constitution is that it creates a moral community among government personnel within a society that knows no political orthodoxy. In the United States, citizenship of itself carries no obligation to support the Constitution. Indeed, that very Constitution allows for those who despise it. When the nineteenth century abolitionist, William Lloyd Garrison, denounced the Constitution as a bargain struck with Satan, he may have spoken unfairly but he spoke in the spirit of the Constitution he denounced. Freedom of speech, press and assembly in America carry the right to criticize not only a current policy of "the government of the day" but the more basic right to criticize the most fundamental principles underlying the Constitution itself.

It is this second and more fundamental right that makes the oath of office significant. Surely the oath does not mean the government employee must support the Constitution in some literal sense that would require him or her to oppose all proposed amendments. From what we have learned in this volume about discernment and fundamental options, we can look for a meaning of the oath that deals more directly with a commitment to the fundamental values symbolized in the majestic generalities of the Constitution—e.g. the guarantee that no person shall be deprived of life, liberty, or property without due process of law and that no state shall deprive any person of the equal protection of the laws. Indeed, it is in our *constitutional* law that the distinction between letter and spirit become most meaningful. Although the Constitution is a legal document, only the most hardened nominalist would consider the great court opinions interpreting the Constitution as "law" in the same sense that one finds law in the more mundane areas of torts, contracts, and civil procedure. The Bakke case is only the most recent in a long, long line of cases wherein the Supreme Court has provided an essay on "the meaning of America" in the form of a legal opinion. In pondering the Supreme Court's interpretation of the grand language of the Constitution one cannot help but note that at times the hands are the hands of the legal craftsman but the voice is the voice of the civic prophet.

The oath to uphold the Constitution is of importance to the government employee because it is his initiation into a moral community based on a profession of commitment to a set of vague but meaningful secular values. When one recalls the vast array of activities performed by those "in government," the oath takes on added significance as one of the few things such men and women have in common. It is the symbol of their common commitment to the public interest and is one of the few factors that make it meaningful to discuss problems of public service in normative terms.

In creating a moral community, the oath of office makes a significant inroad on American pluralism. However disparate we are as a people in the values we hold, I think that nearly all of us would recognize the moral obligation to live up to the oaths one has taken. Indeed, even Thomas Hobbes, whose unsentimental, worldly wisdom underlies so many of our institutional arrangements, would allow this much *(pacta servanda)*. The significance of this obligation for our purposes is that it legitimately *structures* discussions of public morality for government employees along constitutional lines. To put the same point negatively and more harshly, the oath provides a principled basis for ruling certain value-laden statements inappropriate and out of order. I do not make this statement to celebrate suppression of speech but to rescue discussions of public morals from the intellectual chaos endemic to a pluralistic society. Just as an oath forms community, it structures debate and makes it more focused, more disciplined, more practical and more likely to influence behavior.

One of the strengths of the present volume is that it involves structured discourse. There was no oath of office required to participate in the discussions but, as John Haughey's introduction noted, the participants were selected on the basis of certain perceived values they shared with the authors of the papers. Again, no religious test was imposed but all the participants shared the basic values of the Judeo-Christian heritage. They did this not in the general sense in which all Western men and women share this heritage but in a more intense and practical way that I am sure is quite obvious to all who have read this volume.

Recall, for example, the discussion of human rights in El

Salvador, or Paul Simon's remarks on world hunger, or Richard McCormick's comments on the plight of the aged. Suppose that one of the participants had asked why we should worry about what happens to the El Salvadorians, or to the hungry or to the aged. Such a question would have been greeted with a polite but embarrassed silence and a fervent hope that either the question or the questioner would go away. It would have been a clear breach of the tacitly structured dialogue of this community. Not even the most ardent enthusiasts for pluralism would fail to see that these discussions were strengthened rather than weakened by restricting the participants to men and women who, though different in many ways, held many ethical values in common.

The same point applies even more to the second part of this book where Christians address Christians. This discussion may have been particularistic but for that very reason it was meaningful to the participants. It was deep because it was narrow. Indeed, for Christian and non-Christian alike, who are free from "illusion and addiction," Part II could stand as a remarkably innovative addition to the literature on decision-making. It might well be examined as a case study in how a group with common symbolic values tries to articulate the relevance of those values to questions of public policy.

The oath to uphold the Constitution can be looked upon as providing in a formal manner and on a massive scale what the invitation to participate in these discussions provided on a more informal and intimate basis. It creates community and structures dialogues.

Having explained the role I see for the oath of office in structuring discussions of public service ethics in general, I shall now give an example to illustrate how a discussion in this volume would have been different had more formal and explicit attention been paid to the fact that the government employees among the participants had a moral commitment to constitutional as well as to Judeo-Christian values.

I believe David Hollenbach's paper on loyalties and the discussion pursuant to it might have benefitted from a careful consideration of the oath to uphold the Constitution. Hollenbach argues persuasively for the public employee's need for extra-governmental loyalties to put his role-specific duties into a balanced perspective. He is vulnerable, however, to Robert Gessert's criticism that questions the usefulness and the propriety of one's family, friends, and church having an influence on one's decision-making in the public sector. Hollenbach fails to provide any principled guidance on what sorts of extra-governmental loyalties are appropriate for the public servant. Will *any* loyalties do? May employees of EEOC join the KKK or employees of NASA the Flat Earth Society? Such extra-governmental loyalties would undermine the very notion of vocation that Hollenbach puts forth.

The strength of Hollenbach's paper is that it warns against the danger of the total politicization of the public servant. He must not become simply the President's man or even the precinct captain's man. Hollenbach's position is that the political must not exhaust the human. This is a sound application at the personal level of the classic distinction between state and society that is at the heart of the best in Christian political thought. His argument would have been enriched, however, had he attempted to evaluate extragovernmental loyalties in terms of their compatibility with fundamental constitutional values. The oath of office would provide a principled basis for making this evaluation.

One might object that a moral obligation to choose one's loyalties in terms of constitutional values limits one's freedom of association and thereby makes government employees second class citizens. The same argument has been made in connection with the Hatch Act and could be made in connection with conflict of interest legislation that limits the types of property government employees can own and the kinds of employment they can enter after leaving government service. Such limitations on individual freedom raise serious issues but they can be met in terms of the vocation that Hollenbach urges rather than in terms of second class citizenship. Indeed, if one looks to religious organizations as the prime analogate of a vocational setting, the moral and legal disabilities our society places on our public servants are not altogether unlike the burdens religious groups put on their clergy. The clergy are not second class citizens within their own denominations, but, because of their high calling, demands are made upon them that are not made upon laymen. This is done not in the name of a job but of a vocation.

A final way in which a consideration of the oath of office could contribute to the nature of the inquiry pursued by these studies is that it would heighten the awareness of the public servant to the difference between the values of the "government of the day"—i.e. the Carter administration, the Ford administration, etc.—and the fundamental values of the Constitution. Ideally, the former are concrete, time-bound expressions of the latter but this ideal is not always achieved. By encouraging the public servant to reflect on the moral implications of the oath of office, one can guide his critical thinking along politically relevant lines and provide him with a principled basis for judging the moral tone of a particular administration.

The oath's value includes its potential for judging a specific policy or administration in terms of broader political values freighted with moral meaning. The inability to make this sort of judgment seems to have been one of the great failings of the Watergate culprits. As far as I know, there was nothing terribly wrong with their extra-governmental loyalties in the area of family, friends, and church. It was their shocking insensitivity to the fundamental tenets of constitutional morality that led to their downfall. Had they asked themselves what difference it makes that they have taken an oath to uphold the Constitution, they might have found themselves more attuned to the nature of what was happening around them. Indeed, the method Richard McCormick suggests in asking what difference it makes to be a Christian might be applied to the question of what difference it makes to have taken an oath to uphold the Constitution.

FUNDAMENTAL JUSTICE

A second direction future reflections might take is a treatment of the fundamental justice of the American political order or "polity". This point is related to our discussion of the oath of office because of the relationship between the moral quality of an oath and the moral character of that which one swears to uphold.

History views generously the German Army officers who conspired against the Führer whose will they had sworn to uphold. This is not because we treat oaths lightly but because we refuse to confer absolute value on the purely formal obligation to honor one's word. The substantive moral content brought about by the effective execution of one's solemn promise cannot be ignored simply for the sake of the promise itself. This is one reason why Dean Rusk's argument during the Vietnam War that we must "honor our commitments" failed to persuade. Indeed, to ignore the substantive aspects of one's oaths is to adopt the morality of Rumpelstiltskin—the queen must give up her baby because she promised she would.

The oath to uphold the Constitution of the United States takes on moral significance in terms of the values the Constitution represents. It is only if the Constitution has established a fundamentally just political order that an oath to uphold it becomes a serious moral event in one's life. The papers and discussions in this volume are by Americans, for Americans, and about Americans. The fundamental justice of our society is presupposed rather than explicitly examined. Such an explicit examination might have taken the book too far afield but if this is the case, then, perhaps, it might have been noted at the outset that it is simply presupposed that this issue has been settled to the satisfaction of the participants.

I should note that I am speaking of fundamental justice in its subjective sense, i.e., how a particular public servant decides whether or not a particular regime (in our case the United States) meets his or her standards of justice. (To essay a discussion of the objective meaning of fundamental justice would involve nothing less than a recapitulation of the history of political thought.) In examining fundamental justice at the subjective level, the public servant might ask himself or herself questions like the following: (1) What are the professed values of the regime? (2) Are the professed values consistent with my personal values? (3) To what extent does the regime achieve its professed values? (4) To the extent that it falls short of its professed values, are there corrective mechanisms that offer some hope of reform?

I do not believe we are so far removed from the critical spirit of the late 1960's that a battery of questions such as these will be dismissed as a mere formalism. The questions are particularly helpful in directing the attention of the public servant away from the actual work he is doing and toward the higher question of the character of the regime in which he serves. It is the *Constitution* he has sworn to uphold not the Navy or the Securities and Exchange Commission or the Office of Civil Rights. This sense of functioning within a moral order whose grand design one accepts as good seems to me to go to the heart of the distinction between a job and a vocation.

The practical, normative result of stressing fundamental justice at the level of the regime is that it can provide a principled, moral framework for addressing many of the morally questionable situations that inevitably arise in a public service career.

A challenging example is the argument that arose during the Vietnam War on whether that war was a temporary, well-intentioned aberration from a basically decent foreign policy or whether it was a concrete expression of the real meaning of a violent and racist America. Abortion raises a similar issue for those who see it in terms of the taking of human life. Is the severe constitutional limitation on governmental authority to regulate abortions a well-meaning but myopic effort to respect a woman's privacy—as the Supreme Court would have it? Or is it the legal expression of a fundamental American acceptance of the plastic-power model of man that Richard McCormick has described in Chapter 6?

These are the sorts of threshold questions that should be addressed before one commits oneself to uphold the Constitution because, once the public manager has made this commitment, it is virtually certain that at some time in his career he will be called upon to participate in a policy or process he finds morally questionable. High profile issues like war or abortion may not be involved but, as the discussion of Brian Smith's topography of decision-making has shown, morally significant judgments can arise in the routine administration of public policy. When the public servant is confronted with a morally questionable policy, he can find in the fundamental justice of the regime a principled basis for deciding whether he should tolerate or even actively cooperate in such a policy. Regime justice softens the dichotomy between resignation and abdication of moral responsibility.

The fundamental justice of the regime overshadows and compensates for the injustice or many of its specific policies. The orderly, authoritative formulation and execution of public policy in a just regime has an *inherent* moral value that can offset many of the imperfections and injustices of the policies themselves. One of the reasons why men and women in government at times seem to be so cynical about questions of public morality is that they think in terms of the specific policies of their agencies rather than in terms of the values of the regime. This, of course, is quite understandable because at a behavioral and self-conscious level it is a program or policy, not the Constitution, that they are administering. What I am suggesting is that the educational task at hand is to encourage busy practitioners to reflect seriously on the broad regime values (e.g. equality, property, freedom, representative institutions, limited government and due process of law) that undergird specific policies—both good policies and bad ones. It is by retreating to this high ground that they can get the perspective necessary to weigh prudently the moral trade-offs endemic to their calling. They must, however, be sure of this higher ground and that is why it is so important that they be convinced of the fundamental justice of the regime they are sworn to uphold. Without this conviction there can be no trade-off for unjust policies because there is nothing to trade. If their personal convictions will not allow them to find the regime fundamentally just, it seems to me the honorable course is not to enter into government service in the first place. Hence, the crucial importance of this moral judgment on the fundamental justice of the regime.*

It seems safe to assume that the practitioners who participated in the discussions in this book share a common, if unexam-

---

* Elsewhere I have argued that Supreme Court opinions are the most helpful means for understanding regime values. See John A. Rohr, *Ethics For Bureaucrats: An Essay on Law and Values* (New York: Marcel Dekker, 1978), chapter two; and "The Study of Ethics in the Public Administration Curriculum," *Public Administration Review* 36 (July-August, 1976) pp. 398-406.

ined, presumption that the American regime is fundamentally just. A discussion of fundamental justice in the American political system is no small task but it would be particularly interesting to combine religious and civic commitments and examine in an orderly way what the Judeo-Christian understanding of a fundamentally just *American* regime might be.

BIOGRAPHICAL DATA

PART I CONVERSATIONALISTS

Janet Ellen Breslin, Political Scientist, Executive Assistant to Senator Lloyd Bentsen (D-Texas). Has served on Commission on the Operation of the Senate to study institutional problems of the contemporary Senate, Ph.D. Candidate, UCLA ("The Senator as an Organization—Power and Politics in the Personal Offices of United States Senators"). Has worked as Associate Instructor, UCLA, and as a profile writer for Ralph Nader Congress Project.

Ralph A. Dungan, U.S. Executive Director, Inter-American Development Bank. Formerly Chancellor of Higher Education, State of New Jersey, '67-'77; U.S. Ambassador to Chile, '64-'67. In government service since 1952, his roles have included Special Assistant to President Kennedy and then President Johnson, Professional staff work with the Senate Committee on Labor and Public Welfare and assistant to the Director of the Bureau of the Budget.

Robert A. Gessert, Principal Scientist, General Research Corporation, McLean, Virginia. Expert on military and political implications of arms control measures for European environment and specialist on NATO problems. Has directed major studies of readiness and deployability of Army reserve components for a NATO contingency; implications of European theater force balance and asymetries for NATO's nuclear posture (Defense Nuclear Agency); NATO standardization for the Departments of Defense and State.

Joseph W. Lowell, Jr., Assistant Executive Director, U.S. Civil Service Commission. Responsible for coordinating the

Government-wide equal opportunity program. Formerly Deputy Director, Bureau of Training and Director, Civil Service Commission's ADP Management Training Center. Has served as President, Washington, D.C. Chapter, American Society for Training and Development, and later as a Board member of the Society's National Board and Chairman of its Government Affairs Committee.

Dr. Harold Margulies, Deputy Administrator, Health Resources Administration, Department of Health, Education and Welfare. Has had distinguished careers in medicine and medical administration. In addition to his present position, he has held posts as Acting Director, National Center for Health Statistics, Acting Director, Bureau of Health Services Research, Secretary, A.M.A. Council of Health Manpower. Has published results of his research on cardiac disease, medical education and medical administration in a wide range of medical journals.

John Paul Salzberg, Staff Consultant on Human Rights, U.S. House of Representatives, Committee on International Relations (assigned to Donald M. Fraser [D-Minn], Chairman, Subcommittee on International Organizations). Was Representative to UN International Commission of Jurists and Executive Secretary, American Association for the International Commission of Jurists. Has published on human rights issues in numerous law journals.

Jonathan Silverstone, Chief, Civic Participation Division, Bureau of Program and Policy Coordination, A.I.D. Was visiting professor of Political Development, Fletcher School of Law and Diplomacy, Tufts University and has been Deputy Assistant General Counsel, International Cooperation Administration, Assistant General Counsel, A.I.D. and Attorney Advisor to the Secretary of the Air Foce.

PART II CONVERSATIONALISTS

John F. Ahearne, Physicist, recently appointed a Commissioner on the Nuclear Regulatory Commission. Formerly

Deputy Assistant Secretary for Power Applications, Department of Energy. Has had major role in formulation of administration's radioactive waste storage proposal as well as the National Energy Plan and the National Energy Act. Formerly Defense Department analyst on military force structure and tactical weapons, planning of volunteer force, and reform of military promotion system.

Dr. Harold P. Ford, Professional Staff, Senate Select Committee on Intelligence. Formerly CIA analyst and executive; Legislative Assistant to Senator Joseph Biden (D-Del). At Georgetown University has been Research Fellow at the Woodstock Theological Center, 1974-5; Program Director, Institute for Study of Ethics and International Affairs. Has published articles on ethics and public affairs. Member, Board of Directors, Churches' Center for Theology and Public Policy.

Francis A. Hennigan, Jr., Director, Office of Planning and Budget, Legal Services Corporation. Formerly Special Assistant and Chief Legislative Assistant to Senator Roman Hruska; Minority Staff Director Select Committee on Equal Opportunity; Staff member, Senate Budget Committee; Assistant Director, Center for Community Planning, Office of Secretary, Department of Health, Education and Welfare.

Joseph W. Lowell, Jr., Refer to Part I Conversationalists.

Honorable Paul Simon, (D-Ill.) U.S. House of Representatives, 24th District, Illinois. Has been described in political circles as an austere liberal, honest to a fault and noted for his legislative skill. He serves on the Budget and Education and Labor Committees of the House. Representative Simon came to the House in 1974 following a wide-ranging career in newspaper publishing and public service in the Illinois Legislature, as Lt. Governor of the State of Illinois and as a college professor.

Elizabeth Reichert Smith, Chief, Center for State Mental Health Manpower Development, DMTP, National Institutes of Mental Health. Worked in nursing education, mental health program development and health science administration. Has published many articles related to nursing education, sociometry, community mental health needs and the role of social sciences in public health nursing.

Rev. Kenneth Trickett, Episcopal priest. Has extensive experience in the nuclear industry in Government and industry. He has been with the U.S. Government since 1966 in the field of nuclear technology development and related energy policy analysis. Is currently in the Nuclear Reactors Evaluation Branch of the Division of Nuclear Power of the U.S. Department of Energy.

EPILOGUE

John A. Rohr is professor of public administration in the College of Business and Public Service at Governors State University in Park Forest South, Illinois. Ph.D. in political science from the University of Chicago. As an Associate Director of the General Management Training Center of the U.S. Civil Service Commission, Dr. Rohr designed a training manual on ethics in public management. He is the author of *Prophets Without Honor: Public Policy and the Selective Conscientious Objector* (1971) and *Ethics for Bureaucrats: An Essay on Law and Values* (1978) as well as other numerous articles and reviews in various journals.

AUTHORS OF ESSAYS

Thomas E. Clarke, S.J., S.T.D., Gregorian University; Research Associate, Woodstock Theological Center. Theologian, specialist in discernment process, systematic theology and Christology; author of three books.

John C. Haughey, S.J., S.T.D., Catholic University. Research Associate, Woodstock Theological Center; formerly a member of the theology faculties at Georgetown and Fordham Universities; a member of the editorial staff of *America* magazine since 1968; author of several books and numerous articles on theological subjects.

David Hollenbach, S.J., Ph. D., Yale University; Assistant Professor, Theological Ethics, Weston School of Theology; specialist in Christian social ethics; author of articles on human rights, corporate social responsibility, population policy and the relation between religion and economic development.

John P. Langan, S.J., Ph. D. in Philosophy, University of Michigan; Research Associate, Woodstock Theological Center; specialist in history of ethical and political theory; author of articles on philosophy of religion, religious ethics and current politics.

Richard A. McCormick, S.J., S.T.D., Gregorian University. Rose F. Kennedy Professor of Christian Ethics, Kennedy Institute for Bioethics, Georgetown University. Specialist in general moral theology, applied moral theology and bioethics.

Robert A. Mitchell, S.J., D. ès sc. rel., Universite de Strasbourg. Director, Woodstock Theological Center; theologian; former President, National Jesuit Conference.

Brian Smith, S.J., S.T.M., Union Theological Seminary; Ph.D. Candidate in Political Science, Yale University; Research Associate, Woodstock Theological Center; a specialist in political affairs concentrated on Latin America; dissertation on Chilean Church State relations.